African Theatre
Women

Editors
Martin Banham
James Gibbs
& Femi Osofisan

Guest Editor
Jane Plastow

Reviews Editor
Jane Plastow
School of English, University of Leeds LS2 9JT, UK

Associate Editors
Eckhard Breitinger
Forststr. 3, 95488 Eckersdorf, Germany

John Conteh-Morgan
Dept of French & Italian, Ohio State University, 248 Cunz Hall, 1841 Millikin Rd,
Columbus, Ohio 43210-1229, USA

Hansel Ndumbe Eyoh
PO Box 8222, University of Buea, Buea, Cameroon

Frances Harding
SOAS, Thornhaugh St, Russell Square, London WC1H OX9, UK

Masitha Hoeane

David Kerr
kerrdavid42@yahoo.co.uk

Amandina Lihamba
Dept of Fine & Performing Arts, PO Box 35051, University of Dar es Salaam, Tanzania

Olu Obafemi
Student Affairs Unit, PMB 1515, University of Ilorin, Ilorin, Nigeria

Ian Steadman
Faculty of Arts, University of Witwatersrand, PO Wits 2050, Johannesburg, South Africa

Titles already published in the series:
African Theatre in Development
African Theatre: Playwrights & Politics
African Theatre: Women

In production:
African Theatre: Southern Africa

Contributions are invited for the forthcoming title:
African Theatre: Young People & Performance

Articles not exceeding 5,000 words should be submitted preferably on disk
and always accompanied by a double-spaced hard copy.

Format: either IBM or Apple, 3.5 inch floppy disks, preferably in Word for Windows,
Word (DOS) 6, Word Perfect 5.1 for DOS or WordStar 5.5. If using Apple format
please save all files as Word for Macintosh version 6.0.1 or lower if possible. Please label
all files and disks clearly. Typewritten submissions may be considered in exceptional
circumstances if they follow the standard double-spaced format.

Style: Preferably use UK rather than US spellings. Underline titles of books or plays.
Use single inverted commas except for quotes within quotes. Type notes at the end of
the text on a separate sheet. Do not justify the right hand-margins.

References should follow the style of this volume (Surname date: page number) in
text. All references should then be listed at the end of article in full:
Surname, name, date, *title of work* (place of publication: name of publisher)
Surname, name, date, 'title of article' in surname, initial (eds) *title of work*
(place of publication: publisher).
or Surname, name, date, 'title of article', *Journal*, vol., no: page number.

Reviewers should provide full bibliographic details, including the extent, ISBN and
price.

Copyright: Please ensure, where appropriate, that clearance has been obtained from
copyright holders of material used. Illustrations may also be submitted if appropriate
and if accompanied by full captions and with reproduction rights clearly indicated. It is
the responsibility of the contributors to clear all permissions.

All submissions should be accompanied by a brief biographical profile. The editors
cannot undertake to return material submitted and contributors are advised to keep a
copy of all material sent in case of loss in transit.

Editorial address
8 Victoria Square, Bristol BS8 4ET, UK • james.gibbs@uwe.ac.uk

Books for Review & Review articles
Jane Plastow, Reviews Editor, *African Theatre*
School of English, University of Leeds, Leeds LS2 9JT, UK
plastow@english.novell.leeds.ac.uk

African Theatre
Women

Editors
Martin Banham
James Gibbs
& Femi Osofisan

Guest Editor
Jane Plastow

Reviews Editor
Jane Plastow

James Currey
OXFORD

Indiana University Press
BLOOMINGTON & INDIANAPOLIS

Witwatersrand University Press
JOHANNESBURG

First published in 2002 in the United Kingdom by
James Currey
www.jamescurrey.com
is an imprint of Boydell & Brewer Ltd
PO Box 9, Woodbridge, Suffolk IP12 3DF, UK
and of Boydell & Brewer Inc.
668 Mt Hope Avenue, Rochester, NY 14620, USA
www.boydellandbrewer.com

and in North America by
Indiana University Press
601 North Morton Street
Bloomington, Indiana 47404-3797

and in South Africa by
Witwatersrand University Press
PO Wits 2050
Johannesburg

Manufactured in Great Britain

British Library Cataloguing in Publication Data
Women – (African theatre)
   1. Women in the theatre – Africa – History – 20th century
   I. Banham , Martin   II. Gibbs, James   III. Osofisan, Femi
   IV. Plastow, Jane
   792'.082'09045

   ISBN 978-0-85255-596-5 (James Currey paper)
   ISBN 978-1-86814-387-0 (Witwatersrand University Press paper)

Library of Congress Cataloging-in-Publication Data
A catalog record for this book is available from the Library of Congress

ISBN 978-0-253-21539-0 (Indiana University Press paper)

Typeset in 10/11 pt Bembo by Long House Publishing Services, Cumbria, UK
Transferred to digital printing

Contents

Noticeboard

Playscript

Book Reviews

Notes on Contributors

Dina Amin is Lecturer in Theater at Barnard College of Columbia. She holds a PhD in dramatic literature from the University of Pennsylvania. She is an award-winning director, and directs in both the USA and Egypt. She has published papers in major academic journals and has translated a number of plays from Arabic to English.

Laura Chakravarty Box is currently the Irving D. Suss, guest artist in the Department of Theatre and Dance at Colby College. Her PhD dissertation was entitled 'A Body of Words: Strategies of resistance in the dramatic texts of North African women'. Her research interests include theatre history, global performance studies and gender studies. She has worked in Morocco, Tunisia, France and India, and is an actor, translator and dramaturg.

Fatima Dike was the first black South African woman to have a play published when she wrote *The Sacrifice of Kreli* in 1976. She has since written a number of plays on liberation and township themes, including *So What's New?*, 1991 and *Streetwalking and Co*, 2000.

Esi Dogbe is Assistant Professor of pan-African literatures at the University of Louisville in Kentucky. Her teaching and research interests include African and African Diaspora literatures, women's performance arts, and African popular culture. She is currently working on a study of Ghanaian video films.

Chris Dunton has taught extensively throughout Africa, including periods in Nigeria, Lesotho, and most recently South Africa, where he is Professor of English at the University of the North-West. His writing includes *Make Man Talk True: Nigerian Drama in English Since 1970* (Hans Zell, London, 1992) and *Nigerian Theatre in English: A Critical Bibliography* (Hans Zell, London, 1998).

James Gibbs teaches at the University of the West of England (Bristol) and has a particular interest in Ghanaian, Nigerian and Malawian theatre. With Jack Mapanje he co-edited *The African Writers' Handbook* (1999).

Mike Kuria graduated from Moi University, Eldoret, Kenya with an M Phil in literature. He teaches English at Daystar University, Nairobi, Kenya, but is currently on study leave to pursue PhD studies at the University of Leeds where he is in his final year. He has published and presented conference papers on African literature, language, philosophy, media and communications.

Christine Matzke is studying for her PhD at the Workshop Theatre, University of Leeds. She lectures in post-colonial African literature at the J.W.Goethe University, Frankfurt/Main, and has published on African women's writing, representations of West African music, Eritrean performance arts forms and Eritrean visual arts.

Mercy Mirembe Ntangaare holds an MA in Theatre Arts from Makerere University and has contributed to theatrical productions and the teaching programme at the Music, Dance and Drama Department of Makerere University, Kampala. She wrote this article while on a DAAD Scholarship at the University of Bayreuth, Germany, studying for her PhD in Theatre Studies.

Jane Plastow is Senior Lecturer in Theatre Studies and deputy director of the Centre for African Studies at Leeds University. She has written extensively in the area of African theatre, and works on community theatre projects in Ethiopia and Eritrea.

Omofolabo Ajayi teaches in the Departments of Women's Studies and Theatre at the University of Kansas, Lawrence. She is the author of *Yoruba Dance: The Semiotics of Movement and Body Attitude in a Nigerian Culture* (Africa World Press, 1998). She is also an active theatre practitioner, whose many credits include the choreography for the premiere of Femi Osofisan's *Many Colours Make the Thunder-King* at the Guthrie Theater, Minneapolis, in 1997.

Esi Sutherland-Addy is a Research Fellow at the Institute of African Studies at the University of Ghana. From 1986–1993 she was Deputy Minister in charge of Higher Education in the Government of Ghana. She is a member of the Federation of African Women Educationalists and serves on a number of national and international education committees.

Obituary
Joel Adeyinka Adedeji
1932–2001

FEMI OSOFISAN

On 5 November 2001, Professor Joel Adeyinka Adedeji, the first African professor of Theatre Arts, passed away in New Jersey, USA, after a brief illness. As was demonstrated on the 'Night of Tributes' organized in his honour on 5 December in Ibadan, Adedeji will be much missed by colleagues and friends all over the world, and especially by his numerous former students at the University of Ibadan, where he taught from 1964 until 1987, and served as departmental chair for over a decade. In the Programme Notes for the occasion, the department described him as 'a scholar of great repute, a devotee of African arts and culture, a rhetorician, an untiring teacher and leader, a singer, an actor, a dancer, an educationist, a humanist, a religious leader and a committed ameliorator of the sufferings of the disabled.'

Those words more or less sum up his career. Born in Aboso, Ghana of Nigerian parents, Adedeji spent most of his early years in Ghana. Then he went abroad to England on a Nigerian government scholarship – the first in that discipline – to study at the Rose Bruford College, graduating with a diploma in Educational Drama in 1962. After this, he proceeded to New York University where, in the years 1962 to 1964, he obtained both his bachelor and masters degrees. Five years later, while teaching in Ibadan, he obtained his doctorate.

The thesis he submitted, on 'The Alarinjo Theatre: the Study of a Yoruba Theatrical Art from its Earliest Beginnings to the Present Times', catapulted Adedeji to the frontline of scholarship in the field. His findings were so startling and original, that they became an instant reference point. Thereafter Adedeji established his authority very rapidly, with a stream of seminal publications on the origins of Yoruba theatre. Through this brilliant rediscovery of the alarinjo, an itinerant theatre which was very active in feudal Yorubaland in the late eighteenth to nineteenth centuries, and whose beginnings he traced to succeeding mutations in the egungun funerary masques of the ancient Oyo kingdom, Adedeji was able to proceed to the formulation of a general theory on the origin of theatre in black Africa as a whole. Of course his conclusions have since then been challenged by a number of scholars (Owomoyela for instance is a strong critic), but none of them has, in my opinion, really succeeded in overturning Adedeji's authority on the subject.

Natural then that his status as a pioneering researcher brought him considerable recognition, in form of awards and honours, as well as membership of numerous national and international organizations. He also served during his long academic career as external examiner to a number of universities on the continent, including the universities of Dar es Salaam in Tanzania, and of Ghana in Legon, Accra.

Professor Adedeji retired from the university in 1987 to found a ministry for the handicapped, a task to which he devoted himself with customary zeal until his death. May his soul rest in peace.

Wale Ogunyemi 1939–2001

As we go to press we learn of the death of Chief Wale Ogunyemi, playwright, actor and Yoruba scholar. Ogunyemi was a major figure in Nigerian theatre from the 1960s to the present, a charismatic actor for stage, film and television, a prolific playwright and a scholar of the Yoruba world who brought its history, myths and lore dynamically into his writing. Now the ancestors will cherish his rich talents. May he rest in peace.

MB

Introduction

JANE PLASTOW

Women have struggled to be heard in the world of modern African theatre. Traditionally they had secure roles as dancers, singers and story-tellers within a community context. However, as theatre and performance became profession-alised and commercialised, and as control often came to lie in the hands of literate elites, women all too often lost their equal standing with men in the realm of performance. The series editors of *African Theatre* and I wished this volume to contribute to the discussion and understanding of women's place in the development of modern African theatre, to analyse their difficulties in working in theatre and to celebrate both past contributions and the present work of women as performers and playwrights.

I hope this book will be particularly valuable because there is still a paucity of critical work on women's contribution to African theatre. There are a few women playwrights who have been given significant critical space; most notably perhaps the Ghanaians Ama Ata Aidoo and Efua Sutherland. Tess Onwueme and Zulu Sofola from Nigeria, and the South Africans Gcina Mhlope and Fatima Dike, have also been the subjects of a number of scholarly essays. In recent years there have been two publications highlighting women's contribution to South African theatre (*Women, Politics and Performance in South Africa, Contemporary Theatre Review*, 9: 1–3 and *Black South African Women: An Anthology of Plays*, 1998), but I think this is the first book devoted entirely to considering women's roles in theatre across Africa, and one of very few con-tributions which looks beyond women playwrights or the representation of women on stage to include a number of articles (Matzke, Sutherland-Addy, Dogbe) which consider the conditions of women's participation in performance.

My intention in including the range of articles in *African Theatre: Women* has been largely to make accessible work from previously under-represented nations, performers and playwrights, so that others may follow on and deepen the debate and understanding of the possibilities and difficulties of women in African theatre, whilst, at the same time, hopefully encouraging new par-ticipants in the field. With this in mind some of the articles included (Dunton on Stella and Ntangaare on women in Ugandan theatre) are necessarily introductory. The desire is to provoke further debate and interest in the whole range of women's activity in theatre in Africa.

All the essays in *African Theatre: Women* raise, in one way or another, the multitudinous problems women have experienced in participating as equals and in gaining respect for their work in theatre. Mike Kuria's essay on Kenyan women playwrights lists three main factors which he considers have held women back: the commonly held belief that women performing in public spaces cannot be respectable; the domestic demands, particularly in relation to child-rearing, which often prevent women being able to tour or to work the anti-social hours which performance commonly demands; and women's lack of equal access to educational opportunities which means they struggle to gain a voice as playwrights or directors of theatrical work. These factors have been equally important throughout most of the continent. During research in Zimbabwe in the early 1990s I interviewed many women performers. These women fell into three categories, they were young and single, divorced or married to others actors – no ordinary man would allow his wife to perform on stage. During the same trip a theatre lecturer at the University of Addis Ababa in Ethiopia told me that he would never go out with an actress, they could not be trusted not to go off with other men.

This stigma is of course by no means limited to Africa. Women performers, contrary to much actual evidence of women's respectability (although it would be disingenuous to deny the links between some areas of performance and the sex-trade worldwide – see Matzke and Ntangaare), have often been seen as licentious and dangerous; mainly, I would argue, because they work in the public sphere and outside the domestic control of a husband or father. I was very interested to see in these essays in how many countries women's roles had been played by men when the first modern stage plays were performed. I already knew this was the case in Ethiopia, but the interview by Esi Sutherland-Addy with Ama Buabeng from Ghana and Christine Matzke's essay on Eritrean women performers from the 1950s confirm that women either weren't allowed on stage or could not be persuaded to perform in those countries too.

The often critically neglected women playwrights brought to the fore in this book have a common passion. Although their subject matter is by no means limited to the question of women's oppression, articles concerned with Algeria, Egypt, Kenya, Nigeria and Uganda, demonstrate the centrality of the issue of gender inequality to contemporary African women playwrights. Some of the women concerned take considerable personal risks by writing. Box points out the dangers to Algerian women who write plays critical of either the religious or political establishments; while from Egypt, Nawal al-Sa'dawi's radical revisioning of the Isis myth in her play of the same name puts her on a collision course with the patriarchal establishment which she continually challenges in all aspects of her work, and which has led to her imprisonment in the past. What, for me, shone through these texts from across the continent, varied as plays and playwrights are in terms of technical accomplishment and renown, was the passion for justice which seemed to be a driving force behind the need to write.

Taking another angle, both Dogbe and Ntangaare look at how women are represented on stage. Ntangaare's essay from Uganda describes a polarised view of women, which I recognised from other nations. In a raft of mainly male-authored plays women are seen as either angelically virtuous or, more often, as dangerous, duplicitous and rapaciously greedy. Ntangaare points out that either portrayal is of little use to 'real' women. Dogbe's article looks at women and theatre for development in Ghana, an area of theatre work one might think would be especially gender-sensitive. However, the writer argues that even here the complexities of women's lives are seldom taken into account by play-makers, and that in performance the women characters tend to be relatively silent and passive, without agency over their own lives.

The two remaining essays, from Eritrea (Matzke) and Ghana (Sutherland-Addy), are fascinating investigations/interviews with women performers covering a period from the 1940s to the present day. These essays provide unique insights from an older generation into how women have seen themselves as performers, how they lived and loved their work, and their struggles against an often censorious outside world.

It should be noted that nomenclature in the whole area of African performance remains fluid. I prefer to most often refer to theatre as an inclusive term which can embrace more than literary drama, and performance when I seek to describe live art which includes the widest range of theatrical activity, but readers of this volume will see references to a whole range of terms: traditional performance, populist theatre, drama, concert, theatre for development, classical African theatre, etc. I have in no way sought to smooth out these terminologies. I think the articles give enough explanation for the reader to plot a route through the book, and it is part of the dynamic and diverse heritage of this discipline that the naming of forms remains part of the debate about just what makes up the world of African theatre.

Finally, besides our *Noticeboard* and *Book Reviews* sections which describe much recent work in the area of African Theatre, we are delighted to publish Fatima Dike's revised version of *Glass House*. This play examines inter-racial relationships between women in South Africa, and is prefaced by a short introduction from Marcia Blumberg.

AFRICAN LITERATURE TODAY
James Currey Publishers & Africa World Press

After more than 30 years Eldred Durosimi Jones is retiring from the editorship of *African Literature Today*. Eldred & Marjorie Jones tell the story of their involvement with ALT in the last volume to be edited by them:
ALT 23 *South & Southern Africa*

The announcement that Ernest N. Emenyonu has taken on the editorship has been widely welcomed:
'A very good omen for African Literature' – Wole Soyinka
'It is a most appropriate and logical development, and a very happy event for African literature.' – Chinua Achebe
'African Literature Today is part of the tradition from the Alan Hill, Keith Sambrook & James Currey days...Eldred performed wonders for African literature & literary scholarship with it...I cannot think of a better successor to him than Ernest Emenyonu...the time has come for us to do a Nigerian edition.' – Aigboje Higo, Heinemann Nigeria

Editor: Ernest N. Emenyonu
Assistant Editor: Patricia T. Emenyonu
Associate Editors: Simon Gikandi, Francis Imbuga, Nnadozie Inyama, Emmanuel Ngara, Charles Nnolim, Ato Quayson, Nana Wilson-Tagoe
Reviews Editor: James Gibbs

CONTRIBUTIONS ARE INVITED FOR FORTHCOMING TITLES
ALT 24 *New Women's Writing in African Literature*
ALT 25 *New Directions in African Literature*
ALT 26 *War in African Literature*
ALT 27 *New Novels in African Literature*

Articles should not exceed 5,000 words and should be submitted double-spaced on hard copy and disk to:
Ernest N. Emenyonu, Department of English
St Augustine's College, 1315 Oakwood Avenue
Raleigh, NC 27610-2298, USA
email: eemenyonu@hotmail.com

Books for review and review material to:
James Gibbs, 8 Victoria Square, Bristol BS8 4ET
email: james.gibbs@uwe.ac.uk

BACKLIST TITLES ALSO AVAILABLE
ALT 1-4 Omnibus edition
ALT 9 Africa, America & the Caribbean
ALT 10 Prospect & Retrospect
ALT 13 Recent Trends in the Novel
ALT 14 Women in African Literature
ALT 16 Oral & Written Poetry in African Literature
ALT 18 Orature in African Literature
ALT 19 Critical Theory & African Literature
ALT 20 New Trends & Generations
ALT 21 Childhood in African Literature
ALT 22 Exile & African Literature

James Currey Publishers 73 Botley Rd, Oxford OX2 0BS, UK   www.jamescurrey.co.uk
Africa World Press PO Box 1892, Trenton, NJ 08607, USA   www.africanworld.com

'I Will Not Cry'
Women's theatre in the Algerian diaspora

LAURA CHAKRAVARTY BOX

In our country, at the present moment, a woman writer is worth her weight in gunpowder.

Kateb Yacine, 1979 (Tahon 1992: 39)

The phenomenon of Algerian women writing for the theatre is a recent one, and women's participation as actors in Western-style productions since the turn of the century has been, and continues to be, fraught with difficulty. This is true of the Maghreb in general, where the idea and some of the practical aspects of women performing in public clash with deeply rooted social and religious convictions which believe a woman's proper sphere to be the home. There are very few Maghrebian women stage directors, and denial of women's theatrical accomplishments in the region runs high, particularly with regard to play-wrights. Indeed, one highly placed official of a government theatre in Morocco said to me that the women of his country, with the exception of one univer-sity-educated playwright, are writing nothing of consequence. He is quite wrong, but proving it is an uphill struggle. Publishing houses in the Maghreb favour francophone works over arabophone or tamazightophone[1] works, male over female authors, and novels and poetry over plays.

Women have been active participants in indigenous forms of Maghrebian performance, such as dance and storytelling, for centuries. Space does not permit a discussion of whether or not these forms constitute theatre, or are, as some scholars have claimed, proto-theatrical.[2] What can be asserted here is that women have gradually taken their place in the modern theatres of the region as actors, troupe leaders, directors and playwrights during the period following independence from the colonial power of France. Of all women playwrights in the region Algerians have produced the most plays, particularly if the works of the prolific, Algerian-born, French philosopher, Hélène Cixous, are included in the count. Ironically, they have not written at home, but in the European diaspora. Algerians in the European diaspora are also more active in creating performance art, one-woman shows and collage texts then their Moroccan and Tunisian sisters. Algeria's revolution was the most intense of the three Maghrebian independence wars, and the cultural dislocation experienced by

3

the native Algerian intelligentsia under colonialism, and the nationalist fervour this created, produced an atmosphere in which certain highly educated women, such as novelist-playwrights Assia Djebar and Myriam Ben, had difficulty finding a place in their newly independent society. From the perspective of Western feminism, at least, the war failed Algerian women in general. In its aftermath revolutionary women, who had moved into the public sphere during the war, were encouraged to return to their homes to provide a model of idealised Algerian womanhood befitting the government's nationalist vision of an Arabised, Islamic republic. Many were denied veterans' benefits, their role in the war having been deemed supportive rather than active, despite the fact that some *moujahadites* [female freedom fighters] carried and smuggled arms, were captured, tortured and killed alongside their brethren, and were subjected to a form of torture that the men escaped: rape.

This atmosphere, so hostile to their efforts, forced women artists into a fierce introspection that continues to yield a rich body of work. Djebar, whose play *Rouge l'aube* (1969, written in 1960), the first Maghrebian play to have a woman author, started a small but significant movement of theatrical aspiration. In the 1970s and 1980s women took an active role as actors in the national and municipal theatres of Algeria, which flourished until December of 1991 when the fundamentalist Front Islamique de la Salvation (FIS) won a national democratic election that was subsequently overturned by the FLN (Front de la Libération Nationale). In response, the FIS launched a period of civil unrest, marked by assassinations of journalists, artists, feminists and intellectuals that has caused most of Algeria's artists, particularly women, to flee the country. The FIS, the Groupe Islamique Armée (GIA), and other fundamentalist organisations have engaged the FLN in a bloody civil war, much of it on or through the bodies of women. Despite the efforts of Abdelaziz Bouteflika, Algeria's current president, to make peace, the situation remains unstable at the time of writing.

One would think that, given this chronology, Algerian women playwrights would have steadily increased their production of plays during the 1970s and 1980s, and that the 1990s would have seen a decrease in their artistic output. The reality is somewhat different. It seems that even in peacetime Algeria has not been a congenial place for women to write, to see their plays produced, and to get them published. Only Assia Djebar's *Rouge l'aube* was published in Algeria, and it was not written there but in Morocco. Moreover, its production history was so scarred by post-war politics that Djebar never wrote another play. Myriam Ben wrote plays just after the War for Independence, but did so while she was in France. Cixous and Denise Bonal, also a French author born in Algeria, began their theatrical careers in France during the 1970s. The *beur*[3] movement in France produced a few plays by women in the 1980s, most notably by Nacèra Bouabdallah of Port-du-Bouc, while at about the same time native Algerian expatriates Fatima Gallaire and Fatiha Berezak became active in Paris. It was not until the outbreak of violence in 1992, however, that Algerian women in Europe began to write plays in significant quantity, this time not as expatriates but as exiles.

With this outpouring of work-in-exile has come an opportunity to identify important authors, areas of concern and thematic patterns within the body of Algerian women's dramatic literature. These patterns may be observed by examining the work of several authors as they propose transformations in their native society, Algeria, and in the European world by which they were formerly colonised and in which they now live.

Assia Djebar

Rouge l'aube is the only play that Assia Djebar has written, although she mentioned that she was thinking about writing radio plays when I met her in 1997. Djebar is known in the US – where she currently holds an academic post – and Europe as a writer of novels. Djebar, whose given name is Fatima-Zohra Imalayène, was born in 1936 in Cherchell, Algeria, a place she speaks of as 'a lost Eden'. A brilliant student, she was the first Algerian woman to gain admission to the prestigious École Normale Supérieure in Sèvres in 1955. When she began to write, her fiancé, Walid Carn, suggested the pseudonym by which the world now knows her. She wanted to hide from her parents the fact that she was writing novels (Déjeux 1994: 23; Djebar 1990b: 84, 89; Ripault 1985: n.p.). Djebar produced her first novel, *La Soif*, in 1957. Her compatriots in the FLN considered the story, about the troubled relationship between two women, too personal a work to serve the nationalist cause. They also disliked her second novel, *Les Impatiens*, written in 1958. Their scorn notwithstanding, she was the only Algerian woman writing during the war (Accad 1978: 33, 40; Tahon 1992: 40–41).

In 1955, as Algeria entered its independence war, the FLN formed its own theatre troupe. It operated in Paris from 1955 until 1958, and then moved to newly independent Tunis under the direction of Mustapha Kateb. From there, it toured its revolutionary plays to Libya, the People's Republic of China, The Soviet Union, Morocco and Iraq, where the troupe was playing when it learned that Algeria had won independence in 1962 (Tomiche 1993: 141). Djebar and Carn moved to Tunis to join the FLN in its work. Unfortunately, women in the FLN offices were only for ornamental purposes, tokens for the international press, so there was not much for Djebar to do. She went to work on *El-Moudjahid*, the FLN news organ, with Frantz Fanon. She was forced to censor her writing, refraining from acting on her feminist sensibilities and conforming to the FLN's image of the politically committed woman – that is to say, one who would put the interests of the movement ahead of her own. This engagement lasted a year, after which the couple moved to Rabat, where Djebar taught at the university until the end of the war in 1962 (Gardenal 1987: n.p.; Bernhardt 2000; Déjeux 1984: 10; Tahon 1992: 45).

It was in their Rabat period, still under the influence of the FLN, that Djebar and Carn created *Rouge l'aube*. The socialist wing of the FLN refused to accept the notion that art could be apolitical; performances had to be adequately executed, but imposing standards to do with aesthetics was considered a luxury. After the war two types of Algerian theatre were juxtaposed in tension with each other: theatre inspired by and using traditional Maghrebian performance forms, and documentary theatre, which partook of the socialist realism imposed by FLN ministry directives (Salhi 1998: 70-71). *Rouge l'aube*, written during the war, is significant for its attempt to embody both ideas of theatre. This perhaps reflects its dual authorship, but it is not possible to know which impulse belongs to which author, or whether they tried to bridge the gap between the two styles. *Rouge l'aube* employs a traditional *hakawati* [storyteller] device, but also engages in didactic discussion of social and political problems.

Rouge l'aube represented Algeria in the theatrical presentations at the First Pan-African Cultural Festival in 1969. Carn designed the production, an Arabic translation which Mustapha Kateb directed (Déjeux 1984: 11; Wake 1995: 399). Jean Déjeux states that Assia Djebar disagreed with the adaptation completely, although he does not say why (Déjeux 1984: 11). Perhaps the subsequent production of the piece on Algerian radio in 1970 gives a clue, since it cut all references to women's participation in the liberation struggle (van Houwelingen 1985: 109). If the radio and the Cultural Festival used the same text, Djebar was no doubt disappointed and angry.

Djebar's contribution to Algerian theatre was to place women on the stage as agents of the revolution for the first time. Although she made no further efforts at writing dramatic literature she went on to become an internationally famous film-maker and novelist. She had this to say about the perception that women who write are dangerous:

> The danger is certainly there: the woman who can write, that woman risks experimenting with a strange power, the power to be a woman by other means than bearing children … . After all, if Sheherazade had not told stories until dawn, but had written, would she have killed the sultan? (Djebar 1990a: 70)

Dividing her time between France and the US, Djebar fiercely refuses to mourn for her lost Algeria, rejecting the position of the passive observer:

> That's precisely what we ask of women in our country, of those who are gifted with words and eloquence: to be criers, to carry a certain level of lyricism to misfortune and disaster. That is their traditional role: a word after the disaster. I don't want to bend to that. No, I will not cry for my friends who have died on Algerian soil. (Van Renterghen 1995: 12)

Myriam Ben

Ben was a more active participant in the independence war than Djebar. Born Myriam Louise Ben-Haïm in 1928 in Algiers and 'christened' Marylise in the colonial records, she is the oldest Algerian woman to have written a play, although not the first to do so. Ben is the granddaughter of an Arabo-Andalusian musician who kept the key to the family's ancestral house in Spain in an ebony coffer between copies of the Bible and the Quran. The family was expelled from Spain during the fifteenth-century reign of Isabella and

Ferdinand, a tragic period for Jews and Muslims. On her mother's side, she is descended from the tribe of Ben Mochi, Amazigh converts to Judaism who fled from Christian persecution in their native Constantine to found the city of Aïn Beïda, where some, but not all, became Muslims. Her family was proud of its multiple heritage, and she was raised in an atmosphere of tolerance. This idyll ended at the age of five, when she was sent to a French school where she was harassed for being a native and forced to forget her Arabic (Achour 1989: 11–14).

Because her colonial government identity card betrayed her family's Jewish origins, Ben was at risk throughout the Vichy occupation of Algeria during World War II. She was sent to the countryside to live with a Muslim family for the duration, and survived this ordeal only to find herself in danger from the French again in 1956, this time for her revolutionary activities. She became a rural teacher in 1952 – and obtained her pilot's licence in 1951 – but was forced to give up her career when the colonial police issued an order for her arrest. She was tried *in absentia* and condemned to twenty years forced labour, although the prosecution sought the death penalty. She was never caught, and spent the rest of the War for Independence in hiding. When Ben tried to get her job back after the war, her file had disappeared and a young employee of the Algerian Academy accused her of lying about her teaching diploma and her wartime activities. She threw an empty inkwell at him. It took her two years to re-establish her dossier and salary level, and at that point a bad case of asthma forced her to take leave of absence. She went to France, and did not return for ten years (Achour 1989: 26–40).

During her first sojourn in France, Ben continued her studies and began to write. Simone de Beauvoir helped her to get published. In the period from 1967 to 1974 she published a novel, wrote three plays, obtained a diploma in Russian and wrote a doctoral thesis on Soviet politics. She returned home in 1974, where she became the head of the Department of Languages and Human Sciences at the National Institute of Humanities in Boumerdes up until 1985. She published another novel in 1986. She also paints, and writes poetry and short stories (Achour 1989: 40–43). Although the plays she wrote in 1967 were not published at that time, she has recently begun to work in the theatre again. A volume of two plays, *Leïla*, written in 1967, and *Les Enfants du mendiant*, written in 1997, was published in 1998. Unfortunately, life has not permitted her to rest as she has aged – she went into exile after the violence in Algeria escalated in 1992. She has said of her writing:

> I have not sought to exalt an 'ideal conception' of man, in opposition to the less commendable actions of other characters. I have not made the choice between virtuous characters ... and the 'bad guys', the prevaricators, the traffickers whose actions are passed over by complacent literatures. I think the author's ethic requires him to refuse all complacent literatures, whatever the cost. (Achour 1989: 84)

Three of Ben's plays, *Leïla*, *Karim ou jusqu'à la fin de notre vie* (1967a), and *Promethée* (1967b), were written in response to the overthrow of Ahmed Ben Bella, independent Algeria's first president. *Promethée* is a re-telling of the Prometheus legend which functions as a thinly disguised criticism of the bloodless coup. The legendary, enchained fire-bringer stands for Ben Bella himself, and the metaphor is especially apt since Ben Bella was placed under house arrest by his successor, Colonel Houari Boumedienne (Favrod 2000). In Ben's play, Prometheus' son represents the young people of Algeria, who looked to Ben Bella to rebuild their country after independence. The son has allied himself with a priestess of the Earth-Mother sect in defiance of the Olympians who have imprisoned and tortured his father, and the couple are expecting a child. In this allegory the priestess represents the women of Algeria and their ignored potential to change the country. As the eagle tears out his liver, Prometheus watches his son march into the future, secure in the knowledge that his legacy of fire will not be extinguished. *Promethée* is allegorical, displacing the events of the coup to mythological Greece. The other two plays are less allusive, and although *Leïla* does not admit to being set in Algeria, the disguise is fairly thin. One must remember that after the coup, Myriam Ben returned to Algeria, and had to live under its government for many years. Openly criticising Boumedienne's faction of the FLN would have been extremely dangerous, and while Ben was used to taking risks as a *moujahadite*, she was not foolhardy. *Karim* is a loosely structured 'prequel' to *Leïla*. It is set during the Algerian war, and uses some of the same characters as the latter piece, which was actually written first. In this way, Ben anchored the less overtly historical piece to its companion, letting anyone who knows both works realise her intent.

Karim is a short, straightforward play. The eponymous protagonist is a member of a revolutionary cell, which he supports from his father's farm in the countryside. His father is dead: killed, he believes, by the French. Leïla is his fiancée. He and his widowed mother are alone on their farm when the leader of his cell, Si Slim, arrives with his followers, Leïla among them, and announces that the farm is being appropriated to supply the revolutionary army. Karim considers this a great honour. While bringing his guests some tea, however, he overhears them say that they are the ones who executed his father as a traitor, after a hasty, secret trial. Moreover, Si Slim discovers a love letter Karim is writing to Leïla and abruptly informs him that Leïla is now his wife. As Karim is recovering from this shock, the leader and his party leave and, not realising that he has overheard their admission, they hand him a gun. Karim watches them leave and then lies to his mother, telling her that his father was killed in combat while committing acts of bravery. The play closes as Karim contemplates the gun. We are not sure whether he will use it on Si Slim, the French, or himself.

Leïla does not pick up directly where *Karim* leaves off. It is set in an unnamed kingdom, and Leïla is now the widowed sister-in-law of the king. In a move reminiscent of Shakespeare's Claudius, the king has killed his own brother, and now seeks to marry his brother's widow. Leïla knows that the king is a murderer but can do nothing. She seeks out an old friend, Omar, with whom she had fought in the revolution. Omar tells her not to worry, because he is about to overthrow the king. He offers to protect her, but also expresses his love for her, implying that she must reciprocate as a condition of his help. The king is indeed assassinated and Leïla returns to the palace. When Omar warns her that she will be arrested by his revolutionary comrades she denounces his methods and tells him that a new order will not result from his violence. The play ends with her arrest. In Ben's plays, Leïla stands for both the land over which the men are fighting and the female participants in the struggle. Her acceptance of the perfidious Si Slim in *Karim* demonstrates the *naïveté* with which many women approach revolutionary struggles. In the play which takes her name, she is sadder and wiser, and her ultimate refusal to form an alliance with the man at the top of the power chain is an exercise of agency, maturity and integrity.

As might be expected, *Les Enfants du mendiant* is a more mature work, written under very different circumstances. Ben, who was a visitor to France in 1967, is now exiled there. The early plays were a reaction to the post-war FLN party struggles of the 1960s, whereas *Enfants* is an antidote to the continuing attacks, in Algeria and the diaspora, against women who try to improve their status. Its major themes are literacy and the tacit complicity of women in violence against other women. The protagonist of *Enfants* is Meriem, a beggar's widow, who has struggled to become literate in adulthood. Her mother scorns this skill, and tries to burn one of her books. Meriem's response is to compare her mother to the colonial troops who burned the library of Algiers. As they fight a silhouetted scene in the background illustrates the history of book-burning through time, from the destroyed library at Alexandria to the censors of the modern era:

> For a few sheets of paper written in prison, to get them out of hell, the mother of Abd el Hamid and the wife of Bachir took the risk of being mowed down where they stood, and a complete chain of human beings was formed in order to print them, at the peril of their lives. Peasants hid Abd el Hamid's 'Journal of the March' in their homes. To write his testimony, 'The Question', the author owed a debt to the complicity of the entire cell-block where he was held.
>
> And that is how you, my mother, by throwing that book in the fire, have become like the inquisitors of all the countries and all the centuries. (Ben 1998a: 130)

Meriem's daughter has inherited her grandmother's capacity for cruelty against women. She forgets her debt to her mother's single parenthood as she enjoys her lucrative career as a lawyer and judge, and keeps silent at a trial at which a woman is convicted of adultery, while her male lover walks free. Meriem, who has hidden her husband's shameful occupation from her children during their youth, reveals it at last to teach her daughter some humility.

Latifa Ben Mansour

A more humorous argument for the importance of literacy amongst women is set out in Latifa Ben Mansour's *Trente-trois tours à son turban* (1997). Ben Mansour, one of the new playwrights of the Algerian diaspora, is a novelist, a member of the Linguistics faculty at the University of Paris III, and the author of two plays, the aforementioned satire and *Dounia* (1995). *Trente-trois tours* is a

Djeha⁴ play, a satire that takes on the hypocrisy of the religious establishment in Algeria. In this one-act work, Djeha plays the role of a false scholar whose swollen ego is represented by a turban which gets bigger and bigger as he becomes more and more certain of his ability to delude people. As a money-making scheme he sets up a Quranic school and fools everyone, parents and pupils alike, into believing that he is an academic and religious authority. His perfidy is exposed when a poor woman receives a letter from her husband who is working abroad. She begs Djeha to read the letter, and since he is illiterate he lies in order to escape exposure as a fraud and tells her that it is a notice that her husband has died. Distraught and unable to accept the harsh news, she shows the letter to a literate neighbour. He tells her that her husband is alive and well, and will be home soon bearing gifts. The people of the quarter, outraged by Djeha's duplicity, drive him out. At once an argument for literacy amongst women and a criticism of false authorities, religious and secular, *Trente-trois tours*' light touch and wicked humour make the play more effective in its argument than some of the more serious dramas produced in the Algerian diaspora.

Leïla Sebbar

Another formidable Algerian woman of letters, Leïla Sebbar, is easily mistaken for a *beur* writer, a French writer of North African origin, because she often takes the situation of immigrant children as her theme (Hargreaves 1991: 5–6). In reality she was born and raised in Algeria. She is the child of a marriage between a French woman and an Algerian man, both of them teachers. Shortly after her birth in Aflou in 1944, the family moved to Hennaya, ten kilometres from Tlemcen. Her father, while not a militant, was locked up for several months by the French for showing solidarity with the nationalist cause. Sebbar went to graduate school in Aix-en-Provence and Paris, and eventually she moved to France permanently. A prolific novelist, she has been there for more than twenty years, teaching French literature in a high school, and writing for literary reviews and Radio France (Gaasch 1996: 165; Sebbar 1996: 165–7; Déjeux 1994: 27, 30).

Sebbar has said that she is interested in the condition of 'anyone, man or woman, who leaves a country and a language for the unknown' (Sebbar 1996: 168). She remarks that immigrant women rely on their children, especially daughters, to bridge the space between their native and adopted cultures:

> Invisible in the strange country, more invisible still than in their native land, Maghrebian women who follow their husbands to the country where they work are shut in physically and psychically, they don't know the city, the concrete .... Shut in alone, cut off from their extended family, from the community, from memory ... it is silence and night. ... Daughters ... are the Ones Who Traverse, the ones with the audacity and the liberty to come and go. (Sebbar 1996: 169)

Sebbar has also said that she writes because she feels abandoned by Algeria and because she has a nostalgia for her paternal language, Arabic, which she cannot speak.

> I write because I feel like I am in exile, an exile that displaces my body and soul, even if France is also my country, the country of my mother and my sons, the country of my mother tongue, my writing language, the French language, the only one I have mastered. (Sebbar 1996: 167)

Sebbar has written one play to date, *Les Yeux de ma mère* (1992), and true to form, it is about a young woman, daughter of an immigrant mother, lost in the space between her mother's world and her own.

The female protagonist of *Les Yeux de ma mère* is a rebel *beur* who suffers from cultural dislocation to the point of madness. She has been detained by the police, perhaps because she is a drug addict, and spends an hour spewing invective at her captors while telling stories of familial abuse and her silent sister's suicide. Her stories are extreme, and her certainty that her beautiful, blue-eyed mother will rescue her seems improbable. The police treat her as if she is crazy. In the end, however, her mother appears, exactly as described. This maternal materialisation forces the reader/viewer to confront the idea that the daughter's stories are true, and that the pathology resides in the protagonist's environment, not in her head.

Hawa Djabali

Since Hawa Djabali was born Eve Boucenna in Créteil, France in 1949, one might think she, too, belongs in the grouping of immigrant children of Algerian parents (Déjeux 1994: 48). Her life's trajectory, however, has been too complicated to make such categorisation easy. After Algeria's independence war, which she spent in France 'with an ear towards the radio to follow the news …', her family returned to Algeria and she experienced her parent's country directly for the first time. She found this 'return' to a place she had never known healing, and was immediately immersed in Algerian culture by a group of women who wanted to erase the influence that France had had on her (Djabali 1997a: 219). Djabali was encouraged in her artistic pursuits, and went to the National Conservatory to study theatre, dance and music. At the age of eighteen she began broadcasting on Algerian radio. A year later she married, moved to Constantine, and had three children. Djabali acted with an amateur theatre group in Constantine and started to write plays there, but her early pieces were considered too bold and violent to be presented by her company (Djabali 1997a: 220).

In 1983 Djabali published *Agave*, a novel that explored the philosophies of war and received much critical attention. She has written two screenplays and conducts research into comparative religion and oral storytelling traditions in various regions of Algeria. She has written twelve books for children, one in Arabic, and an historical novel set in Algiers during the Roman and Vandal eras, the manuscript of which was destroyed, against her wishes, in 1986. Since 1989 Djabali has been living in Belgium and working with the Arab Cultural Centre in Brussels. Her Belgian period has been a fruitful one for the theatre. She produced three plays in the 1990s: *Sa Naqba Imrou: Giligeamech ou celui qui a vu et touché le fond des choses* (1995); *Tamouz ou le manifeste de l'éxil: Cinq mille ans de la vie d'une femme* (1996); and in 1997, *Le Zajel maure du désir* (Djabali 1997b: 221–4).

She relies on her sensory memory and her powers of observation to aid her in creation:

> I record everything I can: I possess a formidable repertory of conversational snatches, of mimicry, of observations. I never know if a man had a moustache nor what dress I was wearing, but I can recall the taste of a sandstorm on my lips from twenty-five years ago, or the terrible smell of the city, yesterday, in the cold. (Djabali and Rezzoug 1997: 227)

Djabali's work is dedicated to writing the women who inhabit her:

> It lives, my writing, the lives of all the women who live in me. No possible distance, no platonic love: they have the smell of the earth; of the rotting old city; they have the smell of fear, they triumph in their laughter, in their defiance, in their survival. I carry them, their voices, inside my breast like the tradition of ancient music, so sure of itself that it can improvise the present. (Djabali and Rezzoug 1997: 228).

Djabali's *Tamouz* displaces the woes of Algeria's disenfranchised and embattled women onto Hagar, slave to Ibrahim's wife Sarah and mother of Islam's rescued sacrificial lamb, Ismail. *Tamouz* takes up the cry of 'the long feminine experience of those women who are Black, Arab, Berber, suppressed by religions and by powers...' (Djabali 1997a: 224). *Le Zajel maure du désir* illustrates the painful effects of revolution and independence on two lovers. The couple are separated by the War for Independence, she into exile, he into politics. The woman's memories of herself and the country she left are embodied in a dancer and a singer, respectively. These phantoms provide a counterpoint to the painful Paris reunion of the couple in the 1990s, during the Algerian civil strife. They try to be loving to each other, but their war-wounds are too deep to allow them any peace, and reconciliation proves impossible.

This introduction to the *femmes dramaturges* of the Algerian diaspora is of necessity brief. I have not, for example, mentioned the work of Fatima Gallaire who is perhaps the best known playwright in this category, for the very reason that she has already received considerable attention in the US and the UK. It is my intention to bring the work of other playwrights to a wider readership so that this body of words may be considered for what it is: a literary and theatrical movement. The plays discussed here are not academic exercises or theatrical indulgences. They address urgent issues. At the time of writing, all the playwrights whose work I have discussed are safe, but each time they write or perform they put their security and that of their families at risk. The texts mentioned in this article and the larger study from which it was taken suggest the beginnings of a radical future vision for Algeria, one which takes women into account as agents, rather than vehicles, of culture. The writers call for the safety, economic independence, enfranchisement and legitimisation of women. They are both evidence of, and a demand for, person-hood. They are also a warning: the societies of North Africa and the world at large cannot continue to ignore the needs, and indeed the very safety, of half their citizenry.

NOTES

1. Tamazight is the collective term designating the family of languages spoken by the Imazighen [sing. Amazigh]. The Imazighen, or 'free people,' sometimes called the Berbers, may be descended from the original inhabitants of Northern Africa, although their current self-identification is based on language use rather than race. Self-identified Imazighen may be Black-, White- or Brown-skinned, but they all speak some form of Tamazight, with different groups speaking dialects with various levels of mutual intelligibility. There are tamazightophones in Morocco, Algeria, Tunisia, Libya, Mauritania, Mali, Niger and the Canary Islands. Their numbers are dwindling under state pressure to assimilate into the arabophone cultures which surround them.
2. For an analysis of the discourse about the theatricality of traditional Maghrebian performance, please see Chapter Two of my dissertation: 'A Body of Words: Strategies of Resistance in the Dramatic Texts of North African Women', University of Hawai'i.
3. The word *beur*, like the word Chicano, has political overtones. It is an appellation derived from the phrase *berbers d'Europe*. *Beurs* are the children of North African immigrants to Europe. Not all of them are Imazighen, as the name suggests; rather, *beur* as a self-identification implies a certain politicised consciousness of marginalised status, whether the heritage is Amazigh or Arab. Not all French people of North African heritage self-identify as *beur*. Lately the term has become slightly pejorative, so scholars now hesitate to use it (Hargreaves 1996: 33; Bouraoui 1988: 223).
4. Djeha is a trickster figure, beloved of Arabs and Imazighen alike, known throughout the Levant, the Gulf, Egypt and Maghrebian North Africa. A staple of traditional folktales, he also appears regularly in the modern theatre of North Africa. Algerian Amazigh playwright Kateb Yacine used him as the touchstone for his dramaturgy and his troupe's performance style (Salhi 1998: 75–6). His play, *Poudre d'intelligence*, is composed of a series of Djeha stories (Baffet 1985: 146), and its central character, Puff-of-Smoke, is both Djeha and a *hakawati*.

BIBLIOGRAPHY

Accad, Évelyne, 1978, *Veil of Shame: The Role of Women in the Contemporary Fiction in North Africa and the Arab World* (Sherbrooke, Québec: Éditions Naaman).

Achour, Christiane Chaulet, 1989, *Myriam Ben* (Paris: Éditions l'Harmattan).

Baffet, Roselyne, 1985, *Tradition théâtrale et modernité en Algérie* (Paris: Éditions l'Harmattan).

Ben, Myriam, 1967a, 'Karim, ou jusqu'à la fin de notre vie' (unpublished manuscript, cited with the kind permission of M. Ben).

—— 1967b, 'Prométhée' (unpublished manuscript, cited with the kind permission of M. Ben).

—— 1998a, 'Les Enfants du mendiant', in M. Ben, '*Leïla*' suivi de '*Les Enfants du mendiant*' (Paris: Éditions l'Harmattan).

—— 1998b, 'Leïla', in M. Ben, '*Leïla*' suivi de '*Les Enfants du mendiant*' (Paris: Éditions l'Harmattan).

Ben Mansour, Latifa, 1995, *Dounia*.

—— 1997, 'Trente-trois tours à son turban', in *Breves d'ailleurs* (Paris: Actes Sud-Papiers).

Bernhardt, Jennifer, 2000, 'Assia Djebar' (http://www.emory.edu/ENGLISH/Bahri/Djebar.html, downloaded 24 February).

Bouraoui, Hédi, 1988, 'A New Trend in Maghrebian Culture: The Beurs and their Generation', *Maghreb Review* vol. 13, no. 3: 218–28.

Box, Laura Chakravarty, 2000, 'A Body of Words: Strategies of Resistance in the Dramatic Texts of North African Women' (PhD Diss., University of Hawai'i).

Déjeux, Jean, 1984, *Assia Djebar: Romanciere algérienne, cineaste arabe* (Sherbrook, Québec: Éditions Naaman).

—— 1994, *La Littérature féminine de langue française au Maghreb* (Paris: Éditions Karthala).

Djabali, Hawa, 1983, *Agave* (Paris: Publisud).

—— 1995, 'Sa Naqba Imrou: Giligeamech ou celui qui a vu et touché le fond des choses' (unpublished).

—— 1996, 'Tamouz ou le manifeste de l'éxil: Cinq mille ans de la vie d'une femme', excerpted in *Quinzaine de l'éxpression féminine de la culture arabe* (Brussels: Centre Culturel Arabe).

—— 1997a, 'Hawa Djabali: Création et Passion', interview with Christiane Chaulet Achour, *Algérie Littérature/Action* no. 15/16: 219–25.

—— 1997b, *Le Zajel maure du désir* (Brussels: Centre Culturel Arabe).

Djabali, Hawa and Rezzoug, Leïla, 1997, 'Entre urgence at création: Hawa Djabali et Leïla Rezzoug', interview in *Algérie Littérature/Action*, no. 15/16: 227–30.

Djebar, Assia, 1957, *La Soif* (Paris: R. Juillard).

—— 1958, *Les Impatiens* (Paris: R. Juillard).

—— 1990a, 'Entre parole et écriture', *Cahier d'études maghrébines*, no. 2: 68–70.

—— 1990b, 'Interview', with Michael Heller, in *Cahier d'études maghrébines*, no. 2: 84–90.

Djebar, Assia and Carn, Walid, 1969, *Rouge l'aube* (Algiers, SNED).

Favrod, Charles Henri, 2000, 'Ahmed Ben Bella: Président un peu prisonnier beaucoup exilé sans amertume' (http://www.archipress.org/bb/ts3favrod.htm#top, downloaded 6 July).

Gaasch, James (ed.), 1996, *Anthologie de la nouvelle maghrébine: Paroles d'auteurs* (Casablanca: Éditions EDDIF).

Gardenal, Philippe, 1987, 'Assia Djebar devoilée', *Libération*, no. 6: n.p.

Hargreaves, Alec G., 1991, *Voices from the North African Immigrant Community in France: Immigration and Identity in Beur Fiction* (Oxford: Berg Publishers).

—— 1996, 'Writers of Maghrebian Immigrant Origin in France: French, Francophone, Maghrebian or Beur?', in L. Ibnilfassi and N. Hitchcott (eds), *African Francophone Writing: a Critical Introduction* (Oxford: Berg Publishers).

Ripault, Ghislain, 1985, 'Il était une fois une fillette arabe…', *Le Matin*, 25 June: n.p.

Salhi, Kamal, 1998, 'Post-Colonial Theatre for Development in Algeria: Kateb Yacine's Early Experience', in K. Salhi (ed.), *African Theatre for Development: Art for Self-Determination* (Exeter: Intellect Books).

Sebbar, Leïla, 1992, 'Les Yeux de ma mère' (unpublished manuscript, cited with the kind permission of L. Sebbar and the Société des Auteurs et Compositeurs Dramatiques).

—— 1996, 'Interview,' with John Gaasch, in J. Gaasch (ed.), *Anthologie de la nouvelle maghrébine: Paroles d'auteurs* (Casablanca: Éditions EDDIF).

Tahon, Marie-Blanche, 1992, 'Women Novelists and Women in the Struggle for Algeria's National Liberation (1957–1980)', trans. Ruthmarie H. Mitsch, *Research in African Literatures* vol. 23, no. 2: 39–49.

Tomiche, Nada, 1993, *La Littérature Arabe contemporaine* (Paris: Éditions Maisonneuve et Larose).

van Houwelingen, Flora, 1985, 'Francophone Literature in North Africa', in M. Schipper (ed.), *Unheard Words: Women and Literature in Africa, the Arab World, Asia, the Caribbean, and Latin America* (London: Allison & Busby).

Van Renterghen, Marlon, 1995, 'Je ne pleurerai pas mes amis d'Algerie', *Le Monde*, 28 April: 12.

Wake, Clive, 1995, 'French-Speaking North Africa', in M. Banham (ed.), *The Cambridge Guide to Theatre* (Cambridge: Cambridge University Press).

Yacine, Kateb, 1959, *La Poudre d'intelligence*, in *Le Cercle des represaillés* (Paris: Editions du Seuil).

Challenging the Master
Resisting 'male' virtues of the ancient Egyptian goddess Isis in the theatre of Tawfiq al-Hakim & Nawal al-Sa'dawi

DINA AMIN

Egyptian playwrights, mostly men, have almost always catered to their pre-dominantly male audience. Unless the female roles depicted on stage are sacrificing mothers or highly venerated historical and/or religious figures, male dramatists have perpetually portrayed women as mindless, irrational, jealous, hysterical, materialistic and, at times, downright ridiculous.[1] Enjoyed by both men and women – who are unaware that the jokes are on them – those portraits are often rendered by way of comedy and in the spirit of entertainment. Although gender-conscious spectators have been offended by such portrayals, very few have taken it upon themselves to correct these recurrent patterns and women have, therefore, too often been both misrepresented and under-represented in Egyptian drama. Ironically the role women played in Egypt in the development of Egyptian theatre in general – whether as actresses, producers or patrons of the art – has constantly and consistently been praised and respected by the very voices that, by mistake or design, have misrepresented women on stage. This lack of equality between the sexes in terms of dramatic writing and stage-voice on the one hand, and fictional representation on the other, is indeed an issue that needs to be researched further in the Arab theatre; it will not, however, be the direct subject of this article.

In this study I provide a comparative view of two plays that have the same title and are based on the same myth of the ancient Egyptian goddess Isis.[2] The first was written in the late forties by the leading Egyptian littérateur, Tawfiq al-Hakim, and the second in the eighties by one of Egypt's most radical feminists, Nawal al-Sa'dawi. In my analysis I discuss the kind of 'masculine' values that have perpetually been used (by male dramatists) to assess the virtue and uniqueness of Isis. Those values which assume that power is gendered as masculine have influenced the broad conception of what constitute greatness, distinction and significance in aesthetic constructions. These masculine values have typically placed men at the centre of power and marginalised the essential qualities of female power. This male domination has rarely been questioned. In this study I juxtapose the work of one Egyptian feminist, al-Sa'dawi, with that of one of the most prominent Egyptian playwrights, al-Hakim. Generally speaking, al-Sa'dawi questions, indeed defies, the hegemony of male perception and

15

evaluation of the merit and virtue of women. In her play she defends the legacy of the goddess Isis from this male assessment of virtue. In my analysis of the two plays I focus on al-Sa'dawi's position on patriarchy on the one hand, and her aesthetic reconstruction of the myth on the other. I argue that al-Hakim emphasises Isis's human qualities, while al-Sa'dawi portrays her dual nature as both goddess and woman. Nawal al-Sa'dawi portrays Isis as an unconquerable larger-than-life goddess and human being, who is capable of taking on, by herself, a fight with both men and gods.[3]

In writing her version of the famous myth of Isis, in 1981, al-Sa'dawi does not only attempt to re-write mythology, she also vies with one of the Arab world's greatest dramatists, who is also known for his blatant misogyny. In defence of her own feminist reading of history and mythology, al-Sa'dawi says that fiction and historical accounts of Isis never valued her for herself, she was – and continues to be – only seen by predominantly male scholarship and artistic approaches as Osiris's wife and Horus's mother. Her virtue is, therefore, depicted as a 'male-virtue' since she is solely praised for her loyalty and love for her husband and son, irrespective of her merit as a goddess of wisdom, reason, healing and will.[4] In her play *Isis*, al-Sa'dawi redeems Isis's image as a powerful goddess equal to the male gods in stature and power. In doing so, al-Sa'dawi follows

> ... one project of feminist theory [which] is to look critically at traditional patriarchal culture. This entails a critique of the patriarchal canon and the hegemony of male artists.[5]

In challenging the predominant view of Isis as only a loyal wife and protective mother, al-Sa'dawi defies more than just tradition; she consciously meets the master of Arabic drama head-on. In her preface to the play, al-Sa'dawi proclaims that, '... al-Hakim's patriarchal philosophy, which has no room for a woman except as a shadow of her husband, does not allow him to perceive the multifarious sides to Isis's character'.[6] Therefore her daring project of overturning his portrait of the goddess has two aspects: a challenge to the popular and conventional views of Isis, and an audacious comparison of dramatic style with al-Hakim's. Al-Hakim's stature as a pioneer of Arabic drama would have been enough to intimidate many from such a task, but, known for her confidence, al-Sa'dawi contests the master's portrayal of the goddess on his own turf, drama. In *Men, Women, and God(s)*, Fedwa Matli-Douglas discusses al-Sa'dawi's *Isis* vis-à-vis Tawfiq al-Hakim's, arguing that the former has created an engaging dialectic discourse between both plays by '... distance[ing] herself from her predecessor and rewrit[ing] what she perceives to be his misogynist interpretation of the ancient Egyptian goddess'.[7]

It is important to point out that while al-Sa'dawi succeeds in instigating many provocative ideas and in challenging traditional views regarding women's place in political and social history, she does not achieve the same level of success in constructing her play. Al-Sa'dawi's dramatic structure comes through as weak, her dialogue lacks conciseness and the play, as a whole, is without a dramatic arch to reveal the development of the action. Furthermore, in super-imposing gruesome scenes of rape, circumcision and castration, etc., to support her radical views of the results of male domination, the play becomes virtually unstageable. In *The Voices of Silence*, Nehad Selaiha comments on the play saying, '[it] is perhaps unperformable – not on account of its structural faults (worse texts have been performed), but on account of its iconoclastic message and radical views ... Its dauntless questioning and intellectual audacity remain unparalleled in all the writing by Egyptian women.'[8] In defence of her own feminist dramatic writing and 'reading' of history and popular culture, Nawal al-Sa'dawi declares:

> This play, which I am presenting now, is the Egyptian Isis as I understand her from history. It is the right of every writer and author to interpret history according to her/his rationale and to rewrite it anew. Myths and historical legends do not belong to anyone and do not have one uniform reading. They remain a fertile source of inspiration for thinking minds. History belongs to everyone who possesses an amount of imagination, brains and a genuine curiosity to know the truth. Authors own the right to interpret legends within the framework of established facts.[9]

In her attempt at rewriting the legend of Isis and Osiris, Nawal al-Sa'dawi has also taken up some of her general concerns on the subject of injustice. Although in writing the play she claims to be correcting a faulty (male) percep-tion imposed on the legacy of Isis, she also brings in issues of slavery, female genital mutilation, rape and castration of male slaves who were disfigured in order to guard harems. This weighty grouping of issues more often than not diffuses al-Sa'dawi's main message and leaves the reader and/or spectator bewildered. However, these disturbing aspects of the play have an Artaudian effect, they produce a sense of cruelty and oppression in the world of the play and beyond, which is no doubt al-Sa'dawi's intention.[10] One cannot help comparing the grisly scenes in *Isis* to Jacobean drama, which became famous for its blatant violence.[11] As the play is poignant in its message but flawed in its structure, perhaps al-Sa'dawi's main mistake was in choosing the dramatic medium itself, as *Isis* is her first attempt at writing for the stage.

Conversely, Tawfiq al-Hakim (1898-1986) is one of the greatest literary icons in Egypt and the Arab world. Many consider him the founder of modern Egyptian drama. He was born in Alexandria to a middle class family. As a child he was interested in the Arab tradition of oral poetry recitations and story-telling, and during his high school years he joined a number of musical theatre troupes in Alexandria. His family sent him to France to obtain a doctoral degree in law. Instead, he spent his time in that country studying the western theatre tradition. On returning to Egypt he took up writing for the stage. His dearest wish was to establish a modern Egyptian dramatic tradition based on western notions of the unity of space, time and action. He spent five decades of his life trying to enrich the Arab dramatic tradition, and enrich it he surely did.

Even though al-Hakim wrote numerous short stories, novels, poems, auto-biographies and essays, he is chiefly known for his dramatic writing. Having written over seventy plays of exceptional variety, he has experimented with dramatic form and offered plays in a range of dramatic styles. He also presents a variety of dramatic themes, which he categorises as theatre of ideas, theatre of social themes, theatre of the absurd, etc. Throughout his life and after his death, al-Hakim was repeatedly described as artistic, cynical and anxious; he was known to be a devout lover of modern art and music, and curious about anything new or unfamiliar. He has frequently been labeled misogynistic and miserly. In spite of the depth of his contemplative nature, which is reflected in many of his short stories and plays, al-Hakim had a subtle sense of humour that reflected his love of scrutinising human follies and idiosyncrasies.

While al-Hakim devoted his life to the establishment of an Egyptian dramatic heritage, Nawal al-Sa'dawi continues hers in defence of women's rights and freedom. Both a medical doctor and radical feminist, al-Sa'dawi has raised more opposition and controversy than appreciation in her native Egypt. Outside Egypt her fiction and social commentaries are, as Fedwa Matli-Douglas puts it, 'devoured … with seeming insatiability', by scholars of cultural and women's studies.[12] As a result of her audacity and daring in both her fiction and non-fiction writing, al-Sa'dawi was removed from her post as Director of Health Education in the Egyptian Ministry of Health in 1972, and was briefly imprisoned in 1981 by order of Egyptian president Anwar al-Sadat. This incarceration affected her profoundly; after her release she wrote an autobiography based on that experience entitled *Memoirs from the Women's Prison*.[13]

Nawal al-Sa'dawi's inner rebelliousness and rage regarding social and gender injustice, exacerbated by her work as a practising psychiatrist which gives her constant access to people's troubles, have made her embrace women's causes with a vehemence that has often rebounded against her as she lashes out at figures of authority and power. However, she is not one to bow out of a good fight nor to be intimidated by it. Her adversarial spirit is evident in *Isis* as she provides a 'feminist' reading of the legend of the goddess. In doing so she engages in a (feminist) debate with the master of Egyptian drama over perceptions of Isis. Thus, she places herself in the same situation as Isis in the play, where Isis (al-Sa'dawi) battles with the male hegemony of Ra and Seth (al-Hakim).

Before discussing two different approaches in viewing Isis's legacy, it is necessary to provide a concise account of the original myth. In 'Osiris and Isis: An Egyptian Narrative of Re-Creation', Egyptologist Ann Macy Roth provides a fine account of the myth which she has compiled and organised from the different versions available.[14] She explains that, 'Isis and Osiris were … among the nine gods who, according to one Egyptian creation myth, were the first beings to appear out of the chaotic undifferentiated primeval waters that filled the universe before its creation.'[15] Isis and Osiris were not only the most popular lovers in ancient Egyptian mythology, they were also brother and sister. Their parents were Geb (the god of the earth) and Nut (the goddess of the sky). They had two other siblings, who married each other but had no offspring, namely Seth (the eldest of the four children) and Nephthys.

Geb bequeathed the earth (Egypt) to both of his sons, giving the red land of the desert to Seth and the black land of the Nile Valley to Osiris. Known for his violence and disruption, Seth was jealous of his brother. Osiris, on the other hand, was absorbed by his responsibilities as a god and king of the land as he, 'taught Egyptians the arts of agriculture, and the domestication of both plants and animals. And while Osiris travelled around his domain, his wife Isis ruled Egypt as his deputy. His sister was his protector, she who drives off the enemies.'[16] Seth's hatred for Osiris had deeper roots than ambition. He was very much in love with Isis and had continuously failed to make her reciprocate.

To gain total control of the land, Seth conspired to have his brother Osiris killed. He arranged that an elaborate coffin be made, then tricked Osiris to sleep in it for fun. Once Osiris was inside Seth's followers sealed the coffin and threw it into the Nile.

When Isis learnt of the crime she looked for her husband throughout the country. She finally found the coffin adrift by the shore at Byblos on the Mediterranean Sea. She pulled it on land and stayed next to the coffin in order to guard it and remain close to her husband's body. On a hunting trip Seth found the coffin. To make sure that the body was no longer retrievable he cut his brother's body into fourteen pieces which he then distributed around the country thinking that it would be impossible for Isis to recover them. Nevertheless, she managed to collect thirteen pieces; all except for Osiris's sexual organ, which legend has it was eaten by the fish of the Nile. When she had made her husband's body whole again, she turned herself into a bird and hovered above him. She then embraced him and became pregnant with their son Horus. In a 'Hymn to Osiris', the events of Horus's conception are described as follows:

> Great Isis, who protected her brother
> Who searched for him without tiring
> Who wandered the land mourning for him,
> And never rested until she found him.
> She sheltered him with her feathers
> And gave him new breath with the beating of her wings.
> She rejoiced and joined herself with her brother,
> Raising the tiredness of that Weary One.
> She received the seed and gave birth to his heir,
> Rearing him alone in solitude, in an unknown place.
> And she brought him, when his arm was strong
> To the broad hall of Geb.[17]

Hiding Horus in the marshes of the Nile for many years, Isis brought her son up on her own. When he came of age she presented him to the Council of the Gods and requested that he inherit his father's throne. Seth vehemently denied the request, and he and Horus fought over the throne for eight years. Finally the Council consulted with Osiris in his underworld residence. Osiris threatened to send demons to destroy them if the Council did not give the throne to his son. In the face of such a threat Seth conceded to Horus and retreated to the sky, 'where his violence can be heard as thunder'.[18]

In her account of the original myth, Ann Macy Roth refers to the importance of Isis as a religious figure, not only to ancient Egyptians but also to the Greek and Roman invaders of Egypt in later periods. She expresses the opinion that Isis's influence extended up until the days of early Christianity, as many Christians drew parallels between the Virgin Mary and Isis. Roth declares that

> [Isis] is important in many Egyptian myths and stories, and is always portrayed as an intelligent, powerful woman. Time and time again she uses her wits and her magical powers (which were based on her knowledge and her ability to manipulate language) to deceive and overcome her enemies. Her victories were never for herself, however, but were always won for her helpless dependents, either her absent or murdered husband Osiris or her infant son Horus.
>
> This strong and loving goddess was much beloved by the Egyptians, particularly in later periods. At the end of the pharaonic state, when the Romans ruled the lands surrounding the Mediterranean Sea, the cult of Isis became a wildly popular mystery religion, and she was worshipped along with her husband in the farthest corners of the Roman Empire. It has even been suggested that the well-loved figure of the persecuted young mother nurturing and protecting her infant son was compared by early Christians with Mary, mother of Jesus, and that the popularity of Isis thus helped facilitate the acceptance of Christianity in the Roman world.[19]

It is clear from this account that Isis has always been looked at as a larger-than-life human figure and as an exceptional deity. Her human qualities are expressed in her love and sacrifices for both husband and son; her superhuman traits are shown in her single-handed challenge to the strongest (male) deities and in her power to recreate life (Horus) from death (Osiris).

The myth of Isis and Osiris is a love story where love conquers all. It is also a story about the eternal battle between good and evil; the famous couple being representatives of everything good and virtuous, and Seth personifying evil. The combination of these two popular themes, of romance and political intrigue, is possibly what made the myth survive at the popular as well as the scholarly level. On the popular level it has circulated orally for centuries as a saga depicting a heroic dimension of love, sacrifice, deception and triumph. Roth reports that

> because the ability to read and write was not very widespread, the oral traditions of story-telling and myth-making almost certainly continued to flourish alongside the elite literature of the royal court. Many of the stories and myths that were eventually written down by the elite scribes probably had their birth and development in this oral tradition. These stories were told and retold in villages and city streets by ordinary Egyptians, who found in them explanations for the events and processes of earthly life and who, through them, became familiar with the characteristics and power of their gods.[20]

On the literary level the Isis myth has been reconstructed in such artistic forms as drama, poetry, novel and dance. The myth embodies the essential cycle of life and death, as Osiris is the God of the underworld and death, while Isis is the Goddess of healing, and hence life. Their love symbolises a joyous embrace between present and future, transience and eternity; their union (represented in their offspring, Horus) is essential for the maintenance of humanity itself, for without death there can be no rebirth and without birth there will be no notion of death. On this subject Roth comments that

> Many of these stories were concerned with death and the afterlife that followed it, a very important subject to the Egyptians, since they devoted a great proportion of their resources to building and furnishing their tombs. The Great Pyramid of King Khufu at Giza (dating from about 2500 B.C.) and the sumptuous treasures found in the tomb of King Tutankhamun (about 1325 B.C.) are only two examples of this kind of expenditure. Given this cultural preoccupation with death, it is not surprising that one of the major Egyptian myths was the tale of Osiris, god of the realm of the dead, and his loyal consort, Isis.[21]

Horus, who is born after his father's death, continues to fight evil and conquers it by prevailing over his uncle and reclaiming Osiris's earthly and heavenly kingdoms. From this point of view Horus is regarded as the salvation of humanity from annihilation for, 'the myth tells us that ... Horus was conceived after [Osiris's] death, so that life sprang anew from death, just as the (apparently) dead seeds of wheat are buried in the ground and then sprout and bring forth new life ... Osiris and Horus are thus not simply father and son, but also represent different stages in the existence of the same person.'[22] Today, the shrines of the three gods, Isis, Osiris and Horus, stand among the ruins of the temple at Abydos. Their place in ancient Egyptian history is more than just as rulers or gods; they form a unique trinity, the only one known to include a woman.

The myth contains another important element that makes it particularly attractive for fiction writers. The gender roles of Isis and Osiris are not played out in the traditional manner. During his life Osiris spent his time inventing tools for Egyptians to advance their agricultural skills and productivity, while his wife acted as the 'protector' of their domain. Customarily, protection has always been the business of male members of the family; they are the gender that is more known for its violent and aggressive nature than women. Women's role has typically been to raise children and keep house. In this legend, however, Isis is both the aggressive protector and patient homemaker. Moreover, Isis is a model of single-parenthood. She takes on her duties as the only parent of Horus with grace, courage and self-sufficiency. When looked at from a traditional perspective, Isis appears to be an 'exceptional' woman, but from a feminist one, she stands out as a role model and a quintessentially independent woman who refuses to be exploited by men.

From this viewpoint one could argue that the difference between al-Sa'dawi's dramatic treatment of the myth and that of al-Hakim is gender-based. While al-Hakim perpetuates the traditional (male) view of Isis as the good wife who sacrifices her own comfort and status as queen/goddess in order to reconstruct the fractured image of her husband/king/god, al-Sa'dawi overturns this popular self-sacrificial image in favour of a feminist approach in which she portrays Isis as a figure of power with a personal agenda. While both plays are entitled *Isis*, al-Hakim's is really about Osiris, whereas al-Sa'dawi focuses strongly on the struggles of Isis and creates a larger-than-life dramatic persona for the Egyptian goddess.

Al-Hakim's play, although artistically superior to al-Sa'dawi's, is more traditionally constructed. It is basically a struggle between good and evil in three acts, and unlike its counterpart it presents no controversial issues or shocking scenes. In this play, al-Hakim pays homage to the legendary Isis, portraying her as a paragon of strength and viewing her as a powerful and admirable 'woman'. Yet the play's focus is essentially on Osiris. This is a capital offence to a radical feminist such as Nawal al-Sa'dawi as it typifies a 'male' view of women and goddesses. In her opinion, Isis should be first and foremost idolized for her remarkable qualities, not on account of her actions as a wife. Isis's deeds and accomplishments should not be regarded as 'duty', but as by-products of her good judgment as a 'goddess' of wisdom and healing. According to al-Hakim, Isis's struggle is confined to her attempts, as a woman, to give support to Osiris. Isis's principal sense of loss, in al-Sa'dawi's version, is that she is deprived of her most cherished role; helping her dependants and worshippers. In al-Hakim's play, Isis's role is essentially to preserve Osiris in order for him to continue generating Good. She is an agent in the fulfilment of his role, but there is no mention of what her own role might be.

Although al-Hakim remains loyal to the original myth, he humanises the characters of both Isis and Osiris. He characterizes them more as a human royal couple than as god and goddess with supreme abilities. This portrayal leaves one with the question why reconstruct a myth at all if all the characters and events are presented on the level of realism? This is a weakness in al-Hakim's version of the legend, for in rewriting the myth for the stage he has reduced it to a simple story.

In al-Hakim's play Osiris is portrayed as an inventor; his inventions bring prosperity to his people. However, while focusing on developing agricultural tools and teaching farmers to boost their production he neglects his kingdom, leaving an opportunity for his evil brother to usurp the throne:

> **Mustat** Only his (Osiris's) knowledge and creativity have yielded prosperity to the country. If it weren't for him, farmers could not farm; indeed, our very civilization would not be ... but what we cannot deny either is the fact that he has left the business of governing to his sly conniving brother. Seth has formed a circle of schemers around him, and has conspired with the village Headmen to steal the population.[23]

Al-Hakim's Osiris is obviously not a politician; rather he is a life force to his people by virtue of his creativity and deep compassion. There is nothing superhuman about his abilities or stamina. He is a democratic role model and popular figure who wants to live in peace and transcend political machination. Seth is also presented as a human figure, a vindictive ruler, not an all-powerful god whose fury could be ruinous to all. In contrast, al-Sa'dawi maintains the aura of the myth by presenting the main characters as essentially gods, Osiris represents the underworld, Seth, malevolence and Isis, life, wisdom and healing.

One major difference between al-Hakim's play and the original myth is the relationship between the three siblings. There is no mention in his *Isis* that Isis, Osiris and Seth are siblings, possibly because of al-Hakim's fear that his play could be thought of as promoting incest. Seth and Osiris are depicted as brothers, Isis as the wife of the latter. Seth always refers to her as 'Osiris's wife', not as sister nor as the object of his desire. In fact his love for Isis is barely mentioned. Without the concept of jealousy or male rivalry for the attentions of the same woman the central conflict is less complex than that of the original myth or of al-Sa'dawi's play. Seth is not envious of Osiris as a better man, nor as a more venerated god, but only as a better ruler. The element of competition between men and gods in the play is thus submerged under its one-sided political message. It remains at the level of a struggle between a virtuous king and his usurping brother, which embodies one angle of the plot of the myth and represents one relationship, but excludes other important tensions. That is not to imply that the play is without a tragic and effective edge. Al-Hakim's *Isis* skilfully follows the rules of tragedy insofar as it induces pity and fear regarding its major characters, Isis and Osiris. He has chosen to recreate the myth in a way that was acceptable to the traditional Egyptian society in the first half of the twentieth century; the audience for whom the play was written. To al-Sa'dawi this is not a concern at all as one of her goals, it seems, is to generate shock.

Al-Hakim's play opens with an old peasant woman crying for help. The Village Headman has stolen her only possession, a goose. In al-Sa'dawi's play, the parallel scene has a woman whose only daughter has been kidnapped and raped by the chief of police. Obviously in al-Sa'dawi's version the situation is more explosive and dangerous. She means to point out that there is much at stake when women are oppressed by religious or political corrupt patriarchies. She does not only quickly escalate the conflict, but also makes it particularly dangerous to women. Al-Hakim, on the other hand, is concerned more with a general state of poverty and oppression than with discrimination against a minority or repressed group. Although the initial evidence of corruption and aggression in both plays is directed towards women, al-Hakim's scenes of violence against women are considerably more benign than those of al-Sa'dawi. While in al-Hakim's play the women face both violence and deliverance at the hand of men, in al-Sa'dawi's version of the myth men are the instigators of violence and women the protectors of the oppressed.

In defiance of all previous literary creations based on the Isis and Osiris saga, al-Sa'dawi boldly reinvents the character of Isis as she places her centre-stage, marginalising Osiris. She depicts Isis as a noble and wise fighter who struggles long and hard for her dignity and place in history as much as she fights for husband and son. Al-Sadawi's Isis is depicted as equal – if not superior – to her male foes and friends.

al-Sa'dawi's play opens with the emergence of a new religion, that of the god Ra. He announces that he has usurped the rule of the goddess Nut. Thus, the play starts with a world in transition. Matriarchy has been superseded by patriarchy, which translates in Nawal al-Sa'dawi's idiom into a world that has moved from utopia to dystopia. Since the play begins with a male god taking power away from a female goddess, women are presented from of the start as a colonised breed. They are second-class citizens, while a ubiquitous male culture and outlook have become dominant.

The play depicts the lowest point in the life of a famous goddess, Isis, and indicates that with the destruction of matriarchy her only hope for reclaiming her old status is through the resurrection of the slain husband/brother/god, Osiris. She is not solely motivated by her love for Osiris, but also forced, in that patriarchal world, to reinvent herself through him. Her battle is, therefore, like al-Sadawi's own, primarily with patriarchy, and only secondly with the evils embodied by Seth.

Nawal al-Sa'dawi has concrete and irreconcilable differences with patriarchy in general, and with religious patriarchy in particular. In this respect she does not differ from other radical feminists around the world, as

> feminist theory is directly and predominantly political. Its purpose is to struggle against the oppression of women as women. This oppression, which is seen to be historically extremely common and widespread, is the result of patriarchy, the supremacy of masculine power and authority most firmly entrenched in the figure of the father (thus the inevitable relations between feminism and psychoanalytic work). Feminism, therefore, works towards the unraveling and overthrow of patriarchy.[24]

From al-Sa'dawi's social commentaries and fiction, it is clear that she is openly cynical about religions as a whole, and regards them all as fundamentally sexist and biased against women. This scepticism is expressed in her play, *Isis*, and can be easily detected in her portrayal of the highest god, Ra. In many ways he is the alternate representation of 'God', whom she portrays as a woman-hating patriarch. Where al-Hakim confines his observations to human weaknesses and strengths, al-Sa'dawi extends her criticism to the metaphysical Being himself and His divine law which, according to her, has created gender disparity and placed men above women in an illogical hierarchy.

In her play Nawal al-Sa'dawi creates a structure of oppression and domination that demonstrates all forms of male dominance, from religious authority to earthly powers. All these patriarchies are ultimately and subtly connected with the Abrahamic God who is the founder of all forms of patriarchy. She mocks the scriptures which represent God's word and power on earth:

> **Ra** My orders and divine law must be written. To be feared by my subjects, I must never appear before them or deliver sermons to them. My voice is sacred and no human ear can have the privilege of hearing it. The written word is a consecrated one and has a strong impact over people. I command my word to be revered. It must be above dispute, discussion and beyond human comprehension.[25]

In this passage it is quite clear that al-Sa'dawi's greatest criticism is directed towards the Islamic scripture itself, the Qur'an. She means to question and ridicule the Muslim belief which holds that the Qur'an is the word of God himself and is therefore immutable. Her aim is to express her discontent with and sarcasm at the male gender that God has chosen for himself. Generally speaking, al-Sadawi also finds in the application and interpretation of all religions, especially Islam, great injustice towards women, and demonstrates her position by attacking – albeit subtly – the Qur'an and its doctrines.

Unlike Tawfiq al-Hakim, who has constructed his play as a battle between two male opponents, leaving Isis out of the central conflict, al-Sa'dawi's play is constructed as a love triangle, and it is this triangle that propels the action forward. Seth loves Isis, who loves Osiris, therefore Seth kills Osiris, but Isis's eternal love for Osiris resurrects him. Seth's extreme selfishness and sense of disinheritance result in the suppression of the general good (Osiris). He upsets the paradise that Osiris aimed to establish on earth and turns Egypt into a war zone.

Amid this extreme malevolence (Seth) and uprightness (Osiris), Isis emerges as the most sensible and level-headed deity among the three siblings. She controls her feelings of both love and hatred throughout the play, and never falters where she knows that she is in the right. Although capable, by virtue of her position as goddess of harming others if she wished, she always holds back her anger, and while she can be all goodness she is also aware of her desire to cause damage. In contrast Seth is portrayed as an emotional and near hysterical character, driven by a lust for revenge. Osiris is characterised by excessive meekness. He is portrayed as defenceless, frail and eccentric. He is not by any means an admirable character even if he is essentially good.

al-Sa'dawi consciously constructs a world of reversed stereotypes – women are rational beings and men emotional and greedy. Upsetting the notion inherited from Judaism and Christianity, but not in Islam, that Eve was the reason for the expulsion of Adam from Paradise, she creates a situation showing man as the destroyer of Paradise (peace and prosperity), while women are the protectors of life. The wisdom which al-Sa'dawi's female characters possess in the play challenges the traditional view of women, that regardless of their profession or status they are irrational beings. She presents Seth as a paranoid and neurotic angry figure. He is in love with Isis to be sure, but will this love improve him as it does in the case of Isis's love for Osiris? On the contrary, it increases his evil nature and paranoia:

Head of Army There are many women available. Isis is not the only women on earth. There are many like her.

Seth To me, she outweighs all the women on earth. She is not only a woman, a female. She represents intelligence. She inherited intelligence and wisdom from our mother, Nut, goddess of the sky. I inherited the body, greed, desire and possessiveness from our father, Geb, the god of earth. I was made of the clay of earth; she was made of the light and intelligence of the sky. Yes, Isis is better than me. She is better than Osiris and all of my other siblings. That is why I love her and hate her. I don't like anyone to be better than me, yet, I only love those who are better than me. This is how I am torn between my love and hatred for her. When I feel my love for her, I hate myself. How can I love her while she is in love with another man, with Osiris.[26]

Seth constantly refers to Isis as both goddess and woman. He loves her as a man but hates her too, as one powerful god detests another on the basis of competition. There is also another dimension within the love–hate relationship; Seth's pride as a 'man' and male deity mean that he cannot accept that a woman is better than him.

> **Head of Army** (Confused) But majesty, what exactly is the source of her [Isis's] power?
> **Seth** I don't know. This is precisely the problem, no, the dilemma. The dilemma of my life is to be born with a more powerful woman next to me. I do not know the source of her power. I love her because she is more powerful than me. I can never possess her; she has total sway over me.[27]

Another aspect to al-Sa'dawi's interpretation of Seth's love for Isis is jealousy of Osiris. She portrays his love as an egotistical sentiment that is tarnished by political desire for kingship on earth. Seth's pride is challenged over and over again as he watches Isis and Osiris's love develop.

> **Seth** Osiris was both kindhearted and stupid, nevertheless, she favored him over me ... He was weak, lacking in manliness. He was soft, shy as virgins, yet she fell in love with him. I don't know how. She is a strange woman, mysterious.[28]

Seth is controlled by his excessive pride and comes across as small-minded. He is enraged that Isis does not love him, so he scoffs at his brother's sexual (in)abilities. He reports to the Head of the Army:

> **Seth** Shall I tell you something? I used to sneak into her room at night. I would see them [Isis and Osiris] together in bed. He would lie between her arms like a baby in his mother's bosom. She used to breastfeed him and nothing more.[29]

Clearly in al-Sa'dawi's play Seth considers himself a more able lover, god and statesman than Osiris. Yet Isis continues to reject him. Seth's desire to dominate Isis is an example of the oldest form of male exploitation of women, to serve their own selfish needs. After all, by gaining Isis's good opinion and love Seth could become the dominant god and ruler he wishes to be. He could rule heaven and earth secure in the knowledge that he was the better man and superior patriarch. So long as Isis favours Osiris, Seth will always have doubts about himself; he will continue to feel inferior and worthless. Isis's rebuff is not comprehensible to him, and his attempts at reversing the situation in his favour are what propel the action of the play forward. But no turning points occur to mark a shift in the dramatic action. Seth never reaches any form of self-realisation regarding his excesses. Even at the end of the play when Horus overpowers him, Seth never attains catharsis but is simply forced to abdicate his throne.

al-Sa'dawi's definition of masculinity is associated with the strong male lust for power. The final moment of the play demonstrates al-Sa'dawi's belief that men's power is derived first and foremost from their genitals. The final defeat for Seth is when his nephew, Horus, cuts his uncle's testicles with his sword. Castrating Seth takes away his awesome patriarchal image, and reduces him from ruler of heaven and earth to the sound of thunder. Castration is a recurrent symbol of emasculation in the play, and by ending the play with such a gruesome sight al-Sa'dawi means to make her last word a strong statement on both the visual and symbolic levels.

This manner of viewing masculinity (as a political and sexual hunger) is not paralleled by a conventional view of femininity (women as good mothers and wives) in al-Sa'dawi's *Isis*. In her play, women do not yearn to be dominated, instead they aim to rule; they are also independent, wise and fair. In a clear comparison of leadership amongst men and women, male power is portrayed as detached, brutal and based on producing fear, whereas female leadership is pictured as democratic and just.

In conclusion, the use of stereotyping in relation to masculinity is what weakens the message and art of al-Sa'dawi's play. While al-Hakim, who has stayed loyal to the plot of the legend, portrays corrupt leadership as non-gendered, al-Sa'dawi shows corruption as an inseparable element of the inner make up of the male. Her play can, therefore, be viewed as anti-male more than pro-women. In her *Isis* all men are essentially bad and women are models of wisdom, inner power and charisma. Moreover, the popular 'virtuous' image of Isis is itself questioned in al-Sa'dawi's version of the legend; she portrays her as neither a loyal nor a patient wife. After all, al-Sa'dawi perceives loyalty and patience to be 'male' virtues that have been imposed on Isis by male interpreters of the legend. What al-Sa'dawi considers as 'female' virtues are integrity, justice and strong determination, all of which Isis possesses in abundance in this version of the legend. The difference in Isis's character as portrayed in these plays is huge. While al-Hakim portrays his cast of characters, including Isis, as 'people' with limited abilities and many flaws, al-Sa'dawi presents them as both gods and human beings, with Isis superior to all.

NOTES

1 Alfred Farag, 2000, 'Questions Laid at the Doors of Theatre', *Al-Ahram* [Cairo, Egypt] 19 November.

2 This comparison has also been looked into by Fedwa Matli-Douglas in *Men, Women and God(s): Nawal El-Saadawi and Arab Feminist Poetics* (Berkeley, Los Angeles, London: University of California Press, 1995). However, her premise is different from mine as she focuses on how *The Thousand and One Nights* operates as a subtext in al-Sa'dawi's *Isis*.

3 In her autobiography, entitled *The Daughter of Isis: The Autobiography of Nawal al-Sa'dawi* (trans. Sherif Helata, London and New York: Zed Books, 1999), the author draws parallels between

herself and Isis. She particularly views their sense of justice and stamina for tough fighting as analogous.

4 This point has also been made by al-Sa'dawi in her Preface to the play, and by Fedwa Matli-Douglas in *Men, Women and God(s)*.

5 Mark Fortier, 1997, *Theory/Theatre: An Introduction* (London and New York: Routledge), p.71.

6 Nawal al-Sa'dawi, 1986, *Izisz: Masrahiyyah min Faslayn* (Isis: A Play in Two Acts). 'Introduction' (Cairo: Dar al-Mustaqbal al-'Arabi), p. 11. Al-Sa'dawi's play has not been translated, al-Hakim's play has only been translated into French. All translations from the Arabic text into English are my own.

7 Matli-Douglas, *Men, Women, and God(s)*, p. 146.

8 Nehad, Selaiha, 1993, 'Voices of Silence: Women Playwrights in Egypt', *Egyptian Theatre, A Diary: 1990–1992* (Cairo: al-Hay'ah al-Misriyyah al-Ammah li-al-kitab), p. 304.

9 Al-Sa'dawi, *Izisz*, p. 8.

10 One definition of Artaudian theatre is that it is, 'a primitive ceremonial experience intended to liberate the human subconscious and reveal human nature'. 'Artaud', *Merriam-Webster's Encyclopedia of Literature* (1995). Al-Sa'dawi no doubt meant to reveal the brutal nature of man, not only toward women, but also towards their own gender.

11 Jacobean dramatists, 'became preoccupied with the problem of evil; the plays of John Webster, Cyril Tourneur, Thomas Middleton, and William Rowley induce all the terror of tragedy but little of its pity', 'Jacobean', *ibid*. Likewise, al-Sa'dawi prefers to project the tragedy of male injustice and its consequence without leaving any space for pity in regards to their gender.

12 Matli-Douglas, *Men, Women, and God(s)*, p. 9.

13 Nawal al-Sa'dawi, 1986, *Memoirs from the Women's Prison*, trans. Marilyn Booth (London: Women's Press).

14 Roth, Ann Macy, 1997, 'Osiris and Isis: An Egyptian Narrative of Re-Creation', in *Broad Sympathy: The Howard University Oral Traditions Reader* (Needham Heights, MA: E. W. Traylor, A. Frost, and L. S. Lawrence).

15 Roth, 'Osiris and Isis', p. 4.

16 Ibid., p. 6.

17 Ibid., p. 7.

18 Ibid., p. 9.

19 Ibid., p. 4.

20 Ibid., p. 2.

21 Ibid.

22 Ibid., p. 3.

23 Tawfiq Al-Hakim, 1985, *Izis* (Isis) (Cairo: al-Matba'ah al-Namuzagiyyah), p. 20.

24 Fortier, *Theory/Theatre*, pp. 70–71.

25 Al-Sa'dawi, *Memoirs*, p. 22.

26 Ibid., pp. 64–5.

27 Ibid., p. 67.

28 Ibid., p. 65.

29 Ibid.

Of *Suwa* Houses & Singing Contests

Early urban women performers in Asmara, Eritrea

CHRISTINE MATZKE

To the late Amleset Abay who had wenni.

Amleset Abay's[1] last performance was on 15 January 2000, in the small market town of Segeneiti, some 60 km south of the Eritrean capital Asmara, as part of an international conference celebrating African languages and literatures. Two weeks later she died, and with her a powerful voice that had contributed to the musical kaleidoscope of Eritrea for forty-five years. Amleset had been the last active female musician and singer of her generation, together with Tsehaitu Beraki, the grand old lady of Tigrinya song.[2] Both women had shared similar life histories, their artistic origins rooted in the *suwa* houses or *enda suwa* of Asmara, modest drinking places where home-brewed sorghum beer (*suwa*) was served to the music of a lyre-like instrument, the *krar*. Later they had left – Amleset briefly to Addis Ababa, Tsehaitu to join the first armed liberation movement, the Eritrean Liberation Front (ELF) – followed by twenty-odd years of exile in the United States and the Netherlands respectively. Only as older women did they return to Eritrea, Amleset to settle in the mid-1990s, Tsehaitu on a visit in summer 1999 to help boost the nation's morale in the latest military conflict with Ethiopia. It is arguable that field and exile experience enabled these women to continue their careers for nearly half a century when their contemporaries had abandoned the work at a much earlier stage, some settling into the secluded roles of homemakers and mothers, others simply vanishing from the scene. It is the story of these seemingly 'ordinary' women, mapped against the backcloth of Eritrea's theatrical and political history, which I am trying to reconstruct in this article. Given the social climate in the 1940s and 1950s, when the first indigenous urban performers emerged, they were 'extraordinary' not only for daring to defy convention by going public on stage. They also helped pave the way for contemporary female artists and, in their own way, contributed to the unique historical narrative of Eritrea.

This essay is based largely on interviews with one-time performers and their contemporaries, for the most part conducted by myself in 1999 and 2000, with some by the Eritrea Community Based Theatre Project (ECBTP) in summer 1995.[3] The data was triangulated with published secondary sources and unpublished material in the national Research and Documentation Centre (RDC) in Asmara. The initial reaction when I approached the informants was often one of surprise: 'I never dreamt that this material might be relevant', a former teacher, *memher* Lemlem Gebregziabhier replied. 'Then [in the 1950s], I was not careful enough to record these things. If we had written everything down, it would have been helpful.'[4] Memory, as we all know, is an unreliable narrator, especially after fifty or sixty years, causing obvious problems for researchers with dates, chronology and constant contradictions. In Eritrea where politics and performing arts have been so intricately linked, it is also important to bear in mind that accounts of whichever history have also always served someone's personal or political agenda: the colonial regimes (Italy, Britain and Ethiopia), the Eritrean Unionists or the Independence Bloc, the two warring liberation movements, ELF and the Eritrean People's Liberation Front, EPLF (the latter of which led the country to independence in 1991), to say nothing of individuals who chose or were forced to change sides. The following narrative, then, is the product of my own selection and interpretation in the attempt to engender critical debate and, above all, further research into urban theatre arts in Eritrea.

Suwa houses – social, musical and political roots

Eritrea as a geopolitical entity came into being in the late 1880s when Italy established colonial rule in the Horn of Africa. Italian control lasted until 1941 when defeat in the Second World War brought Eritrea under British Military Administration (BMA). Italy had planned to transform Eritrea into a settler colony – expropriating farmland, establishing infrastructure and a sizeable manufacturing industry – yet it was not until the rise of Italian fascism and Mussolini's war preparations against Ethiopia in the mid-1930s that the influx of Italian settlers increased. More than ever Eritreans were driven from their means of livelihood and forced to sell their labour power, and this resulted in rapid urbanisation (Selassie 1980: 53; Firebrace and Holland 1985: 17). By 1941 Asmara had 'changed from a comparatively small administrative centre into a large modern town which was housing some 50,000 Europeans and 120,000 Eritreans' (Trevaskis 1960: 46), the majority of the latter being Christian Tigrinya.

Urban migration had a dramatic effect on the lives of women. Educational prospects for girls had been virtually zero, and the fact that under Italian rule some male children were 'granted' a limited primary schooling to prepare them for low-grade clerical jobs or the colonial army, did not enhance female opportunities (Teklehaimanot 1996: 5; NUEW 1987: 110–13). Hence women began to join the menial work force or the informal labour market. Factory and domestic work were the main options, as was employment in bars; but often women opened their own *suwa* houses which had begun mushrooming with the ever-expanding influx from rural areas. These were modest drinking places in the Eritrean quarters of Asmara which also served as accommodation for the owner's family. Songs and *krar*-playing were part of the amusement and played an enormous role in attracting and keeping customers. In fact, for a long time this was the only live entertainment available to Eritreans. Public performances of Eritrean song and dance were unthinkable, given that the colonial power deprecated anything that could have instilled pride in the people's identity. Italian operas and film shows were barely accessible, due to rigid race segregation; and Cinema Hamasien, the only 'native' movie theatre which opened in 1937, merely showed Italian propaganda films.[5]

There is no doubt that growing urbanisation generated unprecedented dynamics in Eritrea. Women, as part of the emerging working class, were exploited even more than the men, earning less than their male colleagues in the manufacturing industry and being sexually abused as domestic workers or *baristas* – waitresses – in bars. Commercial sex was certainly on the rise during this period; but claiming that prostitution was only introduced with Italian colonisation means turning a blind eye to the fact that concubines and courtesans had a long tradition in the highland cultures of Ethiopia and Eritrea, which is well documented in popular stories and songs.[6] There is a striking similarity of conflicting discourses on travelling singers and courtesans from the earlier periods and entertainers in *suwa* houses emerging in the 1930s and 1940s, a conflict applicable to stage performers until the present day. On the one hand they were looked down upon for their purported though not necessarily actual licentiousness,[7] and on the other they were highly revered for their artistic and social skills. While serving as objects for male gratification – from the admiration of beauty to the possible rendering of sexual services – they did not conform to the societal ideal of a woman. Studies on urban migration and female singers in Eastern and Southern Africa have revealed that women who went to the metropoles, or into the performing arts, were often considered 'uncontrollable' (Obbo 1981: 27–8, 87) or 'loose' because they were moving in 'unmarked territory' (Chitauro et al. 1994: 111) beyond the boundaries of patriarchal control signified by concepts of 'wife' and 'daughter'. In Eritrea, where young girls were primarily raised to submit in marriage, this too was the case. The majority of entertainers in *suwa* houses were single parents, widowed or divorced – some had been orphaned in their early childhood – and most were unusually independent. Those who eventually married immediately left the job. Despite a certain social stigma, *suwa*-sellers were nonetheless appreciated, their lifestyle condoned for the benefit of their work. *Suwa* houses, after all, were people's *homes*,[8] where only local drinks and *taita* (*enjeera*) – sourdough pancakes – were served, not hard European liquor. Compared to bars, cabarets and other public houses, many of which were out of bounds for Eritreans, they still seemed to operate in line with 'tradition' – the drinks, the food and the music – the old family structures merely replaced by a female support network. When asked about people's attitudes towards women performers in the 1940s and 1950s, Ghidey Rustom, a striking woman with an impressive life history (divorced in her early teens she never re-married, she is mother to twelve children, a *krar* player and has been a *suwa* publican for forty years) explained that, after all, 'We were playing in our houses, under our mothers, not in theatres or bars' – 'mothers' not necessarily being the biological parent, but an older female chaperone. 'We were not singing in public', another performer claimed in a similar vein. 'In my sister's place clients were coming to drink, but we did not charge them any money for the music. They were dignitaries and

Ghidey Rustom with her krar *in Summer 2000* (Photo: Christine Matzke)

the sons of the then elite' (I5). Though well-remembered for her skills in the 1940s, the speaker wished to remain anonymous and on the whole did not want to be 'disturbed' by her memories. Carefree and independent days for some, it should also be pointed out that countless other women were forced to sell *suwa* because of financial necessity, not out of choice. Many stories will remain untold and eventually die with their owners, or be moulded into a 'presentable' form. Yet most women I spoke to were not ashamed of their work and saw entertaining customers not only as an economic inevitability but also as the logical conclusion to an artistic urge. 'If I had stopped singing,' Amleset told me three months before her death, 'I would have died. I do not exist without music'. Ghidey, who had listened to Amleset and Tsehaitu Beraki as a child, recounted a similar scenario: 'When we were young we just loved playing *krar*. We never bothered about social or economic problems. We gathered in someone's house, one was pouring *suwa*, the other was making music or dancing or kicking out a drunkard.' Ghidey's venture became successful. Though never internationally known like her famous predecessors, or able to amass wealth, she continued to make music until the early 1990s, later employing other singers, including men, in her growing business. As such she represents the majority of *suwa*-selling women who did not want or get the chance to perform on stage. With the benefit of hindsight, however, their work had an indelible effect on the urban performing arts. '[Modern] music in Eritrea', veteran performer Tekabo Woldemariam insisted, 'was started by women':

We, the men, came after them. For example, Tsehaitu Berhe [Zenar], Fana Itel, Yolanda and Rosina Conti (the daughters of Halima from Keren), Fantaya Gebreselassie, Meriem Ibrahim, Abeba Woldesellassie, Aberash Shifera and others, Tsehaitu Beraki and Amleset Abay. When people say music was first played by men, it is completely wrong. Now with Amleset dead they say that she was the first woman to play *krar*. But it is not true, they were all playing *krar* before Amleset, a lot of them playing in their homes. [...] In our culture [Tekabo is Tigrinya], there is *goila* [a dance event]. There is no *goila*, no entertainment, without the ululating, the clapping and the songs of women. So even traditionally women were the beginners. (I 13, 14)

Catherina Tela (*gual* Mamet)[9] and Letenkial, also known as Teresa (both entertainers in Catherina's bar in Kidane Meheret), Bishat Gebresellasie, Abeba Ashafa, Guae Liay, Nigisti and Alganesh Gerezghier were some of the other performers repeatedly named in conversation. Most of them have died, their art alive only in the memory of their audiences many of whom are advanced in years. Audio records of their songs have not been available,[10] nor are there pictures of the performers. It is difficult, therefore, to elaborate on their music. Tsehaitu based her songs on 'our ancestral [here: Tigrinya] rhythm' as she herself put it, possibly of the *masse* and *melkes* type, the first performed at special social occasions, the latter as dirges for funerals (Negash 1999: 98–9). Amleset too gave preference to these genres, with a penchant for love songs, and it can be surmised that most Tigrinya performers followed similar patterns.

Besides long-established poetry and song forms in Tigrinya and occasionally Tigre, radio seems to have been the second strong influence. Even after the first Eritrean theatre associations had been established in the 1940s and 1950s, and Cinema Hamasien re-opened under the British in 1942 (Anon. 1942: 2), women were unlikely to frequent the shows. 'It was impossible to go out', Amleset recalled her teenage years while living with her mother, also a *suwa* house owner. 'No family allowed their daughters to go to the cinema. We were strictly controlled. So I didn't have the opportunity. The only thing we listened to was the radio. The radio often transmitted Sudanese music, even Amharic was broadcasted very late. There was no television at the time'. Sudanese songs in Arabic were popular in the 1930s and early 1940s, some singers, such as the Conti Sisters, acquiring local fame for their renderings. These songs were usually accompanied by the *oud*, a mandolin-like instrument; its most notable players being Valerina, Teresa, and Zefun Selassie, apart from Yolanda and Rosina Conti (I 3, I 13, I 18).

While I have been unable to trace lyrics of early songs, there was general agreement among the informants that with the beginning of the BMA politicisation among performers and customers increased. This development eventually found expression in popular songs which seem to have had their heyday during the UN enforced federation years with Ethiopia, 1952–62, following a political tug-of-war during the British caretaker regime. In the late 1950s, for instance, a song was popular which spoke of open grass-roots resentment against Ethiopian hegemony: 'I am amazed at what's happening./ I never thought we would go/ backwards in history/ Would Mussolini have been/ better for me?'

(Iyob 1995: 91). After the annexation of Eritrea in 1962 by the Haile Selassie regime, which stripped the country of its relative political autonomy and turned it into an ordinary Ethiopian province, greater caution was in order. Songs became more allegorical for fear of censorship and political repression. Ghidey Rustom recalls that 'these were times of political unrest. Some men still wrote new political songs, but they gave them to women to sing because they did not want to be arrested. So the women sang them. It was only later that men like Bereket [Mengisteab, a former barber whose international music career has continued until the present day] joined us women in *enda suwa.*' From the late 1960s Ghidey actively supported the two liberation movements, hiding fighters in her house or seating Ethiopian clients on boxes filled with ammunition. Yet political activities by *suwa*-sellers did not start with the armed liberation struggle in 1961.

During the Italian colonisation, especially under Fascist rule, Eritreans had been physically and intellectually suppressed, and were not allowed to participate in the government of their country. Under the British caretaker regime, restrictions were gradually removed and a limited policy of 'Eritreanisation' encouraged (Trevaskis 1960: 30). 'Discrimination continued for a long time' (I 10), Osman Ahmed, born in 1927, recalled, the grid of the Italian administration, including its personnel, having been left virtually intact for logistic reasons. Yet unprecedented political possibilities emerged for Eritreans which were readily taken up. Only one month after Eritrea had been placed under the British in 1941, a disparate group of elders and intelligentsia was established 'to communicate Eritrean wishes to the BMA. Above all, they desired an end to Italian domination' (Iyob 1995: 65). This association came to be known as *Mahber Fikri Hager Eritrea*, or Love of the Country Association, and initially operated clandestinely as political parties were banned until 1946. By then it had turned into the Unionist Party which, as its name suggests, favoured the union of Eritrea with Ethiopia. This is not the place to elaborate on the complex political developments that took place in Eritrea under the British Administration. It is, however, essential to note that two opposing factions emerged; the aforesaid Unionists supported by the Coptic Church and the Haile Selassie regime, and the Independence Bloc at the heart of which was the Muslim League. Today, with the latest military conflict between Eritrea and Ethiopia (1998–2000), tendencies to gloss over Unionist links are understandable. Yet there is hard evidence that artists in *suwa* houses campaigned on the Unionist's behalf and that it was notably women who were active. In December 1951 the political adviser of the British Headquarters received a petition for official recognition of the 'Female Society for Union of Eritrea with Ethiopia' signed by ten women among whom was the *krar* player Tsehaitu Berhe Zenar. Further information on the signatories was obtained by the police and, in a confidential correspondence dated 9 January 1952, details on three 'propagandists' were provided. Tsehaitu was identified as the 'ex-mistress of Daedacei, a former Governor of Eritrea [who] now owns a house of ill-repute in the Abbascial quarter' (Green 1952) of Asmara. In Osman Ahmed's view, however, there was nothing disreputable about the artist: '*Gual* Zenar was the greatest *krar* player. She had one song and was famous for it. But she did not play in public. She was a politician and played in her house' (I 11). She was obviously successful in both roles, for on 21 January 1952 the Female Unionist Association was officially acknowledged by the Chief Secretary of the BMA.

Given the social set-up in Eritrea, this can be regarded not only as a political novelty, but also as advancement for women. 'Our families were not only opposed to women singing, they also denied us schooling', Tsehaitu Beraki summed up the social climate of the period:

> All you were required to do was to fetch water, give birth and so on. Social changes seem to have started under the British Administration. Frankly speaking, we [the *krar* players] were some of the few more advanced women at the time. I think growing up in Asmara had a great influence on us.

Cinemas, cabarets and the 'colour bar'

The BMA brought new life into the artistic scene of Asmara. Their main cultural priority was to provide entertainment for their troops and civilian personnel, as well as 'fraternisation' with Italians in an attempt to combat fascist influence. For Eritreans the greatest changes were the gradual removal of the 'colour bar' which allowed access to previously out-of-bounds entertainment,[11] and the possibility of a better education. Missionary schools closed under the Fascist regime were re-opened, and there was an effort at public, including adult, education which comprised lectures, gramophone recitals and Shake-spearean school drama. English replaced Italian as the main mode of instruc-tion, though Tigrinya and Arabic were also being used, manifest in the publica-tion of two weekly newspapers in these languages and the establishment of the Tigrinya Language Council. Demand for education after years of deprivation was high, with people willing to make substantial sacrifices. Initially few schools were opened for lack of textbooks, buildings and teaching staff. The situation began to improve when pupil teachers became available and a system of teacher training was introduced in 1943. For the performing arts in the urban centres of Eritrea this was a decisive moment. Teachers were to become the bedrock of modern Eritrean theatre arts, not only as part of the Teachers' Association which produced educational drama, but also as members of the first national – and nationalistic – theatre associations.[12]

For British, Italians and Allied Personnel a variety of entertainment was on offer: operas, operettas and classical concerts, puppet shows for children, Christmas pantomimes, drama in Hindustani for Indian troops, English and Italian amateur theatre, concert parties, dances at the Garrison Mess or social nights at 'The Singing Kettle'. The list could be further extended. The volunteer Troops Entertainment Committee busily plotted new get-togethers, while the official Entertainment Welfare, under the Information Officer David C. Cousland, was primarily in charge of the cinemas. By 1943 nineteen cinemas operated in Eritrea, seven of which were in Asmara. Cinema

The Croce del Sud, a restaurant during the Italian colonisation, served as a cabaret under the BMA (Photo: Colonial Picture Archive, Frankfurt/Main)

Hamasien, with its English and Arabic-speaking programme, catered solely for Eritreans and the Sudanese Defence Force, while other cinemas became accessible to Eritreans from 1945 onwards (Taylor 1943). All films were 'carefully censored' in the attempt to provide the locals with a 'little relaxation [...] stressing that they are not forgotten in our scheme of things and giving them something tangible to take their minds off political and other issues' (Cousland 1942). However, the incipient politicisation of Eritreans under the BMA would not be contented with 'bread and circuses'. Films were nonetheless an influence on future Eritrean theatre arts. Slapstick of the Charlie Chaplin or Laurel and Hardy type was imitated in comical sketches and playlets, and singers named themselves after Hollywood stars. Sofia Ali, for instance, a participant in the First National Singing Contest, was known as Sofia 'Loren', Tebereh Tesfahunei, popular in the 1960s, as Doris Day. Though, as I will show, purely foreign entertainment forms in non-Eritrean languages were increasingly rejected with the establishment of indigenous theatre associations, the glamour of certain western modes still appealed and was readily appropriated by female performers, possibly also in the attempt to establish a new, artistic, identity in opposition to prevailing attitudes towards women on stage.[13]

The loosening of fascist race laws under the BMA did not genuinely open up European performances to Eritreans. But easier access to performance venues and the legality of Eritrean–European interaction led to unprecedented cultural co-operation. It had always been common in theatre houses for expatriates to accompany film shows with live entertainment. These were advertised as 'Grand Variety' and included musical bands, dances and possibly comedy. Now foreigners began to teach Eritreans European music and included them in their groups. 'There was an Italian music teacher', Osman recalled. 'Everyone paid 10 shillings to study with him' (I 11).[14] Umberto Barbuye, Gino Mini, Dr Mario Forena and Oscar Ramponi were likewise involved in cross-cultural entertainment; that is they worked with Eritreans on European-style shows, comprising mostly Italian songs, dances and comic sketches. Gino Mini is said to have started in 1943 with three of the most popular Eritrean comedians, Alemayo Kahasai, Ali Said and Belay Legesse. A female member of the party was Buzu, also known as Maria, who became famous as 'Donna Electrica'. According to Tekabo Woldemariam she wore a tight-fitting costume similar to a swimming costume that the audience was allowed to touch when she was on stage. The 'joke' of the act was that people then got an electric shock because it was wired to a battery or socket (I 16).

It is likely that these types of shows were mounted in so-called '1st class' ('European') and '2nd class' ('Mixed') cabarets as well as in private clubs, given the evidently seedy character of the performance which made it unsuitable as a family entertainment in venues such as Cinema Asmara. It is also likely that Buzu, like many of her colleagues, was of Italian–Eritrean parentage – liaisons common, and grudgingly tolerated, until the rise of Mussolini. Clubs and cabarets abounded during the BMA, but little is known about the running of their affairs. It appears that Italian and other European performers were brought to Asmara on a contract basis and, on completing their work, returned to their home countries or continued to tour. It is also known that persons of mixed ancestry often found employment in the light-entertainment sector. BMA files from 1944 confirm that clubs like the 'Chez Vous' or bands such as 'Trio Golde' engaged so-called 'half-caste girls' to dance first on the stage and later at the cabarets' (BMA 1944: 'File No. 273, Subject: Colour Bar'). While there was no objection from the authorities to stage performances, they nonetheless suggested that employment of such women as dance hostesses – i.e. dancing partners for punters – might displease the European clientele (so much for liberal attitudes and daily practice). The decision, however, was ultimately left to the proprietors, and no records exist of these. Given the shortage of European women as 'befitting' dance partners for officers and lower ranks in Asmara,[15] it is likely that mixed-race and other Eritrean women were brought in to fill the gaps, especially in so-called 'Mixed' venues open to Eritreans. 'Abeba Tewolde', Tekabo Woldemariam recalled, 'danced in a dance place called "Shanghai" near Kidane Meheret Church. Many women went there and danced, like Ghidey Fesehaye, Gabriela, Maria, Zebenesh Gebray. They were the first women to dance.' Most Eritrean women did not frequent the music halls, yet they too wanted a slice of the western culture cake, especially those exposed to British education. 'In my time', Tekabo continued,

> meaning in '44, '45 to around '50, there were teachers who listened to European disco dances. They also began to wear European clothes. They were a whole group which included Nigisti, Mebrahtu [male], Tsadwa [male], Bizen, Tekha Hagos, Lisa Gustafo, Ghidey and Brehane [male]. They were the first to dance European dances

in their houses. European dress was not common at the time, but they still did it and thus set an example. (I 16)

So teachers were at the forefront of embracing what was considered 'modern' and 'fashionable' at the time. Developments, however, did not stop at the mere level of 'apemanship', to borrow from the Ugandan Okot p'Bitek; (the indiscriminate imitation of western forms resulting in a 'kind of slave mentality'; p'Bitek 1973: 1–2). Rather, by copying colonial cultural habits, an introspective self-awareness was engendered. Eritreans began to refuse the cultural leash of Italy and Britain, and started to experiment with transcultural, hybrid performance forms that were to become an expression of Eritrean nationalism. While one group fully immersed itself in the newly found delights of European-style entertainment, another – through its exposure to foreign performance types – began to criticise the lack of indigenous urban theatre arts.

Mahber Theatre Dekabat – the first Eritrean Theatre Association: Tigrinya theatre and singing contests

In 1944 seventeen men – some experienced performers, others newcomers, many teachers – founded the first-ever Eritrean theatre association under the name of *Mahber Theatre Dekabat*, Ma.Te.De., roughly translated as the Indigenous Theatre Association.[16] One of its architects was Osman Ahmed, my principal informer, others included Alemayo Kahasai, Ali Said, Belay Legesse and Tesfay Gebremichael. 'The idea was that all the theatre groups were of Italian nature', Osman recollected in our first meeting. 'We, the people of Eritrea, needed our own. We wanted to narrate our own history. We wanted to oppose oppression. […] The majority of us had nationalist feelings. We therefore only considered those as members who had a high degree of patriotism.'

Ma.Te.De.'s aim was to produce stage theatre predominately in Tigrinya and, later, songs in Eritrean languages to create something home-grown as opposed to Italianised stage performances.[17] Significantly, but not surprisingly, the first show was 'Eritrea's Past Property', *Z'halefe N'bret Eritrea*, a play about the country's history written by Berhe Mesgun.[18] Some nine full-length plays were mounted during the lifetime of Ma.Te.De., mostly with historical, religious or educational content, and some as long as three or four hours. Performance venues were Cinema Hamasien, Cinema Asmara (the oldest theatre house built in 1920), and Adulis School for Girls; the entrance fee was one East African shilling. As theatre training was not available, artists learnt through trial and error, drawing on their experience of school drama and foreign theatre groups. Later, when it emerged that audiences were bored by lengthy dialogue drama, a musical wing, Ma.Mu.Te.De. (*Mahber Musica Tewason Dekebat*) was introduced which played an idiosyncratic mix comprising mostly European instruments and tunes, but also ancestral melodies. Plays were shortened, comical sketches performed, and musical interludes provided. Prior to the federation with Ethiopia, Ma.Te.De. had been an entirely male affair. Women, even *suwa*-sellers, were reluctant to join because stage perfor-mance was still associated with commercial sex. Women just did not 'stage' themselves publicly; if anything, they played in their 'homes'. Out of necessity female roles were taken over by male actors at the beginning. 'We tried to find women, but it was not possible. However, we had handsome boys in the group for whom we made costumes and who acted like girls. [...] The audience took them for women' (I 9, 11). I enquired whether this did not have a comic effect, given that male cross-dressing is not found in long-established Eritrean perfor-mance forms, though part of the tradition for women.[19] 'There was no such thing as comedy', Osman vehemently objected, 'It was a serious show' (I 9).

The problem was eventually solved in 1953 when the association was able to recruit four female members. None had a *suwa*-selling or cabaret back-ground, but all were conspicuous for their comparatively higher standards of education: the aforementioned *memher* Lemlem, *memher* Hiwot Gebre, *memher* Mebrat Gebru, and Amete Solomon, pupil and neighbour of Hiwot. *Memher* Lemlem recalled:

> I joined Ma.Te.De. because they persuaded me that we were doing it to advance our national culture. Hiwot Gebre too was telling me that it was beneficial for our country. At first I did not go openly because there was pressure from my family. I am a Catholic and the church is strict about these things. My parents were also against it. I told them that I took a course in handicrafts when in fact I was going to the rehearsals. It was only when we started to tour that they found out. They were furious.

Hide-and-seek games of this kind have been prevalent in Eritrea up until the present whenever a girl wishes to join a drama club after school. Yet not every woman had problems with her family. Amete Solomon remembered her brother (a teacher) being rather supportive, hoping it would help her overcome her timidity; and *memher* Hiwot had always been of a different kind. A free spirit in every sense, she was the first woman to enter a bicycle race, and among the first to wear trousers. She also refused to get married, dreading the loss of her independence. 'She was a very open person', her students recalled, 'rather unusual. She did not fear anyone' (I 17). 'In many ways, she was like a man, because she participated in activities only men were allowed to' (I 2). Not sur-prisingly, therefore, that she also expended her enthusiasm and efforts unhesi-tatingly on the association.

Initially female Ma.Te.De. members were merely involved in drama, not in musical shows. Amete, for example, recalled an act as 'a mourning Ethiopian', *memher* Lemlem her role as Uriah's wife Bathsheba who King David seduced in the eponymous biblical play. While the women remained the 'executive bodies' on stage, the men also worked behind the scenes, writing, translating and directing plays, arranging for venues and tours, and dealing with the cen-sorship authorities.[20]

In the mid-1950s voices grew louder bemoaning the dearth of modern Eritrean songs. The music scene was still dominated by the foreign market, and the increasingly nationalistic atmosphere – a result of Haile Selassie's attempts

From left to right: Amete Solomon, Hiwot Gebre (with bouquet) and, front, Osman Ahmed, after the first National Singing Contest in 1956 (Photo: Osman Ahmed)

to undermine Eritrea's partial sovereignty under the federation – cried out for something decidedly Eritrean. Hence, Tesfai Gebremichael, then head of Ma.Te.De., organised the First National Singing Contest in 1956. This was the year in which 'Tigrinya and Arabic were replaced by Amharic as the official language' (Pool 1997: 11), and thus a powerful patriotic statement. Ma.Te.De. members and independent artists were invited to perform their work. 'For the first time in Eritrea', Tekabo Woldemariam explained, 'we presented our own lyrics and songs to the audience, nothing copied from a different country!' (I 13). Thirteen songs were performed by eleven participants, five of whom were women. *Memher* Lemlem sang two songs, *Yefqereka Iya* ('I Love You') written by her future husband Gebregziabhier Teka, and *Lemlem Weynoy* ('Lemlem, My Grape'), a duet with *memher* Abebe Iyasu. Amete Solomon presented *Sigemay Zelela* ('My Barley Stalk') and *Zemanawi Fikri* ('Modern Love'); *memher* Hiwot, *Kokhob Tsebah* ('Morning Star') and *Gual Rubai* ('Girl from my River'), again as a duet with Abebe Iyasu. Amsala Woldesakid sang *Fikrina Ina* ('Love Me'), written by herself; and finally Sofia Ali, a *suwa*-entertainer from Aba Showel, presented 'Songs of our Land' by Tesfai Gebremichael.

A small booklet was produced with titles, singer and the lyrics of the songs, and the audience was asked to vote using the page with their most favoured number as a ballot paper. In the end Tewolde Redda, arguably the most famous Eritrean guitarist, won the competition with his song *Zegitsam Fikri* ('Unfulfilled Love'), followed by *memher* Lemlem with 'I Love You'. Tekabo Woldemariam came third. *Memher* Lemlem evoked the atmosphere of the show, which was unlike anything she had previously experienced with Ma.Te.De.:

The first song I presented was written by my husband-to-be. 'You are my companion/ And that is for eternity./ It is your love that has engulfed me/ Please, visit me'. When I sang these lines, the crowd was roaring. 'Are you singing these lines for me?' They were going mad. Some threw flowers, others threw their coats. My eyes were beautiful at the time. So they shouted: 'Lemlem *weynoy* [my grape], give me your eyes!' [...] I did not sing this song because I was in love. Perhaps he was already in love with me when he wrote the song. I understood its meaning only when I saw the reaction of the crowd. Many people came to attend the competition. Isaak Tewoldemedhin, the then administrator of Eritrean schools, brought my headmistress. She was shocked! When I went to school the next morning, she asked me how I survived the crowd. After that people never left me alone. In the streets

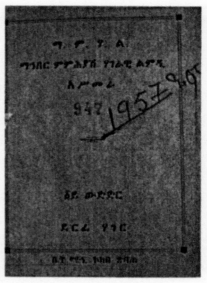

The programme booklet of the second National Singing Contest in 1957, similar to that of the previous year (photo: Osman Ahmed)

people blew me kisses. The rude ones were trying to grab me. [...] I started to feel uncomfortable. It was irritating to hear catcalls in the street. They did not make rude signs to Amleset or Tsehaitu Beraki because they were mature enough to handle it and they also had their *suwa* houses. Moreover, I was a teacher. And for a teacher to sing love songs in public was unbecoming.

Memher Lemlem did not join the second singing contest the following year, 1957 (then organised by a follow-up theatre association due to Ma.Te.De.'s disintegration),[21] nor did Amete Solomon, *memher* Hiwot or Amsala Woldesakid. *Memher* Lemlem found singing incompatible with her teaching career, Amete was moved to a different workplace by her employer, and I was unable to find out much about the other singers. Yet a taboo had been broken that had prohibited women from presenting Eritrean culture on stage. This was later confirmed by the success stories of Amleset, Tsehaitu Beraki and Tebereh Tesfahunei, who were also able to handle, and in fact enjoyed, the public attention.

The Tigrinya language knows an expression, *wenni*, which describes a person who has a natural feeling for music, someone who has musical *esprit*, who can sing and dance the whole night and still go to work in the morning, fresh and relaxed, able to give his or her best. These people are called *wennamat* or, in the singular, *wennam*. *Wennam* also describes an artisan, a person of skilled hands who can manufacture goods seemingly without any effort. To me, this is a wonderfully double-layered wording for a person gifted with the ability of making (and delighting in) music, and a most befitting characterisation for the early women performers I have discussed.

> Hiwot [Gebre] had *wenni*. I think she had the greatest *wenni* except Amleset Abay. Almeset, when she went on stage, she changed completely. Hiwot had it too. There were other singers. They looked on stage as usual. Hiwot, however, changed. Even in a photograph! That was brought about by *wenni*, this feeling of music. (I 17)

Thus it was the *wenni* of these women, their hard work and, above all, their courage, which brought about gradual changes in the urban performing arts and helped pave the way for today's women performers in Eritrea.

ACKNOWLEDGEMENTS

The author gratefully acknowledges the financial support of the AHRB, Cusanuswerk and the German Academic Exchange Service, DAAD. For administrative and office support I am indebted to Solomon Tsehaye, Director of the Cultural Affairs Bureau, Asmara, and to the British Council, Asmara, under its Director Negusse Araya. Special thanks to the following colleagues who worked with me as translators, interpreters and research assistants in Eritrea: Samson Gebregzhier, Yakem Tesfai, Tesfazghi Ukubazghi, Temesgen Gebreyesus, Mohamed Salih Ismail, Tekeste Yonas, Yohannes Zerai and, above all, Mussie Tesfagiorgis.

Picture credits: Amleset Abay, Osman Ahmed, the Colonial Picture Archive at the City and University Library, Frankfurt/Main, at http://www.stub.bildarchiv-dkg.uni-frankfurt.de, no. 020-5105-20, and the author.

NOTES

1 Please note that it is common to address Eritreans by their first name, as you will see in the text, the second is the father's name (the third the grandfather's, and so on) rather than a surname in the western sense. In the reference section, however, authors are listed with their father's name first to comply with international bibliographical standards.

2 Tigrinya is one of the nine languages spoken in Eritrea. Tigrinya and Tigre-speaking communities form the majority of peoples, the Tigrinya being the largest ethno-linguistic nationality with an estimated 45% of the entire population, closely followed by Tigre speakers. Tigrinya speakers live predominantly in the central highlands where most of the urban centres are located and where modern Eritrean performing arts forms have their origins. If not indicated otherwise, all African-language references in this article are in Tigrinya.

3 For further information on the ECBTP see Plastow (1997b) and Campbell et al. (1999).

4 Quotes from interviews will not be referenced in the text except when the informant is not evident or when multiple interviews were conducted with one informant. Then the interview number (I) as listed in the reference section will be cited. Interviews conducted by the ECBTP 1995 are not numbered and will be referred to in full.

5 (I 9), (I 11). Before 1937, some cinemas had 'separate parts set aside for natives (e.g. the Cinema Teatro [...])'. When Cinema Hamasien was opened 'the natives were therefore excluded from all other Cinemas by order of the Governor' (Setton 1941: 1).

6 NUEW (1999: 8), Anon. (1996: 7), Negash (1999: 98), Pankhurst (1992: 68, 261).

7 The nature of my research did not allow me to probe too intimately into people's private lives.

It had never been my intention in the first place, though I tried to find out whether sexual harassment of performers had been an issue. Discussion regarding sexuality is off-limits in Eritrean society, especially to an outsider to the community. Ethiopia Medhanie, one of the interviewees, openly declined to talk about these things, while many politely navigated around the question or declared there had never been any problems. Difficult for the research situation was also the lack of female translators, though my male colleagues proved very sensitive in conducting interviews. Women are still disadvantaged when it comes to schooling in Eritrea, and those who spoke English well either had busy jobs or family responsibilities and were thus not available as research assistants.

8 It took me some time to figure out that 'singing in people's homes' implied *suwa* houses, not private functions such as weddings, baptisms or funerals.

9 *Gual* means 'daughter' in Tigrinya, in this case 'daughter of Mamet'.

10 Tsehaitu mentioned her first recording at the age of sixteen, possibly in 1953. Similarly, an EPLF source referred to a handful of 'traditional songs', such as 'Negusse, Negusse' ('King, King'), which were recorded during Italian colonisation. I could neither trace these records, nor find out whether the singers had been *suwa*-sellers or others (EPLF 1982).

11 In 1942 restrictions were first removed for 'all members of his Britannic Majesty's Forces and the Eritrean Police when in uniform' (Jameson 1942). This probably followed an official complaint that black people working for the BMA, i.e. 'Indians, Sudanese or South Africans of colour or other Allied natives' (Setton 1941: 2), found themselves barred from most places of entertainment.

12 Trevaskis (1960: 22–3, 33–4), Negash (1999: 116), Schröder (1987: 101–5), Lucas (1996), ECBTP Interview with Abebe Iyasu, 6 September 1995, Asmara, Eritrea.

13 Taylor (1943), Temesgen (1956), Tesfahunei (2000) (I 16).

14 It is possible that Italians performed with Eritreans in Cinema Hamasien before the BMA period. This, however, could not be verified (I 16).

15 BMA correspondence of 1943–6 reveals that there was a considerable shortage of European ladies for staff dances and similar occasions, especially as partners for the lower ranks, since only officers were entitled to bring their spouses to Asmara.

16 In other publications Ma.Te.De. has been referred to as Natives' Theatrical Association (NTA). I prefer the Tigrinya abbreviation as it is recognised and widely used in Eritrea; Estefanos (1996: 6), Plastow (1997a: 146).

17 The first Tigrinya plays were not staged by Ma.Te.De. but by *memher* Abraham Redda. According to informants he was a great writer and director, but too advanced for his time. 'It was difficult to make the people understand' (I 11). His principal creative period was from the onset of BMA to the foundation of Ma.Te.De. Only two of Abraham's plays were recorded, his first a religious play 'The Birth of Christ' noted by Alemayo Kahasai, the other 'New World' recorded in 1945 BMA files. Abraham is said to have worked with women actresses, none of whom was to be found in Eritrea during my research period. Kahasai (1977EC), Redda (1945).

18 Some sources claim that 'Eritrea's Past Property' was first mounted by the Unity Association; Plastow (1997a: 148), Kahasai (1977EC). My informants and Yishak Yosief, however, clearly attribute Berhe's play to Ma.Te.De; Yosief (1979). It is likely that a number of Ma.Te.De. members were Unionist. Whether Ma.Te.De. generally had Unionist leanings remains unconfirmed, especially when taking into account that after the 1952 federation artists began to resent Ethiopian hegemony. Perhaps *memher* Lemlem Gebregziabhier came closest to the truth when referring to the political divisions among Eritreans in the mid-1940s and the ensuing mediation efforts of the association: 'The people at the time had divided feelings. Muslims [predominately pro-independence] and Christians [predominately Unionists] were at each other's throats. It was rumoured that even Tsehaitu *gual* Zenar traded blows and punches with Muslim men alongside the Christians. To correct this, Ma.Te.De. came into being.'

19 Cross-dressing can be found among the Tigre during mourning ceremonies, when women dance in the clothes of the (male) deceased, a performance called *difn* or *hebo*. The Christian Orthodox holy day of *Maryam Genbot* is another example. Here, women stage a procession in honour of the Virgin Mary, carrying sticks (a signifier of male authority) and imitating male occupations, such as ploughing and sowing seeds; Kemink (1991: 161).

20 In January 1949, for example, Ma.Te.De. wanted to mount *Tragedi Hatsey Tewodros*, 'The

Tragedy of Tewodros', written by Aba Ghebreyesus Hailu. Permission was initially denied on the grounds that the play 'is likely to excite certain sections of the public and work up racial hatred'; BMA (1948). Later it was given permission according to picture material and Osman Ahmed.

21   The second Eritrean theatre association was known as Ma.M.Ha.L, *Mahber M'Mibal Hagherawi Limdi* or The Association for the Modernisation of Traditional Customs. It was operative approximately between 1957 and 1960. Thereafter followed Ma.Te.A., *Mahber Theatr Asmara* or Asmara Theatre Association (in other publications also referred to as ATA (Plastow 1997a: 150)), the most popular theatre association in Eritrea. It was initiated by Tekabo Woldemariam and Tewolde Redda in 1961 and operated until the mid-1970s when cultural work became impossible under the Ethiopian occupation and many artists went to fight. Ma.Te.A. was revived in the early 1990s but has not been operating since the latest military conflict with Ethiopia.

BIBLIOGRAPHY

Articles published according to the Ethiopian calendar are given with their original date of publication, indicated with EC, and followed by the approximate Gregorian year in brackets. Articles originally published in Tigrinya are quoted in the English translation available to the author.

Anon., 1941, 'Indian Drama', *Eritrean Daily News*, 30 October: 3.
—— 1941, 'Pantomime', *Eritrean Daily News*, 7 December: 3.
—— 1941, 'Teatro Marionette (Bivio Campo Polo)', *Eritrean Daily News*, 24 December: 8.
—— 1942, 'Further Step Towards Advancement of Eritrean Social Amenities: New Cinema Finest of its Kind in Africa', *Eritrean Daily News*, 31 December: 2.
Anon., 1944, 'Teatro Impero: Selezione Delle Poere *Aida*, *Rigoletto* di Guiseppe Verdi, Giovedi 5 Ottobre', *Il Quotidiano Eritreo*, 30 September: n.p.
Anon., 1996, 'The Legend of Wuba Ferede', *Eritrea Profile*, 13 April: 7.
British Military Administration [Eritrea] (BMA) [also: Occupied Enemy Territory Administration (OETA)], 1941–42, 'Clubs and Societies: Cinemas', vol. I, unpublished miscellanies.
—— 1941–43, 'Clubs and Societies: Attendance of Natives in Cinema', unpublished miscellanies.
—— 1942–44, 'Clubs and Societies: Cinemas and Theatres', vol. II, unpublished miscellanies.
—— 1942, 'To Area Commander, Subject: Proposed Dramatic Society or Club', unpublished letter, 25 November.
—— 1943–, 'Amenities: Minutes and Meetings of the Troops Entertainment Committee', unpublished miscellanies.
—— 1944–45, 'Native Administration: Propaganda for Natives', unpublished miscellanies.
—— 1944, 'File No. 273, Subject: Colour Bar', unpublished note, 19 August.
—— 1944–46, 'Clubs and Societies: Cinemas and Theatres', vol. III, unpublished miscellanies.
—— 1945–50, 'Clubs and Societies: Cinema', unpublished miscellanies.
—— 1945, 'To: Mr. Abraham Redda, Subject: A Tigrinya Play at Cinema Hamasien', unpublished letter, 3 November.
—— 1942–46, 'Amenities: Entertainments [sic] Welfare', vol. I, unpublished miscellanies.
—— 1946–48, 'Amenities: Entertainments [sic] Welfare', vol. II, unpublished miscellanies.
—— 1943–46, 'Amenities: Bars, Cabarets, Dancing Halls, etc.', vol. I, unpublished miscellanies.
—— 1948–54, 'Amenities: Bars, Cabarets, Dancing Halls, etc.', vol. II, unpublished miscellanies.
—— 1946, 'Circular No. 22 (Pers) 1946, Subject: Welfare Entertainment', unpublished circular, 29 March.
—— 1948, 'Notice: "The Singing Kettle"', unpublished, 21 January.
—— 1948, 'To: Political Secretary, B.M.A. H.Q., Asmara, Subject: "La Tragedia Di Teodoro" [Compagnia Teatrale Nativa [Ma.Te.De.]', unpublished letter, 18 December.
—— 1948, 'To: Superintendent i/c C.I.D. Eritrea Police, Asmara, Subject: "La Tragedia Di Teodoro"', unpublished letter, 23 December.
—— 1951–52, 'Political Parties: Female Unionist Party', unpublished miscellanies.

Campbell, Ali, Christine Matzke, Gerri Moriarty, Renny O'Shea, Jane Plastow and students of the Tigre/Bilen theatre training course, 1999, 'Telling the Lion's Tale: Making Theatre in Eritrea', *African Theatre in Development*, ed. Martin Banham, James Gibbs and Femi Osofisan (Oxford: James Currey; Bloomington: Indiana University Press): 38–53.

Chitauro, Moreblessings, Caleb Dube and Liz Gunner, 1994, 'Song, Story and Nation: Women as Singers and Actresses in Zimbabwe', in *Politics and Performance: Theatre, Poetry and Song in Southern Africa*, ed. Liz Gunner (Johannesburg: Witwatersrand University Press): 111–38.

Cousland, David C., 1942, 'Ref: Military Administrator's Minutes of 249 (Films)', unpublished minutes, Asmara, 4 September.

EPLF (Research Branch), 1982, *Pilot Survey of Eritrean Culture V: Arts: Literature, Painting, Music and Dance, Theatre and Cinema, Sculpture and Architecture*, mimeograph, translated by Tekeste Yonas (n.p.: Department of Politicization, Education and Culture).

Estefanos, Yonathan, 1996, 'History of Eritrean Drama', Senior Paper, Department of Language Studies, University of Asmara, 13 May.

Firebrace, James, with Stuart Holland, 1985, *Never Kneel Down: Drought, Development and Liberation in Eritrea* (Trenton, NJ: Red Sea Press).

Green, F.G. for Commissioner of Police, Eritrea Police Force, 1952, 'Confidential, Ref: S/17/36, To: Deputy Political Advisor, B.A. Headquarters, Asmara', unpublished, 9 January.

Isaak, Angesom, 2000, 'Amleset: First and Last on Stage', trans. by Tesfazghi Ukubazghi, *Trigta*, 1 February: 1, 7.

Iyob, Ruth, 1995, *The Eritrean Struggle for Independence: Domination, Resistance, Nationalism, 1941–1993* (Cambridge: Cambridge University Press).

Jameson, Colonel F.R.S., 1942, 'Notice: [Colour Bar Cancelled for BM Forces and Eritrea Police]', unpublished, 14 October.

Kahasai, Alemayo, 1977EC [1984/85], unpublished manuscript, Ministry of Culture for the Province of Eritrea, trans. by ECBTP 1995, 15 February.

Kemink, Friederike, 1991, *Die Tegreñña-Frauen in Eritrea: Eine Untersuchung der Kodizes des Gewohnheitsrechts 1890–1941* (Stuttgart: Franz Steiner).

Lucas, Elias, 1996, 'The Development of Eritrean Theatre: From Where to Where?', trans. by Mussie Tesfagiorgis, *Adulis*, 1 January: 25–33.

National Union of Eritrean Women (NUEW), 1987, *Eritreische Frauen*, ed. Ingrid Haller (Kassel: Gesamthochschule).

—— 1999, *Eritrea: Women and their Tradition of Resistance* (1985; Asmara: NUEW).

Negash, Ghirmai, 1999, *A History of Tigrinya Literature in Eritrea: The Oral and the Written 1890– 1991* (Leiden: Research School of Asian, African, and Amerindian Studies (CNWS), University of Leiden).

Obbo, Christine, 1981, *African Women: Their Struggle for Economic Independence* (1980; London: Zed Books).

Pankhurst, Richard, 1992, *A Social History of Ethiopia: The Northern and Central Highlands from Early Medieval Times to the Rise of Emperor Téwodros II* (1990; Trenton, NJ: Red Sea Press).

Parker, Lt Colonel G. Stanley (S.C.A.O. Asmara & Hamasien), 1944a, 'To: Supt of Police, Asmara, Subject: Employment of Half-Cast Girls on the Stage', unpublished letter, 9 August.

—— 1944b, 'To: Chief Secretary, H.Q, BMA, Eritrea, Subject: Employment of Half-Cast Girls on the Stage', 15 August.

p'Bitek, Okot, 1973, 'Pop Music, Bishops and Judges', *Africa's Cultural Revolution* (Nairobi: Macmillan Books for Africa): 1–5.

Plastow, Jane, 1997a, 'Theatre of Conflict in the Eritrean Independence Struggle', *New Theatre Quarterly*, 13.50: 144–54.

—— 1997b, 'The Eritrea Community-Based Theatre Project', *New Theatre Quarterly*, 13.53: 386–95.

Pool, David, 1997, *Eritrea: Towodros Unity in Diversity*, Minority Rights Group International Report, 97/1 (London: Minority Rights Group).

Redda, Abraham, 1945, 'To: Political Secretary, Subject: *New World*', unpublished letter, 3 November.

Russom, Eyob, 1997, 'Interview with Amleset Abay', trans. by Yakem Tesfai, *Setit*, 28 November.

Schröder, Günter, 1987, *Bildung in Eritrea* (Kassel: Gesamthochschule).

46   Christine Matzke

Selassie, Bereket Habte, 1980, *Conflict and Intervention in the Horn of Africa* (New York: Monthly Review Press).

Setton, Captain Maxwell, A.L.A., Eritrea, 1941, 'To: Lt. Col. A.A. Baerlein, L.A., Eritrea: Natives in Public Places of Entertainment', unpublished report, 13 October.

Societa Italiana degli Autori e Editori, 1944, 'To S.C.A.O. Asmara and Hamasien, Director Customs & Excise Dept., Subject: Amateur Theatrical Companies', unpublished letter, Asmara, 13 January.

Taylor, [?], 1943, 'Film Situation in Eritrea', unpublished report, 28 January.

Teklehaimanot, Berhane, 1996, 'Education in Eritrea during the European Colonial Period', *Eritrean Studies Review*, 1.1: 1–22.

Temesgen, [?], 1956, 'First Singing Competition Performed [...]: Ato Tewolde Redda wins First Prize with a Vote of 269', trans. by ECBTP 1995, *Zemen*, 3 October.

Tesfahunei, Tebereh, 2000, *A Short Autobiography of Tebereh Tesfahunei (Doris Day)*, 2nd edn, translated by Mohamed Salih Ismail ([Asmara]: n.p.).

Trevaskis, G.K.N., 1960, *Eritrea: A Colony in Transition: 1941–52* (London: Oxford University Press).

Yosief, Yishak, 1979EC [1986/87], 'Do You Know Much Asmara? The Indigenous Theatre Association (Ma.Te.De.)', trans. by Tesfazghi Ukubazghi, *Voice of Asmara City Dwellers' Association*, 1 October.

INTERVIEWS

Eritrea Community Based Project (ECBTP) 1995, Abebe Iyasu, 6 September 1995, Asmara, Eritrea.

—— Tekabo Woldemariam, Abebe Iyasu, Jabre Mahmoud, n.d., Asmara, Eritrea.

I 1   Abebe Iyasu, 23 September 2000, Asmara, Eritrea.
I 2   Amete Solomon, 21 July 2000, Asmara, Eritrea.
I 3   Amleset Abay, 24 September 1999, Asmara, Eritrea.
I 4   Arefaine Tewolde, 13 October 1999, Asmara, Eritrea.
I 5   Anon., 23 March 2000, Asmara, Eritrea.
I 6   Ethiopia Medhanie, 25 March 2000, Asmara, Eritrea.
I 7   Ghidey Rustom, 22 April 2000, Asmara, Eritrea.
I 8   Lemlem Gebregziabher, 4 April 2000, Asmara, Eritrea.
I 9   Osman Ahmed, 27 January 2000, Asmara, Eritrea.
I 10   —— 2nd interview, 18 February 2000, Asmara, Eritrea.
I 11   —— 3rd interview, 1 August 2000, Asmara, Eritrea.
I 12   Tekabo Woldemariam, 11 March 2000, Asmara, Eritrea.
I 13   —— 2nd interview, 13 March 2000, Asmara, Eritrea.
I 14   —— 3rd interview, 15 March 2000, Asmara, Eritrea.
I 15   —— 4th interview, 21 March 2000, Asmara, Eritrea.
I 16   —— 5th interview, 6 September 2000, Asmara, Eritrea.
I 17   Tekeste Yonas, 28 September 2000, Asmara, Eritrea.
I 18   Tsehaitu Beraki, 13 September 1999, Asmara, Eritrea.

Contextualising Women's Theatre in Kenya
Alakie-Akinyi Mboya's *Otongolia* & Ari Katini Mwachofi's *Mama ee*

MIKE KURIA

Kenya is perhaps best known in literary circles because of Ngugi wa Thiong'o's and to a lesser extent Grace Ogot's fiction. In terms of drama, no Kenyan has risen to the ranks of Wole Soyinka in West Africa, Mbongeni Ngema in South Africa, Ebrahim Hussein in Tanzania, or John Ruganda in Uganda. Although David Mulwa and Francis Imbuga have been in the field for many years and have had several of their plays published, their works are yet to gain as much international acclaim as fiction from both men and women in the region. If men have performed dismally in the arena of drama, women have faired even worse. Micere Mugo co-authored *The Trial of Dedan Kimathi* with Ngugi wa Thiong'o but did not proceed to write any play on her own. Rebeka Njau, whose novel, *Ripples in the Pool* is, in my opinion, the most sophisticated treatment of women's plight in Kenyan novels, wrote a play in the 1960s, *The Scar*, but has yet to publish another. At least three factors seem to be involved in the entrenchment of male dominance in Kenyan theatre: politics, academia and the place of performance. Political repression is by far the most culpable in driving women away from participating in theatrical activities. Theatre in Kenya has very much been like the Mau Mau movement that employed overt and covert subversive activities to undermine the colonial government, only this time the target has been a post-colonial black government. In spite of the lack of international acclaim, however, theatre activity in Kenya since the days of Ngugi's *Maitu Njugira* and *Ngahika Ndeenda,* has continued to be informally vibrant in defiance of fierce opposition and repression from the government. The pace set by Ngugi wa Thiong'o's *Ngahika Ndeenda,* which explored issues of alienation in reference to land rights in a post-independence Kenya, has only slightly slackened. Because of indicting Kenyatta's government for being as repressive as the colonial government and for forcefully taking away land from the peasants, Ngugi was arrested and detained in 1977. In the early 1980s theatre activity was still very strictly censored by the government which refused to give licences to plays, such as Joe De Graft's *Muntu* (1977), that were considered too political. Even high school plays performed in drama competitions were closely monitored, censored and even banned if considered political. This happened to Kenya Science Teachers College's performance of a play entitled

Human Nature. Engagement in drama therefore meant engaging with the government. Given the brutal nature of government responses, and viewed against the background of traditionally defined roles of women, primarily homemaking, drama was not a genre conducive to women. When I interviewed Rebeka Njau in 1998, she indicated that one of the reasons that Kenya had not produced a woman Ngugi·was the fear of reprisals from the government. Reading Kenyan women's fiction/short stories, such as Kabira's 'I Cannot Sign', and Grace Namai's 'The Spider's Web' it is clear that motherhood has a very powerful influence on the choices that women make, and that almost always they choose whatever appears to be beneficial to their children. Women, for example, choose to endure domestic violence in the attempt to shield their children from the pains of divorce or being brought up by a stepmother. In this context it is hardly conceivable that women would have been willing to participate in theatre activities for which they would risk being detained and leaving their children unattended. This is not to say that women did not participate in theatre activity, but rather that it explains the relatively lesser representation of women in the field in comparison to men.

In the late 1980s and early 1990s, Kenyans became increasingly vocal about their dissatisfaction with the Moi regime. They paid a heavy price with many being arrested and subjected to prison sentences on fabricated charges. Numerous lecturers, students and journalists were charged with being in possession of seditious documents such as *Pambana* and *Mpatanishi*[1] or failing to report the existence of subversive clandestine organisations such as *Mwakenya*.[2] By 1992 when Kenya reverted from a *de jure* one-party state to a multi-party state, there was increasingly more freedom of speech. Cartoonists could caricature president Moi and get away with it. Thespians such as Wahome Mutahi could ridicule Moi in such plays as *Mugathe Mubogethi* which ran in Kenyan bars across the country for a record nine months. By the end of the century political satire had made its way from the bars to NationTV, a privately owned television station, with such productions as the immensely popular sitcom *Readykulus* which ridicules and makes fun of government functionaries. This is something that no Kenyan would have dreamt of in the 1980s when people did not dare criticise Moi in public for fear of arrests and harassment. In terms of theatre, productions in the vernacular, especially in Kikuyu, the most widely spoken ethnic language in Kenya, dominated performances in and around cities in the late 1980s and early 1990s. The resurgence of vernacular theatre, which for all practical purposes was a continuation of what was begun in the Ngugi wa Thiong'o-led Kamiriithu project did not, however, make it easier for women to participate. In the first place, most of these plays were performed in bars where waiters criss-crossed the audience serving alcoholic drinks in between scenes. It meant that performances would take place either in the evenings or at weekends when most white-collar workers could afford to be away from their desks. Unfortunately this is also the time when children are away from school and hence need someone to be with them at home. The responsibility of child care largely falls on women in Kenya. Culturally, women are not usually linked to drunkenness or being in the pub. Needless to say, the bars in which these performances take place are in the city or urban centres while most women are to be found in the rural villages. Theatre in Kenya is, in this context, not gender friendly as far as women are concerned.

Finally, theatre in Kenya is closely related to academic institutions and specifically to the university. The centrality of the university in the development of theatre in Kenya is reflected in the fact that although Kamiriithu was a people-based project, the brains behind it were university-trained intellectuals. Rebeka Njau published her play *The Scar: A Tragedy* when she was a student at the University of Makerere. Equally, Ngugi's first play, *The Black Hermit*, was written and produced at the University of Makerere. The most prolific dramatists in Kenya, David Mulwa and Francis Imbuga, are both university lecturers and had their plays first produced and performed at the university. Nairobi University is central to the development of theatre in Kenya, not only because it was the first fully fledged Kenyan university and because Kenya's pre-eminent writer, Ngugi wa Thiong'o, lectured there, but also because many pioneering productions took place on the campus. Ngugi's *Maitu Njugira*, for example, was first performed at the Education Theatre II at the University. This was after it was refused performance at the Kenya National Theatre, only a stone's throw from the University. In Kenyatta's as well as in Moi's government, the university fraternity, prior to 1986, was on various occasions allowed political liberties prohibited outside the institution. Statistics show that even as late as the 1990s women were less than 40 per cent of the university population in Kenya. Eddah Gachukia, a leading gender activist and educationist as well as founder member of FAWE,[3] as quoted in the *Daily Nation*, 3 January 2001, argues that current university enrolment of girls compares with that of boys in the proportion 2:3. This means that the centrality of the university in the development of theatre also means less women's involvement. Connected to the university and the development of drama in Kenya have been the annual drama festivals involving colleges, high schools and primary schools. While this is a good forum for women to participate in given that teaching is a popular profession with women, drama festivals also involve travelling and sometimes staying away from the family for several days, especially at provincial and national levels. In general then, conditions operating in Kenya were not conducive to women's participation in theatre.

The two plays that I examine in this paper, Ari Katini Mwachofi's (1987) *Mama ee* in Kiswahili and Alakie-Akinyi Mboya's (1986) *Otongolia* in English, should therefore, in my opinion and in the context of the foregoing arguments, be seen as these two women's achievements in the face of immense obstacles. Although both of these writers were university products, with Mboya's first play *Radi*, as John Ruganda informs us in the introduction to *Otongolia*, having been read and hotly discussed at the University of Nairobi, and Mwachofi having been a Kiswahili teacher for many years in Kenya, I suggest that their writings should also be understood in the context of the UN Decade for Women International Conference that took place in Nairobi in 1985. Significantly, *Otongolia* was performed during the conference at Nairobi in July 1985. The play had previously been performed in May and June at the Tom

Mboya Labour College in Kisumu, at the University of Nairobi, and at the French Cultural Centre in Nairobi, showing its close relationship to both academia and the city. As will become apparent, it is significant that Mwachofi's play was published two years after the conference. *Mama ee's* subject matter is centred around the issues central to the International Women's Conference held in Nairobi in 1985.

The two plays are markedly different not only in terms of subject matter but also in their approach. *Otongolia* is primarily about politics, specifically about the abuse of power by Otong who, as the head of state in the mythical kingdom of Otongolia, appoints his family members to run the country. It is family members who hold all the top posts in the Illo, the country's governing council. The plot is made a little more complicated by the introduction of neo-imperialism personified in Kalap who, though a foreigner, has influence in all industrial holdings in the country. Further complications emerge when it turns out that Otong's wife is engaging in subversive activities aimed at dethroning her husband and installing her son whom she thinks she can better control. In a reworking of an oedipal relationship, mother and son find themselves pitted against father and daughter as Lia, Otong's daughter, is not only very close to her father but is also his chief adviser. The women in this play are not mourning patriarchal dominance but as John Ruganda (1986) says in the intro-duction, they are 'as fiery, vicious and ambitious as the men against whom they play'. Unlike in *Mama ee*, the discourse involved here is not one of victimhood, with women as victims and men as the aggressors, but one of women's active engagement in the manipulation of socio-political forces that shape the lives of both men and women.

Mama ee, however, does explore women's victimhood in modern day Kenya where men insist that women adhere to traditional rules and regulations while they, the men, dispense with their traditional responsibilities. In this play, Mwavita's husband Kinaya is an irresponsible drunkard civil servant who leaves the business of providing for his family to his wife and subjects her to domestic violence. Although the women in the play resist modern-day male oppression, they are portrayed as victims. In the prologue, presented as dramatised verse, the writer uses the refrain '*Dunia hii ya mawi, dunia ya wanaume*' (this is a man's world), to emphasise that women live in a man's world and that the only way to survive in it, as women, is to unite. In essence, like feminism in its early stages, this plays inscribes Kenyan women as united in a sisterhood of suffering and therefore obliged to engage in a sisterhood of resistance. In spite of the different approaches to issues, however, the two plays are similar in the way that they question conventional understanding of women's politics of liberation in Africa.

In scholarly discourses on Africa it is generally assumed, culturally speaking, that the modern is necessarily progressive and better than the traditional. The rise of gender politics in Africa has also generally been consistent with this practice. The modern is associated with individuality and freedom, education and economic empowerment, monogamy and an appeal to less culturally controlled legal systems. This is supposed to be in contrast to communalism, illiteracy, economic dependence, polygamy, wife inheritance and a culturally controlled legal system; repressive cultural practices such as female circumcision, usually referred to as female genital mutilation, wife beating, and so on. It appears to me that though not denying a certain measure of legitimacy to such an approach, these two plays present a much more dynamic view of the African experience. Obioma Nnaemeka's (1997) argument that '[a] gender analysis of patriarchal and imperialist structure shows how women simultaneously affirm and disrupt such structures' succinctly captures the message of these two plays.

There is no denying, for example, that *Mama ee* is openly and explicitly feminist. As has already been noted, the writer uses the prologue to diagnose society as male dominated to the detriment of women. She then calls upon women to join hands and fight against their oppression and exploitation by men. In reference to women's condition Mwachofi uses such strong words as *kunyonywa, kunyanyaswa, utumwa, ubeberu* and *ukoloni* among many others. These words can be translated roughly as exploitation, oppression, slavery, imperialism and colonialism. The first word needs elaboration as it carries with it nuances of sucking as in the suckling of babies as well the sucking of a leech. In this word, men are accused of not only nourishing themselves from their mothers as suckling babies but that as grown ups they become like leeches and suck women to death. Men's domination of women is likened to enslavement and colonialism. The final part of the prologue is a call to arms, women against men, as well as the issuance of a stern warning that unless men mend their ways, women will extract vengeance. The following excerpts with their rough translations are examples of the militancy that the play advocates:

Ole wenu waume, mnyanyasao wake zenu,
Mlio mapaka shume, itafika zamu zenu,
Mshike jembe kiume, kuauni mama zenu,
Mlowanyonya bila haya, karne nenda,
Karne rudi, AMKENI MJITEGEMEE (emphasis in text)

Woe unto you men, who oppress your wives
You macho men, your time is coming
For you to hold weeding hoes like men, and provide for your mothers,
Whom you have unashamedly sucked/exploited for generations
WAKE UP AND BE INDEPENDENT.

Hatatukubali tena, kunyonywa twaapia
Tuliponyonywa sana, na mkoloni mlaaniwa,
Pamoja tulipigana, uhuru kuunyakuliwa,
Leo tumepata uhuru, imekuaje mtuangamize?
ONDOENI WENU UBEBERU.

We shall never accept again, we swear to you, to be exploited,
When we were intensely exploited, by the accursed colonialist,
Together we fought, to gain our freedom
Now we have our freedom, how is it you dominate us?
AWAY WITH YOUR IMPERIALISM.

The excerpts suffice to demonstrate that the author inscribes women as men's victims in a post-colonial Kenyan/African society, and that she calls upon women to engage in militant resistance to male oppression and exploitation. Indeed her stance is not different from Hélène Cixous' argument in her article 'The Laugh of the Medusa' ((1975) 1977), that women are unfairly blamed for everything that goes wrong in society. This position is articulated by none other than Mwavita's mother when she says: '*uke tupu laana, kwa vyote alaumiwa*' which translates as 'being a woman is nothing but a curse, in everything she is blamed'.

While I therefore grant that Mwachofi's ideas are consistent with feminism, my argument is that she does not cast women's oppression as mapped by such oppositions as traditional/modern, rural/urban or illiterate/educated. Rather, she presents a much more complex situation with women occupying both sides of these divides and experiencing varying degrees of marginalisation/oppression whose intensity is not determined or necessarily relative to what space, traditional or modern, rural or urban, illiterate or educated, they occupy. Mwavita, the lead character in this play, is subjected to domestic abuse even though she is educated, financially independent, an urban dweller and married to an equally educated urban husband. Her advantage is that modernity enables her to choose divorce in a less painful way than traditional African women in this particular society would have had to. In traditional culture, divorce was not encouraged as an option. Instead, emphasis was placed on conflict resolution and re-union between couples. In extreme cases, when a woman completely refused to be re-united with her husband, her toe would be tied with a string and tightened progressively until the pain subdued her into agreeing to return to her husband. Even in such cases some women chose to lose their toes rather than return to their abusive husbands, in which case divorce was granted (Mwachofi 1987: 44). In this case, Mwavita's financial independence enables her to set up house on her own and, perhaps due to her education and hence knowledge, she seeks divorce through a neo-colonial legal system. Although the legal system is male dominated and given to making recourse to traditional values which decree that children always belong to the man, and which therefore leads to Mwavita being denied custody of her children, the fact that Mwavita is granted divorce without being subjected to the painful process of tying her toe might very well be interpreted as a valorisation of modernity against tradition.

However, that conclusion is subverted by the process through which Mwachofi takes Kinaya and Mwavita before they finally come to the court. Mwavita at first seeks justice from the traditional legal system. The old men are surprised to hear that Kinaya had beaten up his pregnant wife to the point of knocking out some of her teeth. In the history of the elders present, such a thing had never happened. In spite of acknowledging that Kinaya is perhaps a victim of society's failure to inculcate traditional values by leaving all education to a westernised schooling system, they nevertheless decide to fine him for his wrong-doing. Significantly the elders do not really seem to be fining him for beating his wife, although that is not condoned, but rather for beating her when she was pregnant, knocking out her teeth, and shedding her blood. To their credit, however, the elders do censure Kinaya for beating his wife. In the words of one of them, '*mke si ngoma wala si mtoto. Ukitaka kumkanya, mdomo unatosha. Hakuna haja ya kumkaripia kwa ngumi*', which translates as, 'Your wife is not a drum or child. If you want to warn her about something just tell her. There is no need of setting upon her with blows' (40). The key thing, however, is that a heavy penalty is imposed on Kinaya, and Mwavita is asked to stay with his parents until Kinaya has paid all the fine. Mwavita, however, chooses to ignore the elders and returns to her husband, citing her concern for her son Juma, before the full penalties are paid. This act does not only anger the elders but also makes it impossible for Mwavita to go back to them when Kinaya turns violent again. In effect Mwachofi seems to suggest that neither traditional nor modern legal systems condone wife beating but that both are subject to abuse. By the time a legal separation is enacted, Mwavita's father has already issued a decree that his daughter should never go back to Kinaya. In real sense then, the traditional court does not fail to function because it is essentially sexist but because Mwavita ignores it's edicts. In terms of sexism, the modern court is equally if not more guilty and amenable to manipulation by men. It is instructive that Kinaya continues to harass Mwavita even after the court issues restraining orders against his visiting her. Mwavita and her sister Tenge are so frustrated by the system's inability to protect and listen to them that the only way to have their case dealt with is to resort to physical violence.

In the course of the elders' arbitration process we also learn about the changing nature of dowry in modern times in contrast to traditional customs. Mwavita's father, Baba Mkubwa Mwavita, one of the elders, says the following in reference to Kinaya's violent nature:

> Kuolewa ndiko huku kweli? Zamani sisi tulioa wake lakinin sasa watu wanunua watumwa na ngoma pia wawe wakipiga wasikize mlio.
>
> Is this what marriage means really? In the olden times we used to marry women but now people buy slaves and drums to be drumming in order to listen to their tunes.

What the old man is saying is that in the old days dowry meant marriage and the beginning of a relationship not only between husband and wife but also between their relatives. To the modern African man, if Kinaya be representative at all, dowry commodifies women and makes them the property of their husbands. He argues that once a woman marries, everything she has, including herself, becomes the property of her husband. Asked by Kinaya why their forefathers never thought the same way, he argues

> wao hawakulazimika kulipa pesa zaidi hivi ati kwa kuwa mke ana shahada! Baba zenu, siku hizi wanawauza. Mimi nililipa shilingi elfu mbili zaidi kwa kuwa ulifika kidato cha sita. Wengine hulipa zaidi-si kununua nini?
>
> They were not forced to pay more money because their wives had degrees. These days your fathers just sell you. I was forced to pay two thousand shillings more because you went to form six. Others pay much more, if that is not buying what is it?

In this quote we encounter a situation where tradition and modernity actually combine in enhancing the oppression of women. Rather than leading to the eradication of the dowry system or recasting it in less oppressive terms, education leads to the commercialisation of dowry, leaving men bitter and women being viewed as no more than commodities. I have always wondered why gender activists do not target dowry with as much enthusiasm as other cultural practices such as female circumcision and wife inheritance when dowry is the major culprit in legitimising men's power over women. I suspect that this is one of the areas in which the modern African man would join forces with modern African women to fight against the practice. The reason being that in contemporary terms, where the educated man is usually economically more powerful than his father, the burden of dowry falls on his shoulders whereas in the traditional times his father would have given him cows and goats. If dowry were eradicated, marriage would be contracted on more equal terms and men would have no legitimate excuse for exercising authority over their wives.

In reference to the urban–rural nexus in this play, which also relates to the modern-versus-traditional debate or the new-versus-old, Mwachofi does acknowledge that rural women are more oppressed than those living in cities. However, the reason is not that they are in the rural areas *per se* but that they are married to husbands who take refuge in the city, leaving all the hard work, specifically farm work and rearing children, to their wives. Tenge, Mwavita's sister, argues that owing to rural women's lesser educational qualifications, they are made to work like donkeys. Meanwhile their husbands live in towns with other women. This argument resonates well with Mary Ngecu's (1992) short story *The Other Woman* and Agnes Gathumbi's *Faith Ruined her Life*, in which women living in rural areas have their lives ruined by unfaithful husbands living in the city. While the modern man in urban areas indulges in amorous activities, his counterpart in the rural area is equally indolent and indulgent but this time in alcohol: either way the women are left in charge of the home in every way. That women in both the city and in the village bear the burden of producing for the sustenance of society suggests, once again, that the dichotomies usually constructed around the rural and urban really do not make much sense in the context of gender politics in this particular community, and I hasten to add in Kenya and most of Africa in general. Surprisingly, only the old people seem to think that in their times men and women had specific roles to which they stuck and adhered. Men, according to Mwavita (and her mother seems to support her point), did not engage in drunkenness but rather farmed, hunted, herded both cows and sheep, dealt with construction work, and made sure that their wives and children had enough food. Women on the other hand took care of domestic chores like cooking and taking care of children. In the modern, post-colonial society, this cultural behaviour has now changed with women having to do everything. It is in this context that Mwachofi calls upon women, educated or otherwise, rural or urban, to unite and demand justice.

Like *Mama ee*, *Otongolia* acknowledges the patriarchal nature of society. The play is about power, and power in Otongolia, the fictional community, is passed from father to son. Indeed although this play was first performed in 1985, there is an uncanny resemblance between Otong's and Moi's government in the late 1990s and early twenty-first century. Some of Moi's closest confidants and power barons are said to be his relatives. A good example is Nicholas Kiprono arap Biwott, who in spite of having been embroiled in controversies allegedly ranging from corruption to the murder of the late Minister for Foreign Affairs, Dr Robert Ouko, remains in government. Even donor pressure has not managed to convince Moi to drop him. He is said to be Moi's nephew. Mark Too, widely known as Moi's public relations adviser is said to be Moi's son. Musalia Mudavadi, a Minister for Information, Transport and Communication in Moi's government is also said to be his nephew. Effectively, Musalia holds three ministries on his own. Like Otong, Moi has appointed relatives to positions of power. On 23 July 1999, under pressure from the International Monetary Fund (IMF) to root out corruption in the civil service, Moi appointed Richard Leakey, a white man born in Kenya, as secretary of the cabinet. Leakey and Kalap, in as far as they are seen as representatives of western interests in Kenya and Otongolia respectively, bear resemblance to each other. The VP's troubles in Otongolia bear similarity to the troubles that Kenya's vice-president, George Saitoti, has been experiencing in the run up to Moi's exit from power in 2002. In essence then, Mboya's *Otongolia* is also about Kenya. Beyond acknowledging male dominance in Otongolia, and by inference Kenya, Mboya also seems to make a distinction between occupying the office of power and wielding power. Men, on the basis of their sex, occupy offices of power while women, on the basis of their manipulative, scheming and intellectual acumen, wield power.

This is perhaps where fiction and reality begin to part ways, as in reality Moi and his wife are separated and he (Moi) is not known to have any powerful and close women advisers around him. In his entire presidency, spanning more than twenty years, he has only once, in 1995, appointed a woman to a full cabinet post. In *Otongolia*, however, Otong's wife is not some background house-wife playing second fiddle or waiting to bow in deference to the all powerful Otong. She is a fiercely ambitious and subversive king-maker, not only contemptuous of her husband but also ready to dethrone him from power and join with progressive forces, even imperialistic ones, to establish a kingdom in which she calls the shots. The end of the play testifies to her strength of character when she declares, after being banished from Otongolia for treasonable activities and on her exit, that she will be back. It is obvious that she has not given up on her ambitions of taking over the leadership of the country.

The strength of the women is asserted through contrasts. The weakness of Otong is seen against the strength of Oting (his wife). The weakness of Ongo (Oting's son) is set against the background of Lia's, Ongo's sister's, strength. Oting and her daughter, though working at cross purposes, are the progressive forces in this society. Ongo, the heir to the throne, is indecisive and hopelessly deficient in ambition and vision. Even when his father passes on the mantle of leadership to him at the end of the play he is hesitant about taking over. This is in contrast to his sister who is already planning on ditching Iso, her errant husband who, with the help of Kalap, has been trying to aid Oting in dethroning Otong. Although Lia sides with her father, she is conscious at the same time that 'traditions [can and] should be bent to accommodate progress and individuality without discrimination' (78). She makes this assertion in defence of her decision to divorce Iso and possibly stay single. Given the weakness of Ongo and the absence of his mother's strong influence, it seems that the real ruler in Otongolia will be Lia. Mboya offers two possible endings: in the first one, already discussed above, Ongo takes over leadership with Lia as his personal adviser. The second is a continuation of the first and has two key additions. First is the announcement that a wedding is about to take place between Ongo and a distant relative of the VP. The second is that Kalap and Iso, who had escaped from Otongolia using the only car in the land, are possibly returning. These two events have two possible implications. First, that Ongo will get married and, if his father's hopes are fulfilled, the new wife will make him 'change his ways, stand on his feet and be the heir' that Otong wants him to be. Secondly, that Kalap is on his way back to exercise authority over Ongo as he had done over Oting. The return of Kalap might also mean the return of Oting because Kalap and Oting have intersecting interests. Kalap wants to exercise greater control in the development agenda of the Otongolian community while Oting thinks that she can use Kalap and his people, the Swallows, unambiguously the West, to fashion Otongolia in her own image. It is also instructive that Oting believes passionately that she can control her son, and given his weakness and indecisiveness, his mother's return is not completely unfeasible. Either way the suggestion is the same: Ongo might be taking over the seat of power but he is unlikely to wield power. The women will continue to wield power in this patriarchal society.

Read hastily, these two plays might be interpreted as being, unwittingly or not, in the defence of African patriarchal cultural practices. Mwachofi, for example, might be accused of turning a deaf ear to the abusive relationships that traditional women found themselves in. She refuses to deal with the issue of wife beating in traditional African societies beyond merely recognising its presence. Indeed she seems to argue that it was extremely rare and hardly ever so cruel as to involve pregnant women, in contrast to the case she dramatises. I would like to argue, however, that rather than absolve traditional Africa from charges of cruelty against women, she is actually trying to defend African feminism against charges of blind imitation of western cultural norms. She does this by accusing men of being unfaithful to African cultural value standards in their abdication of their familial duties. In this regard she is doing much the same thing that Grace Ogot does in her stories such as 'The Old White Witch' and 'The White Veil'. Likewise, Mboya is in no way falsifying history or contemporary African experience by vesting power in women, when in fact women occupy the margins of power in most African governments. I think that the strength of her play lies in her refusal either to glorify women as saints or simply to demonise men. She takes the more realistic position, best captured by Obioma Nnaemeka (1997) that African women in society occupy multiple positions and are equally capable of both malevolence and benevolence, sometimes even in regard to fellow women. At the same time, Mboya argues that while African leadership is generally patriarchal, the women are not to be mistaken as passive, silent and ineffectual. Like Appiah (1992) she suggests that individual women can and do wield immense power in African societies. Mboya goes further by arguing that these women are not only ready to dispense power that is conferred upon them by patriarchal institutions, but that they are ready to manipulate patriarchy in order to harness more power for themselves. These two plays should therefore be read as capturing the condition of women in African societies as well as their potential within the dynamics of their cultural and political environments.

NOTES

1. *Pambana* and *Mpatanishi* were publications distributed clandestinely by members of *Mwakenya* in the early 1980s.
2. An underground Kenyan liberation movement whose activities became most visible from 1982.
3. Forum for African Women Educationalists.

BIBLIOGRAPHY

Appiah, Anthony Kwame, 1992, *In my Father's House: Africa in the Philosophy of Culture* (New York: Oxford University Press).

Cixous, Hélène, (1975) 1997. 'The Laugh of the Medusa', in *Feminisms: An Anthology of Literary Theory and Criticism*, ed. Robyn R. Warhol and Diane Price Herndl (Basingstoke: Macmillan Press).

De Graft, Joe, 1977, *Muntu* (London: Heinemann).

Gathumbi, Agnes, 1992, 'Faith Destroyed her Life', in *They have Destroyed the Temple*, ed. Wanjiku Kabira, Muthoni Karega and Elizabeth Nzioki (Nairobi: Longman Kenya).

Kabira, Wanjiku, 1990, 'I Cannot Sign', in *Our Secret Lives: An Anthology of Poems and Short Stories by Kenyan Women Writers*, ed. Wanjiku Kabira, Muthoni Karega and Elizabeth Nzioki (Nairobi: Phoenix Publishers; London: Heinemann).

Mboya, Alakie-Akinyi, 1986, *Otongolia: A Play in Four Scenes*, with an introduction by John Ruganda (Nairobi: Oxford University Press).

Mutahi, Wahome, *Mugathe Mubogethi*, performed 1995.

Mwachofi, Ari Katini, 1987, *Mama ee* (Nairobi: East African Educational Publishers).

Namai, Grace, 1992, 'The Spider's Web', in *They have Destroyed the Temple*, ed. Wanjiku Kabira, Muthoni Karega and Elizabeth Nzioki (Nairobi: Longman Kenya).

Ngecu, Mary, 1992, 'The Other Woman', in *They have Destroyed the Temple*, ed. Wanjiku Kabira, Muthoni Karega and Elizabeth Nzioki (Nairobi: Longman Kenya).

Ngugi wa Thiong'o, 1968, *The Black Hermit* (London: Heinemann).

Ngugi wa Thiong'o, 1982, *Maitu Njugira [Mother Sing for Me]*, unpublished musical.

Ngugi wa Thiong'o and Micere Githae Mugo, 1976, *The Trial of Dedan Kimathi* (London: Heinemann).

Ngugi wa Thiong'o and Ngugi wa Mirii, 1980, *Ngahika Ndeenda* [translated as *I will Marry When I Want*] (Nairobi: Heinemann Kenya).

Njau, Rebeka, 1965, *The Scar: A Tragedy in One Act* (Moshi: Lobp Art Gallery).

Njau, Rebeka, 1978, *Ripples in the Pool* (London: Heinemann).

Njau, Rebeka, 1998, Interview by author, 11 September, Ongata Rongai, Kenya.

Nnaemeka Obioma, 1997, 'Introduction: Imag(in)ing Knowledge, Power and Subversion in the Margins', in *The Politics of (M)othering: Womanhood, Identity, and Resistance in African Literature*, ed., Obioma Nnaemeka (London: Routledge): 1–25.

—— 1995, 'Feminism, Rebellious Women and Cultural Boundaries: Rereading Flora Nwapa and the Compatriots', *Research in African Literatures* 26.2 (Summer): 80–113.

Ogot , Grace, 1968, 'The Old White Witch', in *Land without Thunder: Short Stories* (Nairobi: East African Publishing House).

Ogot Grace, 1976 (1992), 'The White Veil', in *The Other Woman* (Nairobi: East African Educational Publishers).

Portraits of Women
in Contemporary Ugandan Theatre

MERCY MIREMBE NTANGAARE

During the last decades of the twentieth century uncertainties regarding the future of Ugandan theatre have grown, mostly due to the impact of film and video and the development of music-hall and erotic dance enterprises, all of which have burgeoned in the wake of economic liberalisation. These developments have forced theatre proprietors to devise new means of survival. Some have sought to improve technical and professional standards often imported from the amusement industry, while others have expanded their comic repertoire and the use of unusual gimmicks to attract audiences. In particular there has been an increasing wordiness in Ugandan theatre, and a notable increase in punning humour, which often promotes a real exchange between practitioners and audiences, and has been particularly utilised in populist theatre.

The most interesting developments in the theatre, however, have been the growth of interest in 'star' performers and the commodification and commercial exploitation of the female body. The 'star' phenomenon is beyond the scope of this paper, but the issue of women's bodies on stage is central to the article.

Discussing the rather unsettling, recurrent images of Black Africa in the Western world, J. Scott Kennedy listed factors which, significantly, parallel perceptions of women:

> Africa is a woman! She is both the prediction and the promise. She is always the beginning. But never the end. She is a surrealist. Both the image and the object. She is both art and use. She is truly MOTHER AFRICA. Mother of us all. Yet, to some people, she appears as a phantom in the night. As a spirit haunting their existence. As conscience forever standing over you. But to others she is their whore. Their pot to piss in. Their scum. Their woman to be raped, ruined, rationalized, exploited. Their exotic delight! And still to others she is their saint. Their saviour. Their survival. Their ritual of life. Their liberty. Their liberation! *But to all, she is forever an* ENIGMA! (Kennedy 1973: 22)

Woman is at once the most glorious, sweet, adorable creation in the world and the most pitiful, despicable and sad creature to have been created.

In much of traditional and even modern Uganda, a boy gains his social status as a man, or consolidates it if he has already passed through puberty rites, through marriage. Until this time, however old he may be, a man remains not his father's *son* but his mother's *child*; because fathers, as men, reproduce themselves. Culturally men are also expected to *rule* but not to *manage* homes. One might therefore expect, as in many societies, that women performers might be seen as a threat to men's rule. But in Uganda women could traditionally participate in public entertainment. As David Kerr explains:

> Women were just as creative and outspoken as men, whether it was in exclusively female forms such as initiation rituals and maize pounding songs, in mixed entertainment and rituals such as spirit possession dances and oral narratives, or as a chorus for the male dancers. (Kerr 1998: 43)

Nevertheless where gainful employment and politics are concerned, women's femininity remains a threat to men's masculinity. Contemporary Ugandan theatre portrays women, first and foremost, from a traditional social and cultural viewpoint. But a woman's body also has an economic value on the stage, and is an important aspect for calculating profitability in the commercial theatre.

The invocation of 'traditional' femininity

The 'traditional' image of woman in Ugandan literature and society evokes ideas of reverence and admiration, abhorrence and condemnation, vulnerability and docility. Sometimes the woman is the forbearing, tender, life-giving spirit at the centre of the Universe. She is a goddess-like Earth Mother essential to society's well-being. She is the force which brings into equilibrium the human and material worlds with the metaphysical and supernatural realms. Beyond even Biblical and local religious mythology, woman's link with the mystical world is traditionally manifested through her identification with traditional medicine and her power to give birth.

This is the woman whom Uganda's pre-eminent playwright, Robert Serumaga, adores for her strength and courage in his mythological account of the mother of twins in *Majangwa* (1974). Nagaddya, the mother, is the fount of both good and evil, as reflected in the products of her womb; the twin rivers Mayanja Wasswa and Mayanja Kato. While Mayanja Kato, the younger son, grows into a perfect river, his twin brother, Mayanja Wasswa, is a chaotic force. Through the mystic symbols of the rivers and their mother's birth experiences, Serumaga analyses and criticises Ugandan politics in the early post-independence period (1962–7). Mayanja Kato represents the Kabaka (traditional ruler) of Buganda, Sir Edward Mutesa II, who was both president and constitutional monarch of the country between 1962 and 1964, while Mayanja Wasswa represents Apolo Milton Obote, Mutesa's Prime Minister, who organised the coup which led to Uganda's second, and in Serumaga's view, illegal government. As a staunch *Muganda* (member of the dominant Ugandan ethnic group, the Buganda) and a monarchist, Serumaga could not possibly accept Obote, because no-one could be seen as ruling the king.

In the play Nagaddya, as Mother Uganda, struggles over several days to harmonise her offspring. But as the rivers relentlessly diverge, her efforts are in vain. Uganda herself is the victim of this disorder, though Mayanja Wasswa does eventually suffer for his disloyalty to his brother.

The most famous recent depiction of Mother Uganda was created by Rose Mbowa. In her play *Mother Uganda and her Children* (1987), the mother is both a spiritual and a physical incarnation. Mother Uganda gives birth to dozens of children. Unusually in much Ugandan and indeed African writing, evil is embodied in a male. Tabusana is Mother Africa's last-born child, and traditionally would therefore be seen as her favourite. Unlike Serumaga's mother figure, Mother Uganda refuses to give up on her errant child, and dedicates herself to promoting reconciliation and the moral rehabilitation of her son over many years. At the nadir of the play, at Tabusana's instigation, his brothers and sisters undress and rob their mother – a depiction of the physical, moral and psychological rape of Uganda during many years of political turmoil and trauma – but still Mother Uganda loves and cares for all her children equally.

If Mother Uganda represents the positive image of woman in Ugandan theatre, more usually woman has been depicted as a destructive figure who promotes evil. This is the image of woman often shown in legend, proverbs and traditional sayings. It is also the woman portrayed in Erisa Kironde and Margaret Macpherson's *Kintu* (1960). Here Kintu, the mythological father of the Baganda nation, is corrupted by Nambi, the divinely born princess who marries the hero. Nambi not only seduces and corrupts Kintu, she is also the wilful source of disease, death and evil throughout the world.

This evil image of woman is also central to Mary Karooro Okurut's *The Curse of the Sacred Cow* (1994). Nyabwangu meddles in the field of politics, traditionally outside her domain, to such an extent that she provokes an irreparable imbalance in the social order. However, this play also criticises society for denying opportunities to women like Nyabwangu with leadership potential. She makes mistakes because she has not been given a proper channel for developing her political abilities, and she falls prey to egotism and ambition. Consequently Nyabwangu disastrously challenges tradition and custom, leading to a flood that destroys the community. Because of Nyabwangu's evil the whole world becomes disordered, and even her husband, Mutomo, and his blood-brother, Mwamba, are driven to take their own lives.

Political women are commonly seen as dangerous. In The Ebonies' popular television series, *That's Life Mwattu* (1992– present) the important character of Vicky was removed from a powerful management position. She became a housewife, but one who persists in meddling in the lives of others and who jealously monitors her husband's movements. This stereotype of the dangerous interfering woman has become so widespread in Ugandan art that audiences have come to expect wives to be depicted as evil and would probably be disappointed if this was not the case.

Female stereotypes

Women are commonly seen as 'bad'. They are expected to be malicious and envious, ruthlessly exterminating rivals and enemies, often through the use of poison or witchcraft. Women operating outside the societally endorsed roles of daughter or wife are particularly susceptible to such stereotypes; soft targets such as step-mothers, lonely old women, widows, divorcees and spinsters are most often picked on.

Powerful women are also a common target. This extends to women with higher-education qualifications, those in politics, progressive business women, nurses, secretaries and other women in formal employment. The prevalent thesis seems to be that economic independence and too much freedom and education for women corrupts their souls and makes them rebellious in the domestic sphere. It is the professional women who are castigated most strongly for domestic rebellion while nurses and secretaries are seen as especially rude and mean; the former because their profession is so exhausting and the latter because they are protecting bosses whom it is commonly believed they sleep with.

Educated women are, moreover, often shown as unreasonable and unstable, particularly in their dealings with other women. If they are not openly quarrelling and destructive, they work through gossip and innuendo. Women managers are accused of a 'Queen Bee Syndrome', and a woman with a PhD is subject to the phrase – punning on those initials – 'Pull Her Down'. Housewives enjoy power over servants, and servants in turn seek to undermine their mistresses by seducing their masters or discrediting wives with the neighbours.

To return to the character of Vicky in *That's Life Mwattu*, the malicious look that characterises the actress in this role has become so well known that people have come to believe she must be manipulative and dangerous in real life. 'Vicky' was abused and threatened so much in the early days of the show that she has been forced to consider when she appears in public and to buy a car to protect herself from unwanted attention. Her fellow-actress, Harriet Nalubwama, 'Nakawunde' in the series, suffered a similar fate. It would appear that people are only too ready to believe that the stereotypes portrayed on television are very likely to be truthful representations of powerful women in real life.

Interestingly plays have not chosen to focus on contemporary women politicians though there are a number of important women in power. Nor has there been a spotlight on prostitution even though this is commonly believed to be the *only* way for women to acquire independent riches. Contemporary drama has chosen for the most part to study business women; recent prominent characters have been wholesale traders in hardware, foodstuffs and second-hand clothing, women who own hairdressing salons, *Bikubo* (street-alley) restaurants and *Tononnyira* (Don't Step in my Plate) evening food markets. However, these women are usually described as *nakyeyombekedde* (unmanageable), sharp-tongued and sharp-eyed. They are never wives, but divorcees, widows or single-mothers.

In a raft of productions such as *Liz* performed by Theatrikids and the ubiquitous soap *That's Life Mwattu*, prosperous business-women are usually portrayed as large, with well-oiled skin, dressed smartly in *Ganda* traditional dress, eating and drinking soda incessantly and walking and talking in a leisurely manner; all intended to reflect their economic standing and personal independence. At home they hen-peck their husbands who are often young men they had previously employed as chauffeurs or shop assistants. Interestingly, these husbands do not call their wives by name but commonly refer to them as 'mummy'.

This name is derived from the term 'Sugar Mummy', often used locally to describe older, single or widowed women of means who allegedly seduce younger men to satisfy their sexual urges. When the man refers to his wife as mummy the audience is reminded of the disparity in age between such couples. Extended to the ugliest meaning of mummy, as sometimes referring to a dead body lying in state, the 'sugar mummies' are literally in a 'dead' state of woman-hood beyond the possibility of giving birth. Such women are also dehuman-isingly described as 'off-layers' – chickens that have passed the egg-laying stage in life.

Moreover such a designation defines the terms of such a marriage clearly and protects men from ridicule. They are seen to be simply using the women to accumulate their own financial wealth. When the time is ripe such men will 'liberate' themselves into the arms of other sugar mummies or marry beautiful young girls, preferably straight from university, because they now have the means to control a wife. Plays such as Bakayimbira's *Agali Amakula* (1995), Theatre Owen's *Sota* (1997) and Byron Kawadwa's *Makula ga Kulabako* (The Infamous Beauty of Kulabako) (1968), all dramatise situations in which rich, older women seduce and marry unsuspecting young men, and testify to enduring interest in this topic.

The hypothesis behind such plays is that while money is good for men, it drives women mad because they cannot handle riches. Such women's arrogance and uncontrollable nature often leads to the break-up of marriages as the men look for other women who are ready to 'respect' them. Furthermore, despite their riches and independence, the women are still defined as disposable once their wealth no longer serves a man's interests. This fits in with indige-nous wisdom which describes women as 'grass bands used to cushion one's head from the surface of heavy loads sitting on it. Once the grass band grows old, you throw it away and acquire a new one!'[1]

Women who are low in public status but still financially powerful are portrayed as careless in walk, talk and dress. They commonly shout and swear, and at home are constantly nagging and quarrelling, thus driving their husbands into infidelity. In the domestic setting this type of woman is often a step-mother. The most popular production by Mulago Theatre Kings of Kampala, *Omukazi Muka Sebo* (The Woman of my Father), which has been performed every year since 1988, is a good example here. Siime, the child heroine in the play, loses her mother at a very tender age. The step-mother loves her husband but treats his daughter with monstrous cruelty. The climax to the play is when Siime sings her song of despair '*Oooo! ... Siime nayita ani?*' (Woe is me, Siime! Who shall come to my rescue?). The audience commonly sob in sympathy and curse the step-mother, then break into a standing ovation at the end of the song.

Women as commodities and symbols of exchange

Perceiving women as commodities of trade and as symbols of exchange is not a new phenomenon. Throughout the world the female, whether human or animal, has often been valued primarily for her ability to reproduce and produce wealth. The African tradition of trading daughters for bridewealth has in some cases been merged with colonial ideas of a wife bringing a dowry to her husband, so that among the Ugandan elite it is becoming a common expectation that a wife should bring with her the materials for furnishing an entire house.

Formerly, in much of Africa, women were used as objects in peace negotiations between communities. They were also the most important booty to be won by means of war. Today a woman's economic value can be seen most nakedly in the sex trade, and it is commonly believed that in corrupt public institutions in Uganda, such as the police, money and the sex trade are closely inter-related. The theatre has also been interested in the sexual commodification of women.

In the 1970s and early 1980s the profession of prostitution was seen as an evil to be fought. John Ruganda's *Black Mamba* (1973) attributed the exploitative sex trade going on between the white Professor Cox and his numerous black mistresses, and facilitated by his house boy, Belewa, to the Professor's own sexual greed. But Serumaga's *Majangwa* linked the escalation of the problem to the corrupting influence of the cinema, while in Fagil Mandy's *Bush Trap* (1987) the problem is seen to be the erosion of morality and break-up of families amongst upper-class Ugandans due to an indefatigable pursuit of wealth.

In *Majangwa* Serumaga utters dire warnings about the erosion of literary and moral standards in Ugandan theatre. He appears to have been something of a prophet! Today not only fashion and dance are influenced by the likes of the Congolese erotic dancer Shara Muana and her 'Queen dancers all the way from Paris'.[2] In the theatre modern female characters often have minimal costumes revealing large amounts of thigh, stomach and upper breast, because this sells tickets. Furthermore love scenes have become ubiquitous in populist drama. The audience have only to see a couple holding hands or embracing to break out into ecstatic screams. In *Majangwa* the character of Nakirijja expresses a common perception of how women are expected to respond to men and titillate an audience:

> Five lousy shillings in your pocket and your trousers would go down. Like a flame tree sprouting flowers you'd stand before me, and I in my silly spell would prepare to receive you. Then down on the pavement, right down on the concrete, before those gaping eyes, to give pleasure to the crowd. (Serumaga 1974: 13)

If older women in love or a state of sexual desire towards younger men are targets of ridicule, beautiful rich young women may be portrayed in quasi-fairytale style as a means of bridging class divides when they fall in love with poor men. In Byron Kawadwa's *Makula ga Kulabako*, Kulabako, a princess, falls in love with Nyonyintono, a popular dancer. Despite all efforts she will not be dissuaded from her love and the couple finally do marry. Similarly *Rutamirika* (1991), by the Kigezi Kinimba Actors, has the eponymous protagonist courted by the daughter of the hero's rich employer. Once again love triumphs and social and class divisions, still very prevalent in Ugandan society, are defeated.

The modern and truly liberated woman

It would be a misrepresentation of Ugandan theatre if there was no mention of efforts being made by the women's movement and its allies towards change and a positive portrayal of women in society. Beyond a few fairly realistic portrayals of ordinary Ugandan women in plays such as Charles Mulekwa's *The Woman in Me* and *The Eleventh Commandment*, and Rose Mbowa's *Nalumansi* (1986), most plays advocating women's rights and a positive view of women characters have been part of committed conscientisation projects.

The trouble with the portrayal of women in these plays, such as the heroine, Kabayanda, in *Time Bomb* (1994), by a women's rights group, Action for Development, is often that they are too good to be true. They are enlightened and well-informed on the question of personal and human rights, vocal and articulate, responsible, economically independent, politically active and civically competent. They dress, walk and speak in a modest yet smart manner. Such women are stereotypes just as much as the more negative images discussed above, and as they are not credible so they are likely not to be useful.

In the final analysis, despite significant social achievements in Uganda regarding raising issues of women's rights and importance, on the stage women are commonly stereotypes used to reinforce, usually, negative ideas which support conservative patriarchy and male sexual titillation. They are very seldom rounded or remotely realistic characters, being rather idealised dreams or demonic visions of femininity.

NOTES

1. This is a translation of a local proverb from my own mother-tongue, Runyankore-Rukiga of the Banyankore in South-Western Uganda.
2. This is an example of the type of catch-phrase commonly used by entertainment promoters to entice an audience. It is commonly believed that prostitution originated in Paris, that Parisian women are sexual experts, and that the best erotic shows originate from Paris.

BIBLIOGRAPHY

Bakayimbira, 1995, 'Agali Amakula' (unpublished).
Ebonies, The, 1992, *That's Life Mwattu* (television series, Ugandan Television, UTV).
Kawadwa, Byron, 1968, 'Makula ga Kulabako' (unpublished).
Kennedy, J. Scott, 1973, *In Search of African Theatre* (New York: Charles Scribner & Sons).
Kerr, David, 1998, *Dance, Media, Entertainment and Popular Theatre in South East Africa* (Bayreuth: Bayreuth African Studies Series, 43).
Kigezi Kinimba Actors, 1991, 'Rutamirika' (unpublished).
Kironde, Erisa and Margaret Macpherson, 1960, *Kintu* or *The Beginning* (Nairobi: East African Literature Bureau).
Mandy, Fagil, 1987, 'Bush Trap' (unpublished).
Mbowa, Rose, 1986. 'Nalumansi' (unpublished).
—— 1987, *Mother Courage and her Children*, (video tape).
Mirembe, Mercy Ntangaare and Eckhard Breitinger, 1999, 'Ugandan Drama in English', in Eckhard Breitinger (ed.), *Uganda: The Cultural Landscape* (Bayreuth: Bayreuth African Studies Series, 39).
Mulekwa, Charles, 1994, 'The Woman in Me' (unpublished).
—— 1997, 'The Eleventh Commandment' (unpublished).
Mulago Theatre Kings, 1988, 'Omukazi Muka Sebo' (unpublished).
Okurut, Mary Karooro, 1994, *The Curse of the Sacred Cow* (Kampala: Fountain Publishers).
Ruganda, John, 1973, *Black Mamba* (Nairobi: East African Publishing House).
Serumaga, Robert, 1974, *Majangwa* (Nairobi: East African Publishing House).

Drama in her Life
Interview with Adeline Ama Buabeng

ESI SUTHERLAND-ADDY

There is perhaps only one other living actress who can be said to have had as lengthy a career as Adeline Ama Buabeng in Ghanaian theatre. In her thirty-six-year career she has worked at the cutting edge of popular theatre with the Brigade Concert Party and Kusum Agoromba.

Buabeng's relationship with her mentor Efua T. Sutherland provided her with the opportunity to experience the development of research in drama and to participate in the consolidation of the Ghanaian theatre movement. She thus took up roles in scripted plays culminating in the star role of Anansewa in the Twi version of Efua Sutherland's *The Marriage of Anansewa*. Her interpretation of traditional performance culture on stage is one of the hallmarks of her stage presence and style.

Involved in all facets of production, Buabeng has been engaged not only in acting but also in makeup, costume, stage management, directing, production and management. In the wake of the near demise of the Concert Party, Buabeng's talent and experience have made it possible for her to become a pioneering force in the remarkable renaissance of this popular theatrical form in the mid-1990s.

This article is a translation of substantial portions of an extensive dialogue with Buabeng. Our interest is not only in presenting her remarkable life but also in examining with her the implications of the development of drama in Ghana's development and the role of women through it all.

The history of Ghanaian theatre has been quite comprehensively documented both by scholars based in Ghana and elsewhere in the world.[1] In much of this chronicling and commentary there seems to be a dichotomy between 'literary or script-based drama' and Concert Party [popular, or improvisational drama]. One has in mind particularly the seminal essay by Kofi Agovi on 'literary drama' (Agovi 1990) that carefully documents the history and origins of this form on the one hand and the extensive work of researchers like John Collins and Kwabena Bame which seeks to document in profound detail the lives and work of the Concert Party artistes of Ghana. These demonstrate quite persuasively the distinct evolution of these two subgenres of theatre from the point of view of dramatic technique, mode of composition, dramatic tradition, target audience, social function, venue of performance and type of actor.

As regards the question of actors, the history of Ghanaian theatre leads one to expect a similar dichotomy, namely that until recently persons involved with literary drama would be of both sexes, quite highly educated in the formal school system, who did drama as a hobby. The Concert Party actors, on the other hand, would be almost exclusively male, with little or no formal education, and acting either fully or partially for a living.

While it is important to establish the distinctions between these subgenres for the purpose of validation and analysis, it has been clear for almost forty years that some researchers and practitioners of Ghanaian theatrical arts have been intrigued by the possibilities for the creation of contemporary Ghanaian theatre based on the resources offered by both of these tendencies, as well as drama in traditional societies. Scholars such as Sutherland, Agovi and Mohamed Ben Abdallah have documented evolving trends within these discrete forms. Sutherland and Abdallah have, moreover, sought to mediate the evolution of form through their own creative work and the establishment of cultural institutions and programmes which provide opportunities for crossing the boundaries in areas such as dramatic technique, mode of composition, venue of performance, type of actor, target audience, etc.

The mutual respect and admiration between Efua Sutherland – playwright, researcher and cultural activist – and Adeline Ama Buabeng – veteran actress and cultural activist – developed in just such a context. The enormous talent of Buabeng and the artistic vision of Sutherland were among the pillars of a collaboration of thirty-six years' duration during which pioneering strides were . made across boundaries towards the creation of a contemporary Ghanaian drama. As may be seen in the life that unfolds in the interview below, Buabeng's relationship with Sutherland inspires her to break the fetters of parochialism and see herself and her work as being of national relevance.

Esi Sutherland-Addy has for many years been privy to the discourse around this bonding and creative process in reflective as well as activist interventions by both Sutherland and Buabeng. The interview that follows therefore more formally picks up some of the themes of this discourse in a continuum involving not only Buabeng and Sutherland-Addy but Efua Sutherland, as an invoked fore-mother whose presence is palpable. This dialogue is also in fulfilment of a mutual agreement between Sutherland-Addy and Buabeng that her remarkable story and insightful reflections must be systematically documented.

Our approach to the documentation has been, on the one hand, to stimulate a narration of a life story gently prompted to ensure that sufficient detail is provided and, on the other, to engage Buabeng in a dialogue on some of her key concerns. While Sutherland-Addy's intimate familiarity with Buabeng has the drawback of a subtext and set of assumptions that could make the text of the dialogue somewhat allusive and exclusive, an effort was made to compensate for this by a review of major issues to be addressed prior to the recording. The review also involved an affirmation between the two persons involved that the dialogue was to be an oral history which was to be a matter of public record.

In terms of presentation, the following features are worthy of note. Firstly, what has been presented below contains most of a 4½-hour interview held on 15 and 16 September 2000. Secondly, the dialogue took place in the Akan language and therefore appears here in translation. Care has, however, been taken to edit the text for repetition, and explanation of elliptical statements has been provided. Some expressions of the narrator's have been left untranslated or have been literally translated to foreground her style and personality.

We have also taken a number of editorial decisions which include the exercise of discretion in reproducing parts of the dialogue which are pertinent to Buabeng's evolution as an artist and her contribution to the development of drama in Ghana today. To provide a rounded picture of Buabeng as a personality, some of our conversation about Buabeng's life experiences have also been included.

The discussion was guided by questions formulated to trace the trajectory of Buabeng's life in the context of her reflections. It begins with Buabeng's most recent projects and works its way back through her entry into the field of acting into an exploration of the development of her career and its historic import. The discussion is organic and does not follow a strictly linear pattern.

Interview with Adeline Ama Buabeng

ESA We are going to have a brief discussion, 'na daakye asem nti', for the sake of future debates ...

AAB 'na yedi borode a yegya naha han', that when we eat plantain we reserve the skin.

ESA So that if there is a testimony to give you do it in a timely fashion. You do not wait until you have forgotten everything. Firstly, it is amazing that today when you look on the stage you see Key Soap Concert Party at the National Theatre. I know you had something to do with it. How did it come about?

AAB What happened was that we went to the funeral of Kojo Stamp at Abeka LaPaz area of Accra. He was the best comedian. [I had just returned from a trip sponsored by Auntie Efua Sutherland.] The way I found him, I did not like it. That morning when we got there [to take him to the cemetery], there were only about ten people around this coffin, which had been set out on two benches. So we hired a tipper truck, put Kojo Stamp in it and took him to the Achimota cemetery.

Indeed when I got home, I was deeply saddened and I said to myself 'I did not take up a good vocation, if I am going to die and be put on a bench and driven on a tipper truck to the cemetery.' I thought long and hard.

The following day I met some of the Concert Party Union. I told them what I had seen and suggested that we should come together and start something. So every one became very sad and we resolved to raise up the Concert Party.

Sometime after this, I was told one morning that Abdallah [Dr Mohamed Ben Abdallah, then Chairman of the National Commission on Culture] wanted to see me. When I went, he told me you had said something to him and he was wondering how we could rally around the people to do the work. So I undertook to find them, for he had said that some documents needed to be signed.

Soon after we had done this Abdallah left and came here [to the University]. Mr Amoako [Director] and Korkor Amarteyfio [Administrator] came to the National Theatre. They said 'Oh we have heard that you had wanted to revive the Concert Party. So what is happening?' Mr Amoako explained that his enthusiasm dated from his childhood days when he would crawl through holes in the wall to watch Concert Party. He therefore gave us a little money with which we started. When we started it was with 'man's power' [i.e. without the support of microphones and other electronic devices]. It brought us nothing. Sometimes only three or four people came to see us – sometimes there were about ten persons in the audience. Afterwards you could hardly get ¢5,000 [$2.90]. Sometimes there was not even enough for one's fare.

So we continued putting up the shows. The Key Soap people [Lever Brothers Company] offered to sponsor. As we went along we suddenly realized that the whole place was full. After that the place became too small for the audience so we were allowed to use the main hall.

You see at first the impression among ordinary people was that the theatre had not been built for the 'Oman' – the people, but for white people and speakers of English. But the Concert Party show put paid to such comments. Now everyone wanted to come there. They said, 'Ah, so this was not true.' As we played – many people and then more people. The maximum capacity of the hall is 1,500, yet there were more than 1,500 people coming. Indeed when we did the 'Who is Who' [championship competition for Comedians and Groups] – we had to stop the people from coming in. Then more and more Concert Party artists started to come and we began training people. It was not an easy task because some people did not even know how to mount the stage.

ESA So now I would like us to talk about your origins. How it was that you came to take up acting in the Concert Party tradition?

AAB In the past Concert shows, magical shows and all kinds of performance were staged in my home in Mepom. So many Concert Party groups used to come to our place. One day the Worker's Brigade Concert Party group came.

B.K.Afano[2] and co. used to call me their wife – they told my mother 'Maame, this child of yours is going to be a Concert Party actress. We see she has a gift within her.' Araba Stamp,[3] Wofa Kwamena Ampah[4] and all – they said, 'this child will be a Concert Party actress so when she finishes school, she should come and join us'. when I finished school [middle school], my mother did not allow it, so I ran away to become an actress. So I came to stay with Araba Stamp in Chorkor.

ESA So who is Araba Stamp?

AAB Araba Stamp was very gifted and became very popular. She gained popularity when she acted in a play directed by Morriseau [Leroi]. She acted the woman in *Awo Ye* [It is Good to have a Child].

At that time we used to do shows, but we did not have space at the Arts Centre so the leaders decided that they would go and ask for the use of the Ghana Drama Studio. At that time it was nestled among trees with a bungalow on stilts behind it. There was a large park in front of the studio where the Accra Great Olympics football club practised. So the leaders went to see Auntie Efua Sutherland and she agreed that they could come, particularly because a resident company could enliven the Studio. She explained that the Studio had been built for actors to work in so she had no objection.

I was a part-timer in the Brigade group from 1965 to 1966. I used to receive little tips at performances. Also when people got paid, someone would say, 'take this and buy yourself some food'. Whoever sent me, whatever their status, I would go willingly.

As a part-timer, I used to dance – *Atsiaghekor, Adowa* and *Takai.* It was the Brigade Drama Group that started including these dances in their shows. This was why there were many women in the Brigade group. We had a dance band and we had dancers. This was the 'Cabaret' group.

There were a lot of us so we moved by the busload. The dancers heralded the show and then in certain scenes also we danced. In other instances we danced to close the show. In the past audiences preferred female impersonators to the women because they found it amazing that men had dressed as women. There was one called Rosina who entered a beauty contest and won during the Nkrumah regime. Rosina used to work in the Kakaiku Concert Party. He unfortunately died of injuries, sustained in a road accident, which he didn't have enough funds to treat. Then there was also Prempeh and then another whom I can't remember. This one was an undertaker. He used to dress the corpses of all concert party actors who died. So there were about four or five great ones who were difficult to distinguish from women when dressed. Their gait and everything was just like women.

So in my experience it was the Brigade Drama Group that first used women in their show. It was much later that audiences began to accept that women's participation in shows made them more natural, and eventually even began to prefer them to the lady impersonators. So the first group to use women was the Brigade group followed by Auntie Efua's Kusum Agoromba. After this, when we used lady impersonators, we deliberately used them in selected scenes as appropriate.

ESA So now tell us about the pioneer actresses. What were some of your experiences and travails in the early days?

AAB When we began what I saw was that, when a man came into your life, he would end up not marrying you.

ESA Marriage became a problem.

AAB Yes, marriage became a problem. You would have to quit your acting career. He would see you on stage and be attracted to you but once he was going out with you, he couldn't stand to see you on stage. Then he would start pulling back. You wouldn't know what you had done to offend him, but the man would start drawing away and the marriage would begin to develop problems. He would say he would not marry you and allow you to leave him and go on the road because you were likely to be sleeping with your fellow actors.

ESA So that gave you quite a few problems. How about those [men] whom you were with [in the Concert Party business]?

AAB Oh, well. As far as those were concerned they really understood us. When it got to a certain point we were like brothers and sisters. No one was shy. The men were like our brothers. They didn't judge us 'concert women' like the people in town. Indeed, if they heard people talking against us they would defend us.

ESA So tell me about the regulations made specifically for women.

AAB One of the regulations which lasted for a long time pertained to sleeping in town. If you slept in town you were likely to be dismissed because you would be spoiling our name. We had a bad reputation already. Also if something happened to you we would not know about it.

Another regulation was that if you were a married woman and wished to work with the company, you had to bring your husband along to affirm his willingness to allow you to join the group and to go on the road. If he wasn't in agreement, we wouldn't accept you. With the men also there were regulations. You couldn't bring a woman to sleep with you among us. At first the men were also not allowed to go and sleep in town but it was realised that this would create problems for them, so eventually they were permitted to sleep in town on condition that they went and showed another member of the group where they would be sleeping so that in case of any emergency they could be reached. If you contravened this regulation you would be fined.

ESA Now you say you were in the Brigade Concert Party when Auntie Efua saw you and said you liked you. Tell me how this came about.

AAB When she saw me she told Kwamena Ampah that she could see that 'this child had something in her' and that she liked her. We did a show and I danced on stage ... I did the *kurunku* dance. She didn't say anything to me right then.

So one day I was called by Kwamena Ampah and told that Auntie wanted to work with me and would I be willing to leave the Brigade Group?

At that time I was still a part-time worker. I said I would go and inform the elders of my family. So I went and told my elders and they said OK, if I thought the lady could handle me [with care], their concern was that I should be working. After that I did not worry about it any longer. So one day she called me and said we would go to my hometown. She asked Ekua to plait my hair nicely for me. We went with Uncle Kofi [Auntie Efua's uncle], and Nana Atwia,[5] and Uncle Willis.[6] She took along drinks: one carton of beer, one crate of soft drinks, schnapps, whisky … about six different kinds of imported liquor. When we got there my grand uncle was lying in an easy chair and I told him that a certain lady was looking for him. My mother had gone to the farm. The guests were seated in my own father's room.

So Auntie Efua told them that having been with me for some time, she wanted to take me as her child but wanted to come and officially inform my relatives because of the future repercussions of her actions. They responded:

> Alright, if the child herself likes you, we have nothing to say because whatever surface you apply a solution of red clay [for polishing] it will have a red sheen. Wherever you lie, if you will succeed, you will succeed. If you sit there and you will succeed, you will succeed. If this woman says she likes you and you like her we have nothing to say.

My grand uncle then poured libation. So then we came home. And this is how I came to remain in Auntie's hands and how you all have cared for me till this day.

ESA Well speaking of homes and backgrounds, would you not agree that with a family background like yours questions must indeed be asked? After all there is a stool [symbol of traditional political office] on both your mother's and your father's side. Please tell us about the towns where the stools are and also the effect that your chosen career had on matters to do with your family.

AAB Now my mother's clan was the *abusua baatan* or kingmaker's clan. They indicated who should be made chief. We also had the 'whip of office' of one of the Asafo or traditional militia. Also the stool of the village of Oasadu was in our clan. Also the Oyoko stool – the stool of the traditional executioners or *Abrafo* was also in our clan. So there were three stools in my family. So Auntie always used to say 'as for this child, she is royalty'. At one time they were going to capture me,[7] but my grand uncle Akwettey gave me the hint which enabled me to escape to Accra. When I went and told Auntie, she brought me to her house and sent Martin the driver to fetch the Head of Family. Well, when he came he showed her the document [indicating that I had been nominated] which he had signed because he did not want to be accused of refusing to cooperate when it came to someone from his side of the Clan being designated. Auntie, however, explained to him that with my great talent, if I became a traditional office holder all of it would be suppressed and lost and therefore she could not accept the idea. So he said that if that's how she felt then he would also concede to her way of thinking. He therefore asked her to hide me. Thus I stayed in Auntie's home for two to three weeks until such time as someone else was caught. When this person was caught, I was free to move about.

ESA So as regards the royal blood in your family. What sorts of problems did your mother have because of your career?

AAB What the family said was that I was polluting the stools because Concert or popular drama was the work of prostitutes, that is 'those-who-move-about-in-order-to-eat'. I had no idea that my mother had this problem. It is just that every now and then she would make a negative comment. Everyone spoke against it. So every year my mother was obliged to make an offering of one bottle of schnapps to the elders of the clan. When she died in 1974, my uncle came to me and told me that they could no longer continue to pay the propitiation drink and that I should find a proper job and that I should stop this 'concert-concert' which is of no value. What I said to him was that I had had a child and that I couldn't depend on him to look after my child and myself so he should look for another job for me and I would also endeavour to do the same. Nothing more was done or said.

ESA So this was a really big issue at the time. But how about now? What do they think about you now?

AAB What silenced them was the grand performance of bands at the death of my Grand Uncle Akwettey. That was what vindicated me to this day. This is what has made me a name in the Clan to this day. When he died Auntie Efua sent Kusum Agoromba to stay in the town for a week. We put on Concert Shows. We played music. This became a historical landmark in the town of Awutu Bereku. And this is what has 'given me my head to eat in' [given me my peace] to this day.

I really owe a great debt of gratitude to Auntie Efua, otherwise I would have been declared a useless adult and even a child would have been deemed more useful than me. This is also why these days young people in Bereku are anxious to become performers of Concert Party.

In the past my mother must have had a really hard time. She said nothing about her suffering. She wasn't a great talker but she must have had a terrible time. We had immense difficulties. Indeed, it was because of this [these prejudices] that my relationship with Kweku's [her first child] father ended. Because of my talent, I could not endure [his attitudes] so I quit. The direct consequence of this was my relationship with Ajoa's [her second child] father, Wofa Kwamena Ampah.[8] This was because any person I got into a relationship with ended up giving me these problems. So I said, 'No, then why don't I have a relationship with some one who is a performer and have done with it?'

ESA Now can you tell me about how you got women into Kusum? We are talking about the field in general but with a particular emphasis on women. You told me before that some times when you were out performing in rural areas you would see a young girl who you thought would do well in the group, or at other times they would come begging you to take them on. Tell me about how they came on board and the talent that they brought with them.

AAB Ahaa! Well when we go on the road and the band is playing at a show, I, for example, would go and stand in an innocuous place and watch the people [dancing]. Then upon observing a good performer I would enquire about their other skills such as singing. If we offered to take them on they would often rush and pick up their bag in order to come along.

ESA So some are taught and others are simply talented.

AAB Yes, in some cases I bring them in myself. Take Esi Koyobeda [the only female comedian currently in Concert Party circles] for example. I am the one who went and fetched her from Abura Dunkwa [in the Central Region]. When we are out on the promotion tour for Unilever Products I scout for talent.

ESA Tell me about your research processes.

AAB Sometimes we just go and sit somewhere. Like when we are putting a play together. Auntie Efua could give us money and ask us to go to town and study a prostitute or a lunatic. Then you would go and observe long and hard. Indeed we learn a lot of things from lunatics. Even with a sigh for example, a lunatic's sigh could be quite natural and better than what you might have devised. So now if someone is doing something in town, I cannot pass by without watching it closely. That is why people always say I am a very good actress because what people see and ignore, I see and treasure. I use it to enhance my work. It is also because of this tendency that I find it easy to teach novices. When I go to funerals, weddings, arbitrations, or when I am present during a quarrel between husband and wife, siblings or child and parent. Or sick people at the hospital: the different facial expressions that go with various ailments and pain. Sometimes when I am walking with you, I look at your mannerisms without you knowing. I will say nothing unless asked, but I would have picked everything. Also in the market. Pepper sellers, tomato sellers, cloth sellers: all of them.

ESA It would seem that with the revival of the Concert Party tradition at the National Theatre, it would seem that there is a new crop of artistes altogether that has sprung up. It would seem that the old groups sank and new ones have come into being and thus you need to teach them. This is why you have been giving workshops on stagecraft and so on.

AAB Well with the new artistes. Some of them are talented but they do not know how to bring their talents out. If you instruct them and they don't get it, you have to get up and demonstrate.

There is a difference between drama and Concert which the new entrants do not seem to understand. When you are doing drama, you can sit or stand more or less in the same place and talk for a long time and maybe sing only one song. But with Concert, your body is an instrument. We use song in Concert Party. Your hands, your face, your feet. You must be able to sing and dance. You must be able to use proverbs. This is the formula that makes Concert 'sweet' [entertaining and meaningful]. Some people recall trying events in their lives when you use proverbs. You say the proverb, use it in the play, and demonstrate its meaning. People find this really edifying.

ESA You keep emphasizing training a lot. Would you like to elaborate on this?

AAB The reason why you need training is the proverbial nature of Concert Party [language] and the use of song. You have to synchronise the proverbs perfectly with the songs. This is what is beating today's performers. For example, one might say, 'The efforts I have made in life have tired me out', and then the song would start [singing] 'I have made worthless efforts ...', something like that. You need to know when to speak and when to break into song. You must also be able to speak without jumping from one subject to the other. Concert dialogue must not be disjointed. It should flow as a letter on a page.

ESA What would you say to the assertion that scripted drama is more difficult or more important than Concert Party?

AAB My response would be that they are different. For those of you who have been to school, the scripted drama which has been refined by writing and rewriting prior to performance is very good. For those of us who have not been to school it is the improvised one that we prefer. If you take a scripted play to the village they will watch it, yes, but the typical spectator will say you are bothering him/her with too much talking. She will not get what she should out of it because the additional ingredients which would move him/her emotionally have been 'sieved' out. He will not be touched. You know, with the Concert Party sometimes the audience can even be part of dialogue creation because some member of the audience may suggest an alternative line to the actor. I know that with those of you with a high educational level it is only those who know our culture well who will also appreciate improvised theatre. Those who don't know do not appreciate the Concert.

ESA Now tell me what you learnt yourself during your training as regards costumes.

AAB We were taught to mend costumes by hand and even to sew new ones. We learnt to iron, men's cloths for example, women's clothes, men's shirts. All the old members of Kusum Agoromba know how to do these things. We were taught tie-and-dye by Auntie Dora [the artist Ekua Banchie-Eghagha]. Peggy Watts [then at the English Department of the University of Ghana] gave us literacy lessons. So Auntie Efua ensured that all those who had not been to school learnt to write their names. We were taught home management and personal hygiene. It is a fact that some of the newly recruited persons came with bad body odour and bad breath. Auntie Efua one day made a proverbial gesture pregnant with meaning, by buying each one of us Lux soap and Pepsodent toothpaste! Those of us who were matured understood the symbolism and worked with it.

ESA Can we go to training in makeup? What did you learn?

AAB We learnt how to makeup young people as old people and to make older persons youthful. Also how to, say, make a robber look like a really evil person. We all learnt to make up people to look injured or to be crying. We could also change people to look like beasts. We were taught this by a white lady who was paid for by Auntie to come and teach us. She brought makeup for blood and for putting on the eyes to give an impression of blindness. So when we were in Kusum, people used to wonder after the performance who took which part.

ESA This must be the training that made it possible to do your current job [as wardrobe mistress at the national theatre]?

AAB As far as that is concerned, since Auntie Efua took charge of me, I have learnt many things with which I have managed my life until this point where I am entering into old age! She has enabled me to do a lot of work for this nation. The people I have trained, my work with costumes, whatever. All of this I learnt from this woman. So wherever I go I am proud and everyone gives me the respect due me because they know I am knowledgeable in the field.

ESA So let's continue with the things you learnt. You learnt to be a stage manager didn't you?

AAB Yes, and to handle props. You didn't only learn acting. Props were an essential aspect of play-making. We also learnt a little about electricals. A few of us were selected to work with Paul Alibar [the former theatre electrician at the centre for National Culture, Accra]. All the women learnt elementary electricals. Even those who had not been to school at all had an inkling. Our eyes were opened.

ESA Now it is true that Kusum did not only do Concert Party. You also did scripted plays. Given the differences in the two genres and the fact that some of you were not literate, how did you manage?

AAB Those who were not literate were grouped with those who had received some education. None of us had gone very far with our schooling. We were broken into about six groups. Usually those parts that went together in the play formed a group. The literate one would say his/her lines and teach the non-literate ones theirs. Because these plays were in our own language, the non-literate actors picked up the dialogue easily. If there was a scene with some English in it we could teach those who had never stepped in a classroom and could not read 'a' to say those lines without the audience being any the wiser.

ESA Now let's talk a bit about plays in which you took leading roles.

AAB In the Brigade Drama Group, I did not act until one day in 1966 in the town of Prankese [Central Region] when the Brigade people got to know that I had a flair for acting. As you know I was a dancer. So the group knew I could dance but had no idea I could act. On that day the lead actress did not come and all had been set for the performance by the promoter. We would have had to pay the costs or be sued by the promoter if we did not do the show. So we were in trouble. Anyway Kwamena Ampah said the show need not be cancelled because someone, meaning me, could do the part. This suggestion was met with derision by the other leading members of the group, and Kwamena Ampah declared that I should be allowed to do it and that if it did not work, he should be given the sack. So Kwabena Ebo, B.K. Afano and myself did the opening chorus. Wofa played the guitar and we sang and danced in the section called the Duets. The cinema hall where we did the show was packed and our people were backstage predicting that our instruments would be smashed up. As we started the show the audience started showering us with more and more money. I was the leading character. Everyone was pleasantly surprised at my performance. They did not know that I had been quietly understudying the lead character from backstage all along.

ESA Now we want to list all the shows in which you were the leading character and the name of the character you played. Let's go to Kusum.

AAB We started *Anansewa* in Twi even from the Brigade. Then I acted as Foriwa in the Twi version. We sometimes mixed Twi with English in the same play depending on the audience. When we went to Festac in 1977 we did the songs in Twi. That was because the songs did not sound so good in English. In *Wo Hyee Me Bo*, I acted as Dansoaa, Ananse's wife who out of jealousy revealed the origins of his mysterious new wife and destroyed the newly found prosperity of Ananse. Then in the children's play, *Ananse and the Dwarf Brigade*, I acted as Okonore, Ananse's wife. In *Yaa Konadu* [Sutherland's adaptation of Chekov's *Proposal*] I was the lead character Yaa Konadu who was being wooed by the painfully shy Kwame Dapaa.

ESA In *Foriwa* and the plays mentioned above, you acted as young woman and also as a jealous wife. Taking the Concert roles, what characters did you play?

AAB With *Mogya Ye Duru* I was a stonehearted woman who had never had children. In *Mmofra No Nti* I was a woman who had been greatly troubled and then dumped by her husband. Then in *Hena Bedi Made* I played a widow who was subjected to harsh and unjust treatment by her husband's people. In *Abotare* I acted the nagging wife, Agya Badu. Here I was the wife of a philanderer and drunkard so I divorced him. Then in *Nipa Ho Hia* I was the elderly woman who listened to no-one and drove out my pregnant daughter while my favourite daughter became disabled in a car accident. In that play we wept a lot! I was type-cast as a hard woman for quite a while, and Auntie Efua admonished Wofa and all that because I was always grimacing my face was losing its friendliness and that they should give me a part with a 'smiling face'.

ESA So of all the roles you have played, which was the one you liked the most and which was the most challenging?

AAB What gave me the most problems at first was the scripted play. I wasn't used to it so I used to feel too lazy to learn my lines. So one day, Auntie Efua shook me up. I was understudying a certain girl for the part of Foriwa but at some point she did not learn her lines and I was called onto the stage ... and there I was, standing there! So I became very serious with it. After that, when I had lines to learn I would sleep at about 7.00 p.m. and wake up at midnight. Even when I had a boy friend I would ban him from coming to see me for two weeks. My mind was really on my script. I would be so taken with the script that nothing else would be important to me. In fact if I had not been careful I might not have had Kweku. I was even no longer interested in men at some point. This was particularly the case with *Anansewa*. Indeed I was obsessed with acting.

This led to another problem for me when we were changing over to the Concert Party genre. I did not have the ideas for formulating a dialogue when I was given the outline. Wofa and Co. kept having to put words in my mouth. All of a sudden, one day, it clicked and I jumped in. So I would listen to the story, go home, and come back and ask a few questions and then I would need no more prompting.

ESA What other play did you like doing?

AAB One play I really enjoyed doing was *Mogya Ye Duru* because I was able to talk any amount of rubbish without let or hindrance ... And the audience used to rain abuse on me – it was no joke! So the more they abused me the more inspired I got! Sometimes they would throw oranges. When I did *Hena Bedi Made* it reminded me of my own life story. You see my mother went through a heinously difficult patch in her life when my father died. When he died they took all his property away from my mother. When I compare the storyline to my mother's life, in a moment I'll be in tears. I tell you! So my mother was in penury. My mother has really suffered. She only had enough for a hand-to-mouth existence. It was her brother Tetteh who gave her the money for the funeral. So we children were shooed off in a vehicle like chickens and brought to Bereku. There were nine of us but now there are six left. And my mother and other co-wives were put into *Kuna* – the widowhood rites. It wasn't this lightweight stuff that is done today. It was really intense. The person who cooked for the *kunafo* was covered with skin rashes. This was deliberate especially if your husband had been very successful and rich. You were kept for a month and could not go out except through certain byways and alleys. To this day, widows cannot move about freely until the purification rituals have taken place. It is these sorts of experiences that play back in my mind when I am doing such plays.

And indeed my own experiences. For example I used to climb orange trees as a girl. No boy could beat me. Hrrrr, and I was up the tree! I would pluck the oranges for a small fee and then buy some and go and peel them for sale. I also used to cut down palm fruits. Again I would climb the palm tree placing my feet against the sides of the stem till I reached the top and cut the fruit. I did this to see myself through school because my mother could not afford my educational needs most of the time. When she had resources, she would give me some but she often didn't. So I really toiled, my sister. My mother and I really suffered together because all her other children were either married or living with other people. When I started to work, from time to time I would take my mother a piece of cloth or some other present.

ESA So these are the memories which make you portray pathos [to the point of weeping real tears] so convincingly.

AAB Yes. In a moment I can be in tears. So I lecture trainees that when something happens in their homes which is painful, they should hold on to the poignancy of the moment inside them. So as soon as they remember, the tears will flow.

ESA Now there are some things that you know you do well and are able to move your audience profoundly. What are some of these things?

AAB Some of these are: my choice of language because I use proverbial language. We Africans need proverbs. We love them. Secondly, when I do the show, I act very realistically, and am able to evoke the scene and make it immediate. Sometimes, I depict exactly what is going on in someone's home. For example when I weep, people tell me they forget completely that they are watching a play. They feel that they are involved in something that is happening in a real-life setting. This is what the people like about me. Also I sing well.

ESA Let me remind you that you sat at the feet of Nana Atwia quite a bit. Can you explain how this helped you with your work on stage?

AAB Yes, I lived in the same house with her in Ayalolo [a suburb of Accra]. I used to listen to the way she spoke when people came to her. Also when we were taken to Atwia she used to ask me to come and sit down when she was holding court. This was because when she went to my home in Mepom, she realized that I came from a stool house. So I learnt public speaking from her. I learnt how she spoke when she was angry and how she admonished people who were in the wrong. I used to watch her moods and her use of indirection to arrive at what she was really trying to say. Also her singing – as with *Anansesem* – storytelling songs. You just don't sing them just like that. There is a way you lift them or get into them, and a way for the chorus to respond. I also learnt a lot of that from her, because when she is lifting the song she modulates her voice in various tones. I picked some of that up from her. She was a really talented person. Atwia itself as a town also had this gift within it. A lot of the citizens had it. So we started Kusum Agoromba number two in Atwia. I enhanced my own repertoire with what I had learnt from Atwia, particularly with the *Asafo* and *Kurunku* forms and *Anansesem*. That is why I can do many things such as being spokesperson for engagement and other ceremonies.

ESA So, what else makes you a unique actress?

AAB What makes me unique is that I work with my whole body. As I said, if you speak without involving your whole body, you are not convincing, but if you make meaningful gestures and deliberate steps you help the audience to get the full import of what you are trying to say. Some people watch Concert and say, 'Ah, this man, even the way he smiles makes me happy. Each member of the audience comes to the show looking for something and if they do not get it they say the Concert was not entertaining. It is not because it was not good but because you did not act and speak well. Laughter, tears, anger, irrational behaviour, dignified behaviour, ability to change moods and roles. If you don't understand the work well, you cannot do it. If the nation really understood the importance of Concert and treated it like they treat sports, older and really seasoned actors could be given a place at the Arts Centre or the National Theatre to meet the young ones. Some of the old actors have talents but are sitting on them. A lot of them have died with their knowledge. I am so sorry about this.

ESA So in your opinion, what can drama do to help the nation?

AAB Drama can be shown on television. Also performing groups can be asked to perform at certain events. We give people joy and we give them solace. The reason is that after a hard day's work, people need to relax and take their minds off their problems. The people get a lot from us. They are entertained, they are comforted by us. They receive love from us. They are able to compare the situations depicted and conclude that their own situation is after all not really that serious.

ESA Tell me a little about Concert audiences since you have been mentioning them from time to time.

AAB Oh well, with the audiences, sometimes they make comments. For example a person might, say, 'Get off the stage! We don't want this one.' Sometimes, they join in the dialogue. So we've been controlling them in the National Theatre. But when we go out to the usual venues, people can talk. They can say, 'Oh, you have done well.'

Now as you know I belong to the Oyoko Clan [one of the seven major matrilineal clans to one of which each Akan person belongs], so sometimes when we go on tour and I am in a play where I am being treated badly and being labelled a witch, I may dissolve in tears and say, 'Oh, members of the Oyoko Clan come and take me from here for I am in a lamentable condition.' Then you will find all members of that clan in the audience forming a long queue and coming up to sympathise with me. Some might wipe away my tears and say, 'I am your clansman, take this and do not weep.' Or, 'We will take you home' ... And they mean it. In Ayerebi, some boys executed a plan where they poured hot water onto the roof that hung over the stage. Hei! It is not everything that one can say. We were in the middle of the play when some people shouted, 'Get away from there! Get away from there!' And down came the water: Hrrrrrrrrrrrrrrr! The audience got furious. They chased after the boys but never got them. And we also never went there again. So we face a lot of things on trek, but when we get back we say nothing.

ESA Now lets go back to women in the Concert Party. Do you think they will remain? Especially given the situation with highlife music where there hardly appear to be any women highlife vocalists any more?

AAB The way things are now, my opinion is that the situation will not change any more. Women will take on the roles of women and men the roles of men. These days Concert has become like a job. You become popular. People also respect Concert Party artistes these days, so the actresses are also happy that they will be seen on TV. There is now some respect for us and our work. So everyone is proud to be a Concert Party artiste. With the music, I believe there will be a resurgence of highlife music. People will get tired of the church music and return to highlife. Mostly these female gospel musicians do not sing original songs. They do mostly adaptations of old songs. So I Ama, I am upset about the suppression of highlife music. If you ask people to dance the highlife they cannot. With the new Concert Party groups, they cannot sing but these songs are really deep.

ESA I believe it is because of the persistence of the pioneers such as yourself and Araba Stamp that women's involvement in Concert Party has come to stay. If you had given up in the face of the difficulties and discouragement, particularly in the early days and during the period when the entire Concert Party Tradition took a nose-dive in the 1980s, the situation might have been completely different. At this stage is there any lesson you have learnt which you would like to share with the coming generations? Or is there an issue that is really on your chest, which you would like to air?

AAB I want to talk about the fact that it is with your support that I have been able to work to this stage. What I will say to those who are coming up is that I will be willing to help any talented person who wants my support, because if I had not had the support of the Sutherland family, Dr Abdallah and others, my talents would never have blossomed. This way the beneficiaries will also train others and the nation will have something to remember us by.

NOTES

1. The works of Graham White, Martin Banham, Kofi Agovi, Efua Sutherland, John Collins and Kwabena Bame are relevant here.
2. The reigning champion of Concert Party Comedy.
3. A Veteran Concert Party actor and currently member of the Adehyeman group.
4. The late leader of the Kusum Agoromba Group.
5. Nana Baah Okuampah the VI, Lady Chief of the village of Atwia in Ekumfi, Central Region where Sutherland did her most significant research on storytelling in Ghana She also raised funds for a small theatre called the Kodzidan or Story Telling House to be built in the middle of the town.
6. The late Willis. E. Bell was the most prominent photographer to operate in modern Ghana until the early 1980s. He collaborated with Sutherland in publishing many of her books, notably *The Roadmakers* and *Playtime in Africa*.
7. Persons to be placed on stools or given traditional office are captured before being prepared for the rites and requirements of office.
8. Kwamena Ampah, affectionately called Wofa, was a leading member of the Brigade Drama Group and left in 1966 to become the leader of the Kusum Agoromba Group under the direction of Efua Sutherland. He was a talented musician specialising in guitar band music. He was a composer, playwright and director in addition to being a manager of travelling theatre groups.

REFERENCES

Agovi, Kofi, 1990, *The Origins of Literary Theatre in Colonial Ghana: 1920–1939* (Legon: Institute of African Studies Research Review, Vol. 6, No.1).
Sutherland, Efua, 1975, *The Marriage of Anansewa* (London: Longman).
—— 1960, *The Roadmakers* (Accra: Ghana Information Service).
—— 1960, *Playtime in Africa* (London: Brown, Knight & Truscott).

Visibility, Eloquence & Silence
Women & theatre for development in Ghana[1]

ESI DOGBE

Are African women voiceless or do we fail to look for their voices where we may find them, in the *sites* and *forms* in which these voices are uttered? (Ogundipe-Leslie, 1994: 11, emphases added)

A performance sketch

On a breezy late July afternoon in 1994, the rhythm of Kpanlogo music draws an audience of children, women and men to a theatre performance under a big Flame of the Forest tree in Amasaman, a village on the outskirts of Accra (the capital of Ghana).[2] By early evening, a standing-room-only crowd has gathered in a circle around an all-woman cast from Weija.[3]

In the performance, two single mothers find their paths crossing in the most dramatic way. The women are simply called Kofi's Mother and Kotei's Mother. Their lives 'eavesdrop', so to speak, on the bustling life echoing from the nation's capital – a capital sprawling and fast eating up their land. Construction fever is visible all around; everyone seems to be cashing in on the real-estate boom.

The run-away city spreads with a momentum all of its own, aided by the labour of young school drop-outs creatively but precariously straddling the margins of the informal economy – giving a new twist to the term 'free market'. The city, like the country, is an ambiguous symbol of the new modernity; having been nursed on generous doses of the 'Structural Adjustment' palliative under the watchful eyes of ubiquitous twin midwives, the International Monetary Fund (IMF) and the World Bank.

The protagonists' sons, Kofi and Kotei, are lured into the informal economy. More construction projects mean increased demand for sand, and a chance to make quick money. The boys reason that joining the ranks of 'sand winners' is a better alternative than school and the looming spectre of unemployment. They take over their mothers' lands and dig up sand for sale. Being desperately

83

poor themselves, the mothers can do little to stop the boys. However, things turn sour when Kotei's Mother catches her son's friend, Kofi, digging up her land. When she reports the incident to the other mother a bitter quarrel ensues between them. Both women are eventually summoned before the village Chief who chides them for bad parenting, and for failure to heed the government's warning against sand winning. In exasperation, the Chief refuses to settle the dispute between the two women and literally storms off the 'stage', at which point the performance co-ordinator and facilitator step forward to seek the audience's help in resolving the case.

During the spirited post-performance discussion, some local young men involved in the sand-winning trade defended their occupation on the grounds that it provided them with the only opportunity available to earn an income in the face of a failing educational system that did not prepare them for productive employment. Another man talked about the local government's lack of serious initiatives for addressing unemployment and providing basic amenities to the community. An elderly woman, however, quietly pointed out to this writer that

> ... you see, we don't have running water in this village. Yes, the sand digging destroys the land. We know that. But, this is land that is already too poor for farming. The craters left behind on the land collect rainwater and sometimes that is the only source of water, especially for us women. Otherwise I have to walk miles for water. So what are we to do? (Personal Communication, July 1994, translated from the original Ga language)

The preceding sketch is based on a performance facilitated by a third-year Theatre for Development student at the School of Performing Arts, University of Ghana, in July 1994.[4] The performance was intended both to educate and engender community discussion among the people of Amasaman about the environmental problems that result from sand winning.[5] Like other practices deemed 'detrimental to national development', such as teenage pregnancies, or the HIV/AIDS epidemic, sand winning came under media and government scrutiny in Ghana during the mid-1990s. The practice was deplored for its adverse impact on soil quality and flood control, especially in the environs of the capital city. Rapid urban expansion, however, had made the labour-intensive trade in sand quite a lucrative cottage industry dominated by young males who sold sand from private land to middlemen who in turn sell to building contractors.

The performance and the issues it brought to the fore raise pertinent questions about agency, decision-making, gender relations and community empowerment. Was the performance 'successful' in promoting genuine dialogue? Were the issues presented aligned with the internal priorities of the community? What role did gender play in how societal problems were analysed, or development goals defined? Did an all-woman cast from the Weija branch of the 31st December Women's Movement that claims to be at the 'forefront' of women's development agendas, necessarily render Amasaman women's voices 'audible'?[6]

Women, culture and development

Much development literature defines African women as the most vulnerable and disenfranchised segment of contemporary African society. Current statistics show the socio-economic condition of the majority of African women to have declined in ways consonant with the dismal global portrait that emerged out of the 1995 Fourth World Conference on Women in Beijing. Governments, corporations and community institutions have failed adequately to secure real empowerment and parity in decision-making positions for women in their societies ('Platform for Action', Section IV (G) pars 186–9). In Africa, Structural Adjustment programmes, oppressive cultural practices and widening socio-economic inequities have had a far-reaching negative impact on the lives of women. Yet, Ogundipe-Leslie's (1994) question quoted at the opening of this paper challenges existing ways of knowing, representing and interpreting African women's presence in their societies. The portrait of African women as an undifferentiated category, that lacks autonomy and passively accepts oppression from indigenous patriarchal culture, obscures the dynamic (sometimes contradictory) strategies that the women as groups and individuals *actually* cultivate and employ to negotiate the social, economic and cultural constraints that they confront in their lived experiences. Such an image also fails to show the shifting ways in which the prevailing contexts shape whatever choices poor women must make to utilise the intellectual and scant material resources available to them. Women's silence has been defined in terms of the absence or erasure of their voices from a public realm considered to be the locus of social power. Mata (1994) describes this silenced condition as the 'tongue whose "disability" refers to the existence of another more valued tongue' (193). Nevertheless, understanding the often incongruent 'sites' where women create spaces from which to speak, moves the debate from whether African women have voices or not, to understanding *what, how* and *where* they actually speak.

This paper explores Ghanaian women's involvement in institutional theatre for development projects in Ghana as particular performance 'sites' where women's presence is significantly visible yet ambiguous. The aim is to understand what happens during situational uses of indigenous performance genres for development communication, as well as the nature of interaction between communities and the institutional sponsors of these performances. The focus here is to examine how women participants could be simultaneously 'vocal' and 'silenced', 'visible' and 'invisible' in projects that claim to engender grass-roots *participation, empowerment* and *transformation* in the lives of so-called vulnerable groups. Some of the issues to surface include the apparent contradictions and nuances in women's strategies of participation that defy labelling them as either 'total victims' or as 'empowered actors'. In the performance contexts researched for this paper, women's silence sometimes signalled their actual lack of voice, but elsewhere functioned tactically in tandem with non-verbal cues to neutralise institutional directives. Sometimes the women's exuberant participation in the theatre performance yielded no clues about how they actually perceived the sponsoring institutions' agendas. During another performance, women's varied initiatives and responses set in motion conflicting discourses that ran parallel to the institutional script.

Exploring theatre for development performances *in situ* involves moving beyond the two dominant perspectives within the field. On one hand, there is the developmentalist school for whom popular theatre is an alternative 'tool' for communicating and implementing development policies among illiterate rural populations. On the other are to be found activists in the Paolo Freire (1968) and Augusto Boal (1979) tradition who consider institutional appropriations of culture to be an insidious form of 'domestication' (see Kerr 1995; Kidd 1982; Mda 1993; Mlama 1991). Instead, they argue that genuine culture is a revolutionary weapon that should augment people's critical consciousness and dismantle the prevailing 'culture of silence' from the bottom up.[7] Useful as these two perspectives are for charting the differences in ideological orientation and praxis between social activists and institutional policymakers in defining the masses' participatory role in development, they alone do not determine the actual outcomes of institution–community interactions. Among several others, gender dynamics, prevailing fluid social contexts, and how communities themselves value certain cultural forms are all pertinent factors to consider. Theatre for development provides an excellent textured canvass for exploring what Muñoz (1994) calls the 'selves and situation of women' (88), specifically in understanding the myriad ways in which, through performance, women stitch together or 'rhapsodise' (Ong 1982) dynamic relationships between their individual and group worldviews, lived experiences (praxis), and pleasure (affect). The theatre provokes attention to its textures through dialogue, sight, touch, gesture and the body itself.

Culture in development

Ghana's development and cultural-policy documents reflect the trend towards reviving indigenous cultural forms as productive components of development. A second oft-stated mission is the empowerment of women. However, what does it mean, 'to harness' culture for development? Which 'culture'? How can culture-in-development become 'empowering' for women, when aspects of these same cultures have been used to oppress them? Ghana's cultural policy over the past decade has focused on culture's (a) reclamatory, (b) therapeutic, (c) protective and (d) creative potential to transform national development processes.[8] The document's framework is based on the Akan concept of *Sankofa* – symbolised by the bird whose neck is arched back to its tail – and intended to link historical continuity with modern innovation. Upon close scrutiny, recovering hitherto ignored indigenous art forms and knowledge systems to transform stalled national development presents conceptual and practical problems. Conceptually, this view seeks to construct an idyllic image of culture for policy goals rather than recognise the complex and often conflict-ridden histories that produce flux in culture. Such a stance also erases from view the human actors whose conflicts shape and re-shape culture, as if culture were a 'superorganic entity' (Geertz 1973: 11). Even if the intended roles for culture are interpreted progressively, current development policy-making and implementation processes are formulated on the mistaken assumption that empowering women and other marginal groups will not require fundamental changes to the *status quo*. Such policies obscure rather than address fundamental issues such as inequities in access to resources and decision-making.

Integrating culture and women in development

Women have historically cultivated a wide-ranging repertoire of competencies in the nuances of their pliable cultural systems which has enabled them to carve out communication spaces for themselves and devise strategies that both subvert (Riaño 1994) and accommodate the culture, regardless of how oppressive the cultural milieu may be. For example, some performances discussed below portray theatre-for-development (TFD) performers exploiting the nuances of the prevailing culture through coded verbal, symbolic or kinaesthetic cues performed alongside the official script. The effect is neither wholly reactionary nor radically subversive, but meshes humour with conservatism and with social criticism.

Why do the people at the grassroots seemingly co-operate with the development agencies' agenda? Rather than simplistically attribute such participation to a static notion of 'false consciousness' (see also Barber 1987; Waterman 1990), such accommodationist tendencies reflect the communities' pragmatic seizure of what Johnson (1986) terms 'strategic moments' in the face of limited viable alternatives. In an era of Structural Adjustment and down-sized national spending, these 'strategic moments' become prolonged as deprived groups seek ways to lock in their economic and social needs with the funding priorities of policymakers and donor agencies.

Harnessing culture: 'keep it simple and cost effective'

Institution-based uses of TFD in Ghana reflect considerable tension between the desire to cultivate genuine grassroots participation through indigenous cultural media and attaining sponsoring agencies' goals. The agencies operate on a linear communication model that views accessible cultural media as an instrument to achieve specified (quantifiable) goals in order to shape the behaviour of people in local communities 'in the direction that maximizes national objectives' (Ugboajah 1985: 181). The practice is not new in Ghana, but dates back to the colonial era (of the then Gold Coast) when the colonial administration's propaganda was channelled through 'native' performances, radio, mobile information vans and cinema. Currently, popular drama groups are commissioned by such organisations as the United Nations Children's Fund (UNICEF), the UN Fund for Population Activities (UNFPA), and the ministries of agriculture and health, among others, to perform 'edutainment' (education and entertainment) in villages.[9]

Targeting women's behaviour

While women's empowerment remains a stated goal, none of the TFD projects researched actually factored in gender-specific concerns within the framework of their programmes. Nevertheless, the performances overwhelmingly targeted behavioural change among women, with messages to work harder, keep their surroundings clean, develop eco-consciousness and discipline their sexual behaviour. For example, despite the visible involvement of women in the performance of the sketch outlined in the opening paragraphs of this paper on the adverse environmental impact of sand winning, pertinent issues relating specifically to the needs of the women of Amasaman were omitted. The narrow focus on land degradation side-stepped complex relationships between environmental conservation agendas, survival strategies of community groups, and economic constraints among poor women who are responsible for providing the basic needs of their households (water, food, fuel). Secondly, the performance was silent regarding supply and demand factors fuelling the sand winning business, such as poorly regulated construction practices, uncontrolled urban sprawl, and a growing unemployed labour pool. Significantly for a community that had no access to potable water, the short-term 'benefit' that the craters provided as rain-water reservoirs after the sand had been dug was important for the women who have to trek miles for water.

Malaria, witchcraft and women's rivalry

In 1994, the United Nations Children's Fund (UNICEF) Malaria project sponsored a series of TFD programmes to educate people in target towns in the Greater Accra Region, namely, Old Ningo, Prampram and Dodowa. Two performance facilitators from the Theatre for Development Unit at the University of Ghana were commissioned to train nursing staff and local people in the use of TFD techniques to educate the community about preventing and treating malaria outbreaks. The plays' framework was based on three ideas supplied by UNICEF: (a) isolate malaria as a preventable and treatable disease, (b) stress that environmental factors and human behaviour, not witchcraft, are responsible for malaria's transmission and (c) educate community members to rely only on qualified health officials to provide safe treatment.

The performances were intended to supplement other educational programmes of the Ministry of Health in these communities. This enabled the nurses, who also took part as actors, to interest their patients, especially pregnant women and new mothers, coming into the clinics. However, both rehearsals and the final performances of the malaria plays showed that enthusiasm for the project was not uniform in all locations. Sporadic attendance at rehearsals revealed the kind of time and resource constraints experienced by people in communities who first and foremost have to earn a living working at their farms, trading and fishing businesses. The agency staff frequently complained about 'lack of sustained commitment' or 'ignorance' on the peoples'

Malaria play at Old Ningo: A fight breaks out between the co-wives
(Photo: Esi Dogbe)

Malaria play at Old Ningo: A nurse educates the fisherman's family on the virtues of modern medicine
(Photo: Esi Dogbe)

Malaria play at Old Ningo: The 'quack doctor' tends to the sick Paku
(Photo: Esi Dogbe)

Malaria play at Old Ningo: The 'quack doctor' tends to the sick Paku
(Photo: Esi Dogbe)

part, thus revealing the significant gap that exists between institutions' expectations and those of people in rural communities.

Malaria: context, facts and myths

The cast comprised a fisherman, his first wife, their teenage daughter Paku, a second, childless wife, an itinerant 'quack doctor', a teacher, two nurses and the community clinic doctor. The play opens in the home of the fisherman, his two wives and his daughter. The wives are cast as rivals who fight over everything including how to share their husband's fish catch. The husband resolves the constant conflicts by simply sharing the fish equally between the two women. In the next scene Paku has a fever, which her mother immediately attributes to her rival's powers of witchcraft. A fight breaks out between the two women that excites the audience and elicits snide comments about women's innately quarrelsome nature. Paku's father believes that a generous dose of his 'bitters' (a mixture of hard liquor, spices and herbs) will quickly cure his daughter. When the girl's situation deteriorates an itinerant quack 'doctor' is called in who exuberantly administers a deadly concoction of expired tablets, followed by a potion injected into her knee. Paku lets out blood-curdling screams while the audience roars with laughter.

Later, a schoolteacher enters to advise the frustrated parents to take the child to the local clinic; which they reluctantly do. But before they leave Paku's mother reiterates very forcefully that the real reason why her child is slowly 'dying' is because her rival has resorted to sorcery to compensate for her own barrenness. At the clinic the doctor and nurses diagnose Paku's illness as malaria and proceed to giver her 'proper' treatment. In addition they instruct the parents, especially the mother, to keep a clean domestic environment. The teacher returns at the end to deliver a short speech on the virtues of modern medicine while deploring superstition, ignorance and indigenous cures. The nurses and facilitators then invite the audience to share their opinions on the performance.

According to the institutional TFD formula, fights such as those between the co-wives are supposed to function as bait to sustain audience interest (Asare 1994, personal communication). However, were the audience chuckling because they believed women to be stupid, or were they reacting to the 'spectacle' effect of the performance itself? Did the women in the villages find these portrayals to be offensive, normal aspects of their 'culture', or irrelevant? In an interview, the women who performed the roles of the co-wives indicated to this writer that their involvement was just an 'act' that they enjoyed very much for its emotional effect, and that they felt no personal investment in the message itself.

One of the more instructive insights to emerge from the UNICEF-sponsored performances was that no single cultural form or context constitutes a transparent vista into the entirety of a community's worldview. During one of the rehearsals it became apparent that various discourses were occupying contiguous creative spaces that required fluid cultural competencies for their interpretation. Under the same trees where the 'official' UNICEF Malaria–play was being rehearsed, a group of local midwives comprising fourteen women and one man had assembled for its weekly meeting. In the midst of their deliberations they broke into an impromptu skit and bawdy song celebrating their hard-won recognition from the orthodox medical establishment as legitimate health providers.[10] The dialogue, style, depth of knowledge and cultural competency that this group of midwives displayed was much more assertive and compelling than the marginal voice that women possessed in the UNICEF performance. The contrast between the two performance contexts makes it untenable to conclude only from the 'official' performances that the townswomen were 'accepting' of their marginality and state of ignorance.

Changing behaviour: women and verbal duelling

The Ghana Institute of Journalism (an institution for training journalists in Ghana) launched a population communication (GIJ – Pop. Comm) project in 1989, with sponsorship from UNESCO and the UNFPA. The project was intended to enable journalists to become instrumental in the 'development process' within local communities. This focus would supposedly render the nation's 'communication efforts for family planning goals more effective ... with particular emphasis on the related cultural modes of communication and research methods' (GIJ 1989: 3). What follows is content analysis of two of the videotaped instructional materials that GIJ researchers compiled during the first phase of the project after commissioning popular performing groups to 'weave' messages about family planning and other development issues into their repertoire.

The Ewe language play *Where do they Sleep?* was devised by Hesino Torgbe Klu Gborglah's musical group with the collaboration of two facilitators from the TFD Unit of the School of Performing Arts. The popular group first performed the skit in Mave, a village situated in the Volta Region of southeastern Ghana. It features an elderly man (played by Gborglah himself) and his wife, Deviwo Dada, who have several children including a son just returned from Nigeria, their youngest daughter Adugborvi, her husband, his second wife and Adugborvi's four young children. Other characters include Deku, the elderly man's friend who has only two children. The 'stage' is set under a large tree in a clearing in the centre of the village. Before the opening scene, the camera pans across the village highlighting the mostly thatch-roofed mud dwellings, and comes to rest on two barely clothed children playing traditional musical instruments. The action opens with Adugborvi exploding in anger after her parents send her to buy her father some medication from the next village:

> I am not your only child.
> The others have all gone away to Ivory Coast, to Nigeria
> Why should I be the only one here to serve you, to be your slave?
> No! I'll also leave. I'll go to Aflao.[11]

...
I'm going to Aflao to buy myself some silk cloth, jewellery and fine things.

She storms out of the house despite her parents' cautionary words and song about how tough life really is. Next we see Adugborvi in the border town of Aflao sitting dejectedly on a doorstep with four very young children, one strapped to her back. Her co-wife enters to 'sweep' Adugborvi and her children out of the house. Their husband soon joins his new wife and both send Adugborvi packing. While all this confusion is taking place in Aflao, one of Gborglah's sons arrives from 'Agege', and takes over Adugborvi's former room.[12] Adugborvi's sudden return to her parents' household with all her children creates tension. While her mother, Deviwo Dada, worries deeply about how she is going to feed all the new mouths, a quarrel ensues between Adugborvi and her brother over the room he has taken. He tells her

> **Brother** Too bad for you. I am staying here now. It is mine. *Remember that I am the male here.* So get yourself back to wherever you came from; your husband's.

Deku, a friend of Adugborvi's father, visits the family and realising the tense situation offers Adugborvi's brother a room in his own house. The message is that Deku has plenty of room in his house because he has only two sons. Gborglah thanks his friend for his kindness, but loudly laments his own poverty:

> **Gborglah** Hmm ... see how I am suffering. What will happen when the others return? All eight of them scattered out there are coming back. What will happen then?
> **Deviwo Dada** Oh my husband. God will provide.
> **Gborglah** Perhaps he will. *All I have is my song.*

The performance ends with the group singing about life's vicissitudes.

This play opens up a number of significant issues, even though on the whole it is a rather unremarkable piece. The acting is uneven, and the content appears to hang on flawed logic. It fails to establish a convincing causal relationship between having too many children and poverty. The play seems to operate on a wavelength different from the official script, as the issues portrayed in the play are not necessarily family-planning problems. Gborglah's children are casualties of the crises in most African countries suffering from the human and social cost of IMF/World Bank-imposed Structural Adjustment conditions. Gborglah's children constitute a growing breed of the 'nouveau pauvre' class who are returning to the villages because of public-sector wage freezes, reduced social services and employment attrition. Theirs is a classic case of what Göran Hydén (1983) has called 'taking the exit option'. This 'option' is the ingenious art of straddling both the formal and informal economic sectors, since a person who works in paid employment can only survive with supplementary income from the 'informal' economic sector, and with heavy dependence upon kinship and ethnic networks.

Thus the old man's lament is also about the loss of security from remittances that he, as patriarch, once received from his adult children, coupled with the fast-looming spectre of feeding them and their children. His is not a predicament necessarily *caused* by having had eight children, as implied in the TFD performance. The classic family-planning scenario is probably portrayed in the character of Adugborvi whose low level of formal education, unplanned rapid births, and subsequent single-parenthood traps her in misery. But hers is a complex gendered problem. The play exposes, albeit unintentionally, a critical aspect of the intersection of gender and age inequalities. Adugborvi as a *daughter* and the *youngest* of Gborglah's children is subject to forms of age and gender exploitation experienced by women who have to put their own aspirations on hold in order to care for elderly relatives. In other scenarios, urban-based educated people who recruit young female relatives to serve them as unpaid or minimally paid housemaids also exploit such filial bonds. In the play, Adugborvi's protest is interpreted as evidence of her wanton greed (lusting for clothes and jewellery), delinquency and disrespect for elders. Therefore, the consequences of her rebellion – bad marriage, poverty and hungry children – had to be attributed to the gods' retributive justice. Though the gender/class/ age dimensions of her predicament remain officially unacknowledged, they cannot be erased from the margins of the script. Furthermore, men's failure to provide for their offspring as well as complicity in perpetuating polygyny are elided in favour of the more sensational narrative of vain women locked in inane rivalry.

While women were highly visible in terms of numbers performing, theirs was a presence marked by relative silence. Deviwo Dada plays the role of supporting beam of the family. Yet now in old age her plight is about to worsen as she anticipates caring for returning children, grandchildren and an ageing spouse. Despite this primary role, she fades into the background within the dialogue itself until the songs come up, where she is most expressive both within the act and in her interaction with the audience. As soloist she not only moves the *direction* of the songs and the mood, but also plays the contrast superbly between her agency-in-song and her secondary role as Gborglah's sidekick in the dialogue. It is a contrast that effectively captures African women's struggle not so much to speak, but to be heard *seriously*. It would seem that more often than not, to borrow Gborglah's last line, 'All [she has] is [her] song.'

The GIJ Pop. Comm. Project also commissioned the popular Nkontompo Nnwonkoro group in the village of Nkenkansu in the Ashanti Region of Ghana to record *nnwonkoro* performances for its teaching library. *Nnwonkoro* is a recreational song and verbal art form historically performed exclusively by women that continues to serve a variety of social and aesthetic functions. The repertoire covers such themes as 'life, love, courtship, marriage, childbirth, infertility, competition, rivalry, adversity, justice, death' (Anyidoho 1993: 97). Facing inwards in an enclosed circle in an open communal arena, the women take turns to chant solos about myriad themes while the rest sing the chorus, dramatise the message, and sway their bodies in continuous rhythmic motion taking turns to praise, lament, insinuate, abuse, protest and reflect on life (96). Anyidoho's concept of 'verbal duelling' as a 'mechanism of negotiating difference' (245) clearly captures the dialogic nature of *nnwonkoro*. Its relative popularity has made it appealing for political, religious and developmental uses.

In Ghana, HIV and AIDS are feminised in the Ghanaian imagination as prostitutes' diseases, as portrayed in the following excerpt from a dramatised song, entitled 'AIDS':

Cantor Listen to me, Listen to me,
        Listen to me, Ghanaians!
        The twig threatening your eye
        Is uprooted, not clipped
        We vehemently taboo
        What is not good for man
        The night cry of the clock bird is taboo
        The crooked head of the toucan bird
        Is the price of disobedience
        Acquired Immune Deficiency Syndrome
        AIDS for short
        It's a disease without a cure
        The palm branch will not rattle
        If nothing sets it off
        Promiscuity begets the disease
        God is not in favor of a promiscuous life
        This woman is attractive
        See her enchanting eyes
        Her plumb [sic] legs, gap between her teeth[13]
        Beauty attracts no wages
        When the vulture fattens
        It is not for the benefit of man
        Be careful, AIDS will not spare you
        If you fall in its trap
Chorus *Be careful, AIDS will not spare you*
        If you fall in its trap (repeated over and over)
(translated by Kwesi Yankah, GIJ 1989)

These portraits of HIV/AIDS that foreground the prostitute as the primary transmitter of the disease have impacted on public-health policy, adult-education curricula and religious rhetoric. The disease is presented less as a public-health concern and more as a moral issue. This approach has limited prevention education to the avoidance of 'decadent lifestyles', and without mentioning safe-sex methods as the mutual responsibility of *both* men and women. The AIDS song above presents its arguments using three potent reference points: (1) deception, (2) taboo and (3) retribution. Deception is constructed out of deeply ingrained Akan values about the ideal woman's beauty – 'enchanting eyes', 'gap between the teeth', 'plumb legs', and warns the public to beware the lure of the beautiful woman who could kill an unsuspecting man with HIV/AIDS. The message also implies that women's promiscuous behaviour is an abomination likely to cause cosmic imbalances within the transgressor's lineage and wider community.

How then do we interpret these TFD projects if they overtly demonise women and burden them with added responsibilities? To infer from the performance that there was a complete co-option of the performing groups or subordination of the women is to commit an 'instrumentalist fallacy'. The shrewd responses that interviewees gave to researchers' questions offer interesting insights into effective strategies of deflecting hegemonic discourse. In an exchange between a project researcher and a mother of five at Nkenkansu after the performance of another song on birth control, the woman bluntly told the interviewer that she has heard all about family planning but 'prefers the traditional method called *Gye wa home*' (literally meaning 'take a rest'). The research team was surprised that there was such 'evidence that the people were aware of traditional methods of controlling birth' (GIJ 1989).

The village women demonstrated that they *too* had compelling reasons for not glibly buying into the institutional agenda. Although not overtly stated, the underlying question was about how having fewer children would practically fulfil their labour needs in a labour-intensive subsistence economy without the benefit of 'modern' conveniences more readily available to urban women. What kind of development do policymakers envisage when there are more family-planning clinics in rural areas than there are primary health-care facilities or agricultural-credit and -extension services? For women the issues are a complicated negotiation between basic survival needs and a radical emancipatory project.

Conclusion

This paper has attempted to construct a context within which to analyse women's participation in selected theatre-for-development projects in Ghana, and the extent to which these cultural arena portend the possibility of *empowerment for women* in decision-making processes. Both field research and documented TFD material showed that the major constraints that women face in their communities are not physical invisibility, but the *difficulty of being heard when they do speak* and the lack of a critical mass of opinion and action to favour their input. The institutions simply replicated Riaño's (1994) 'participation typology' in which women's participation was a means to an end, to mobilise targeted communities to implement agency agenda without actually conceptualising the gender implications of their projects.

One critical insight gained in the larger research on which this paper is based was the fact that the women did not perceive themselves as a composite category with similar aspirations. They were keenly aware of their 'diversity of experiences' (along class, age, ethnic and educational lines) and 'discursive differences' (Riaño 1994: 34). This diversity made some of them, in some contexts, defend the *status quo* whilst elsewhere resisting co-option. Thus, the issue of women's empowerment can be summed up as the cyclic cumulation of small battles won and others lost. At least TFD performances offered the women performers an opportunity to share the emotive benefits of play, acting and laughter.

NOTES

1 This article is based on research conducted for my dissertation, 'Culture and the Development Process: A Study of Women's Community Participation in Popular Theater Performance in Ghana', University of Texas at Austin, 1996.
2 Kpanlogo is a type of recreational music and dance traditionally performed by the Ga people of southern Ghana.
3 Weija is situated about 15 miles west of Accra, the capital city. It developed into a small town following the construction of a dam and water treatment plant that supplies drinking water to parts of the city.
4 I am grateful to Professor James Gibbs for graciously giving me video recordings of TFD student productions (1994) from his personal library for my use. My personal observations of the Amasaman performance are supplemented with his videotaped record.
5 Young males dominate sand winning. Women, on the other hand, engage in small-scale stone quarrying – a tedious occupation that causes respiratory diseases and other health problems as a result of long exposure to dust and other debris.
6 The 31st December Women's Movement was founded by Ghana's former First Lady, Nana Konadu Agyemang Rawlings in 1982 following the military *coup d'état* led by her husband, Jerry John Rawlings, that overthrew the country's third civilian government. The organisation is currently registered as an NGO that seeks to promote the welfare and empowerment of Ghanaian women.
7 Latin American adult educationist Paulo Freire (1968) coined the term 'culture of silence' to describe the disenfranchisement of masses at the grassroots.
8 As outlined in *The Cultural Policy of Ghana* (c. 1989).
9 Apart from the long tradition of itinerant independent Concert Party theatre groups, there are other precedents of taking 'theatre to the people'. The late dramatist Efua Sutherland was instrumental in initiating a collaborative indigenous performance project during the 1960s with the woman-Chief of Atwaa-Ekumfi, to found the *kodzidan* (story house). Playwright Mohamed Ben Abdallah also toured the country with the Legon Road Theatre in 1969–70 with plays adapted to the concert party format (Gibbs 1972).
10 Hitherto, local midwives, officially called Traditional Birth Attendants (TBAs), had been banned from practising in their communities on the grounds that they lacked formal education and proper medical licensing. However, when economic and health-care crises began to plague the country in the 1980s, the government had no alternative but to recognise formally their vital role in rural areas that lack access to orthodox medical services. Training programmes have been devised to upgrade their skills.
11 A Ghanaian town on the border across from Togo's capital city, Lomé.
12 Agege is the name of a suburb in Lagos, Nigeria that has become a popular shorthand in Ghana to refer to any place in Nigeria.
13 Historically among Akans the criteria for defining a woman's beauty have been large eyes, fleshy firm legs and hips, a slender ringed neck, and most especially a gap between the front centre teeth.

BIBLIOGRAPHY

Anyidoho, Love Akosua, 1993, 'Gender and Language Use: The Case of Two Akan Verbal Artforms', Vols. 1 and 2 (unpublished PhD dissertation, University of Texas at Austin).

Asare, Yaw, 1994, Interview, Old Ningo, 6 July.

Barber, Karin, 1987, 'Popular Arts in Africa', *African Studies Review* 30, 3: 1–78.

Boal, Augusto, 1979, *Theatre of the Oppressed*, trans. C. McBride and M.L. McBride (New York: Theatre Communications Group).

Cultural Policy of Ghana, c. 1989, n.d. for publication.

Dogbe, Mary E., 1996, 'Culture and the Development Process: A study of Women's Community Participation in Popular Theater for Development in Ghana' (PhD Dissertation, University of Texas at Austin).

Fourth World Conference on Women, 1995, Platform for Action, Beijing, Section IV (G), Paragraphs 186–9.

Freire, Paolo, 1968, *Pedagogy of the Oppressed*, trans. M. Bergman Ramos (New York: Herder & Herder).

Geertz, Clifford, 1973, *The Interpretation of Cultures* (New York: Basic Books).

Ghana Institute of Journalism (GIJ), 1989 and 1991, *Folk Media: Population Communication Project. Instructional Media*, Videocassette (Accra: Ghana Institute of Journalism).

—— 1988, 'Project Request from the Government of Ghana to the United Nations Population Fund (UNFPA)', unpublished proposal (Accra: Ghana Institute of Journalism).

Gibbs, James, 1972, 'Mohammed ben Abdallah and the Legon Road Theater', *African Arts*, Vol. 5, No. 4: 33–4.

—— 1994, *Theatre for Development: Performances Facilitated by Students of the Theatre-for-Development Unit, School of Performing Arts–University of Ghana*, Legon, Videocassette, Private Library.

Hydén, Göran, 1983, *No Shortcuts to Progress: African Development Management in Perspective*, (Berkeley, CA: University of California Press).

Johnson, Richard, 1986, 'What is Cultural Studies Anyway?', *Social Text* (Winter): 38–80.

Kerr, David, 1995, *African Popular Theatre: From Pre-Colonial Times to the Present* (London: James Currey).

Kidd, Ross, 1982, *The Popular Performing Arts, Non-Formal Education and Social Change in the Third World: A Bibliography and Review Essay* (The Hague: Centre for the Study of Education in Developing countries (CESO)).

Mata, Marita, 1994, 'Being Women in the Popular Radio' in P. Riaño (ed.) *Women in Grassroots Communication: Furthering Social Change* (London: Sage): 192–211.

Mda, Zakes, 1993, *When People Play People* (Johannesburg and London: Witwatersrand University Press and Zed Books).

Mlama, Penina Muhando, 1991, *Culture and Development: The Popular Theater Approach in Africa* (Uppsala: Afrikainstitutet Nordiska).

Muñoz, Sonia, 1994, 'Notes for Reflection: Popular Women and Uses of Mass Media', in P. Riaño (ed.), *Women in Grassroots Communication: Furthering Social Change* (London: Sage): 85–101.

Ogundipe-Leslie, Molara, 1994, *Recreating Ourselves: African Women and Critical Transformations* (Trenton, NJ: Africa World Press).

Ong, Walter J., 1982, *Orality and Literacy: The Technologizing of the Word* (London: Methuen).

Riaño, Pilar, 1994, 'Women's Participation in Communication: Elements for a Framework', in P. Riaño (ed.) *Women in Grassroots Communication: Furthering Social Change* (London: Sage): 1–30.

Ugboajah, Frank, 1985, 'Delinking the Western Professional Model', in F. Ugboajah (ed.), *Mass Communication, Culture and Society in West Africa* (New York and London: Hans Zell): 179–86.

Waterman, Christopher A., 1990, *Jùjú: A Social History and Ethnography of an African Popular Music* (Chicago, IL: University of Chicago Press).

Contemporary Nigerian Theatre
The plays of Stella Oyedepo

CHRIS DUNTON

I First, this paper tries to correct a misrepresentation – one for which I'm afraid I am responsible. In my 1998 book *Nigerian Theatre in English* I attempted to list as comprehensively as possible published Nigerian play texts in English and Pidgin, annotating and commenting on the bulk of the 500-plus texts in print I had been able to locate. The single entry for Stella Oyedepo – on her play *The Greatest Gift*, published in 1988 – describes her as one of Nigeria's foremost female dramatists, and identities the play listed as her only published work (see Dunton 1998: 218). Since writing that entry, in 1997, four more published play texts by Oyedepo have come my way: *Don't Believe What You See* and *Worshippers of the Naira*, both bearing the publication date 1994, and *Doom in the Dimes* and *See!*, both dated 1997. It is true that in Nigeria published texts are not always made available at the time their publication dates suggest; true, also, that distribution of texts published in Nigeria is generally highly erratic, making it difficult to give a reliable account of what is available at any given time. Nonetheless I do regret that in *Nigerian Theatre in English* I gave only such a slender indication of Oyedepo's achievement; the present paper attempts to fill in that picture a little more fully.

Stella Moroundia Oyedepo's[1] origins lie in Ondo State, south-west Nigeria. Trained as a linguist, she was for some years in the 1980s Senior Principal Lecturer at the Kwara State College of Education, Ilorin.[2] More recently she has been Director of the Kwara State Council for Arts and Culture. Since her first work, *Our Wife is Not a Woman* (1979), Oyedepo has, according to her publishers, written over a hundred plays. Many of these have been performed, under commission, to grace specific occasions (a general trend in contemporary Nigerian theatre). *The Rebellion of the Bumpy Chested*, for instance, was performed in the Ibadan University Arts Theatre to celebrate the tenth anniversary of the ANA (Association of Nigerian Authors). Like Bode Sowande's epic play *Tornadoes Full of Dreams*, Oyedepo's *Burn the Fetters* was commissioned by the French Embassy in Nigeria to celebrate the bicentenary of the French Revolution. *Don't Believe What You See* was given in honour of the participants at a 1992 workshop for Magistrates, Area Court Judges and Customary Court Judges, and *Worshippers of the Naira* as a 'command performance' to celebrate the opening of First Midland Mortgage Finance Ltd, Ilorin (Oyedepo's tongue-in-cheek Author's Note to this play points to the relevance of the theme MONEY to the occasion, even if MONEY – 'the HONEY of life' – is here dressed 'in a seeming MOURNING garb': Oyedepo 1994b: vi). The frequency with which plays are commissioned for performance is worth noting, as it gives some indication of the (not unproblematic) status theatre is accorded in Nigeria by commercial organisations, professional institutions, associations and parastatals. In addition, Oyedepo's work is frequently reviewed in the Nigerian press. Despite the fact that only a tiny proportion of her work is published (apparently!) and the fact she has received little recognition outside Nigeria, within the country she is a prominent dramatist.

That Oyedepo's drama is issue-driven is evident from the titles of her plays. In common with many other Nigerian dramatists, she sees contemporary Nigerian society as fractured, self-destructive, wasteful of its people's energies: her work represents an attempt to identify the symptoms and causes of the national anomy, and to highlight those correctives that might lead Nigerian people – as the title of one of her plays has it – *Beyond the Dark Tunnel*.[3] Titles such as *Mourning for the Land*, *The Days of Woe* and *Survive, We Will* point to Oyedepo's recognition of the severity of Nigeria's problems and the will to overcome these. The fragility of the national economy, the monumental greed that has characterised Nigeria's governing elites and their collaborators, the crass materialism that symptomatises the panic felt by Nigeria's masses and their sense of the failures of state structures to sustain civil society, are examined in plays with titles such as *A Sacrifice to Mammon*, *Doom in the Dimes*, *A Storm in the Purse* and *Worshippers of the Naira*.

In addition, a whole succession of plays such as *The Twelfth Wife*, *Our Wife is Not a Woman*, and *The Rebellion of the Bumpy Chested* deal with marital problems and with the broader recognition that in suffering Nigeria it is Nigerian women who suffer the most harshly. Finally, throughout Oyedepo's work, values traditionally associated with women's conscience and management, in particular the values associated with the loving care of children, are projected as being crucial to the survival of Nigeria: those values identified, in Oyedepo's first published play, as representing *The Greatest Gift* the country possesses.

II Oyedepo's drama is often frankly didactic – as in the case of *The Greatest Gift*, a play that has a highly schematic plot. In the first three scenes of this play, Oyedepo depicts a dysfunctional family, driven to ruin – despite the wife and mother's efforts to hold it together – by the husband's reckless drinking and callous disregard for the family's needs. In the second part of the play, in stark contrast, a successful, integrated, loving family is shown, the husband and wife acting together for their mutual benefit and for that of their children. The single link in the plot between the two halves of the play lies in the fact that the harmonious family have adopted one of the children from the dysfunctional family (a child emblematically named Hope). Other than this slender element in plot continuity, the play's message is driven home by dichotomising the conduct of the two families. In the play's most overtly didactic scenes the father of the harmonious family lectures his neighbours on the constituents of a good marriage.

Clearly there are questions to raise here about the ideology of the text. There is, for example, a facile identification made between loving relationships and financial stability (one response to which would be, in an anomic society you can love as selflessly as you can and still see your children starve). The point I wish to emphasise here is the extent to which Oyedepo succeeds in preventing her drama degenerating into a shallow, lifeless didacticism.[4] In *The Greatest Gift* dramatic vitality is achieved through a series of episodes in the first part of the play, vividly depicting – and so enlivening – familiar and pressing problems: the poverty-stricken family's inability to pay rent, a schoolboy's (inadvertent) drug-taking, a schoolgirl's turning to child prostitution. In each case Oyedepo gives her actors material that enables these episodes to impact sharply. Elsewhere in the play she fleshes out her basic schema, introducing material that gives resonance to the idea of loving mutuality: in, for example, a scene in which the good husband/father confronts his traditionalist mother, who is shocked at the gender equality that thrives in his relations with his wife (Oyedepo 1988: 43–7).

In other plays by Oyedepo that deal, broadly speaking, with marital problems, an essentially didactic approach lies in awkward co-existence with a development of plot that is melodramatic and sensationalist. In each case here an exploration of the ideology of the text would need to examine how the stated concerns of the drama (the issues that Oyedepo problematises) are articulated through procedures in plotting and characterisation that do not always seem adequate to these or that display other, unruly energies that subvert the drama's apparent stated message. This is so in *The Twelfth Wife*, a play on polygamy and adultery, and in another unpublished work, *Our Wife is Not a Woman*, a play that deals, again, with polygamy, and with the stigma attached to childlessness. *Our Wife* boasts the unusual plot-motif of the discovery (in one of the main characters) of 'testicular feminisation' (Kemi, younger wife in a polygamous marriage, possesses 'the external genitals of a female but the internal features of a male'). Less extravagantly, this play, like *The Greatest Gift*, tackles the conflict between traditionalist and modernising preferences, in depicting the struggle between a husband and his mother, to whom he is strongly tied emotionally, but who rejects his household's European lifestyle (a thematic motif developed in a dialogue between Mama and her contemporaries that has a vitriolic quality similar to that of Okot p'Bitek's monologue poem *Song of Lawino*).

These are plays that tackle themes central to the repertoire of the Nigerian English-language theatre. In another play, *Don't Believe What You See* (published in 1994), Oyedepo deals with subject-matter that is much less commonly treated: love between a man and woman of significantly different age – specifically, between a schoolboy and the mother of one of his age-mates. This is a striking subject for Oyedepo to have tackled, and the way she develops it thematically is interesting (and problematic). Much of the tension in the play derives from the mother's son Banky's objections to the love relationship –

objections arising, he claims, from his sense that it exposes him to ridicule, diminishing his name and that of his late father (Oyedepo 1994a: 6, 41). Set against this is the principle of individual fulfilment, irrespective of custom (the mother Doris's young lover Maja proclaims 'We are in a world of our own': p. 23). The Author's Note asks 'is Banky guilty or not guilty' (for challenging the relationship, and indeed causing its breakdown): the factors indicated above are crucial here, and yet these are not sufficiently developed as thematic motifs for the play to emerge as a fully fledged exploration of a conflict of principles.

All the plays discussed so far possess real theatrical flair. Oyedepo is especially skilful, for example, in creating startlingly dramatic opening scenes: the father's drunken arrival in *The Greatest Gift*; the labourer Ashafa's rage at losing his wife to the wealthy Chief Gbadamosi at the beginning of *The Twelfth Wife*; the (initially) unexplained beating of Maja by Banky that opens *Don't Believe What You See*. Yet other, often sensational, elements in the plot are less impressive, for example, the catastrophic denouements of *The Twelfth Wife* and *Our Wife is Not a Woman* (a fatal car accident and a suicide, respectively), both of which represent cop-outs in terms of thematic development. In *Don't Believe What You See* the uneven handling of the play's thematic material runs the risk of leaving the play beached, in a somewhat prurient treatment of the relationship between an adolescent and an older woman, that neither effectively validates their love nor very consistently problematises this in terms of its broader social implications.

III   If Oyedepo's plays on marital problems focus on issues that are very familiar within the repertoire of the Nigerian English-language theatre (which is not to say they are hackneyed: these are matters of perennial concern to Nigerian audiences), much the same is true of her plays focusing on different aspects of a failing and fractured national economy. Like many other Nigerian plays of the 1970s and 1980s, *A Sacrifice to Mammon* (unpublished) deals with the phenomenon of armed robbery. As in *The Greatest Gift*, though here less plausibly given the complex and critical nature of that problem, the thematic focus is on a loving and integrated family environment as a bulwark against anti-social tendencies. *Doom in the Dimes* (published in 1997) is a stronger play, though again one in which the stated thematic premise doesn't seem entirely convincingly articulated through plot and characterisation. The somewhat awkwardly phrased publisher/author's synopsis suggests 'The didactic message of the ephemerality of the mundane and the futility of material acquisition is but too evident in the play' (Oyedepo 1997a: ii). What emerges is a drama with two focal points that are not entirely happily related: first, the social divisions caused by inequality in wealth – most vividly depicted in the main character, the businessman Owoeje's, treatment of a group of beggars and of his impoverished first wife; second, the source of Owoeje's wealth, namely a pact with the devil culminating in the sacrifice of his daughter and ritual murder.

Once again, much of Oyedepo's material is dramatically viable. The opening scene has an emblematic quality, as the group of beggars, suffering extreme physical degradation (one has guinea-worm infesting his testicles), come face to face with Owoeje, whose vanity is being boosted by a praise-singer (Oyedepo's characterisation of Owoeje here has the same Ubu-esque quality as Kole Omotoso's treatment of Chief Alagba in a notable theatrical success of the mid-1970s, *The Curse*: Owoeje uses a chewing-stick as big as the stem of a sapling; when he is depressed he drinks only one calabash of palm wine rather than his usual ten). The details of Owoeje's ritual practice are depicted in unsparing detail: a feature of Nigerian drama (reflecting an acute preoccupation for Nigerian audiences, constantly faced with press reports of the violence associated with these practices) instanced in plays as diverse as Olu Erinola's *Initiation and Sacrifice* and Soyinka's *The Beatification of Area Boy*. An effective and telling tension is developed between Owoeje and his estranged first wife (no longer able to bolster Owoeje's status; in the days of their marriage, Owoeje explains, 'The agony of poverty was unbearable, Then, money came like a heavy rainfall to wash away all my suffering': 32); this motif is effectively consolidated through the characterisation of the second wife and the daughter, both complacent beneficiaries of Owoeje's wealth (the latter especially ironically, given her function as sacrificial victim) and of the servant Adanri, who anxiously, self-servingly, assures Owoeje 'I know the house of wealth can never be attacked by the termites of sorrow. Nothing else inhabits the honeycomb but honey. I am sure nothing else inhabits the heart of a rich man but happiness' (p. 31).

Despite the play's undeniable theatricality and shocking depiction of Owoeje's use of his wealth, the question remains whether the plot motif of a money pact with the devil provides a wholly effective means of exploring the damage an extreme materialism has inflicted on Nigerian society. I do not want to suggest there is a conflict here between the province of social realism and the apparently sensational nature of the play's plot, since for many of the members of a Nigerian audience ritual practice registers as a commonplace phenomenon, part-and-parcel of a general heritage in which the quest for power and wealth overrides considerations of social good. It is, rather, that Owoeje's pact with the devil has, in terms of its contribution to the play's thematic development, a shallowness about it, a lack of resonance in terms of the play's potential exploration of the social causes and effects of uninhibited 'material acquisition'. 'Once the money charm from the Devil is swallowed', a medicine man advises Owoeje, 'it cannot be easily vomited' (p. 21) – an observation that contributes effectively to the dramatic characterisation of Owoeje (driven yet remorseful) and yet at the thematic level functions only as a dull platitude that has little resonance when it comes to an exploration of the crisis in Nigerian civil society.

IV   This paper has so far discussed plays by Oyedepo in which there is at least a partial disparity between didactic purpose and the choice of subject-matter, scenario or plot devices through which the play's stated message is to be articulated. Three other plays are equally issue driven, but more consistently successful in creating an exciting theatrical experience that persuasively carries the drama's thematic material. These plays are *Worshippers of the Naira* (1994), *See!* (1997) and the unpublished *The Rebellion of the Bumpy Chested*.

In *Worshippers of the Naira* Oyedepo departs from the simple linear structure employed in the plays described above, building her play instead from a series of episodes that are linked thematically but independently of each other in terms of characters, scenario and plot. The dominating theme – in what remains an issue-driven drama – is that of the unbridled materialism that Oyedepo identifies as infecting Nigerian social life and societal organisation. Successive episodes are interspersed with dances around a Naira Idol (the naira being the main unit of Nigerian currency). The episodes themselves depict the impact of avarice in a variety of social contexts, so that the widespread corrosive effects of materialism are revealed. In scene two, for example, an 'opulent man' is seen in the company of a praise-drummer and a news reporter, and it is the sycophancy of the latter, his seduction by the businessman's wealth and his abandonment of journalistic objectivity, that is the source of Oyedepo's concern. 'It is a rare privilege', the journalist begins, 'to have conducted an interview with one of the wealthiest men in the world ... I am filled with immense awe. It is like when a tiny ant beholds the gigantic blue whale' (Oyedepo 1994b: 4). Familiar motifs reappear. Once again Oyedepo here depicts ritual murder as an epiphenomenon of a society obsessed with the acquisition of wealth and power. Dramatic variety is achieved by alternating episodes of realist domestic drama and episodes that have the structure and emblematic devices of a folk tale. But the considerable effectiveness of this play lies not so much in individual episodes as in its cumulative impact. The sense of a loss of civic values being compounded with each fresh act of selfishness, the sense that this barrel is stuffed so full it must surely burst, is powerfully conveyed in the following dialogue between armed robbers:

> **Okiri** The Naira Villa must be seized from Ejanga ... Ejanga, by being smart took over the Naira Villa from Madam Tiogba.
>
> **Alasco** Just like Madam Tiogba smartly snatched the villa from Ibieda her late husband.
>
> **Wawa** And just like the late husband seized the financial empire from his first wife, Inukan.
>
> **Alasco** And I remember the first wife, Inukan, was the only daughter of a petroleum magnate who made huge wealth through bunkering.
>
> **Wawa** Before the magnate went into bunkering, he was a close friend of a top shot in government. The latter gave him a staggering sum of money to deposit in a Swiss bank on his behalf. However, the man smartly deposited the money in his own name.
>
> **Alasco** I learnt the top government shot had an instant heart failure when he discovered the fraud.
>
> **Okiri** (*in a stentorian voice*) Cut your story short! Business first and stories after! (60–1).

Like *Worshippers of the Naira*, Oyedepo's *See!* (first performed in 1988, published 1997) is a large-scale play with an episodic structure. Here again Oyedepo addresses the materialism of contemporary Nigerian society, but in a broader context, in which she surveys the condition of the Nigerian State as a whole. An opening series of mimes, songs and soliloquies, establish the history of exploitation that predates Nigeria's present condition (the cardinal event here being the slave trade) and the recognition that contemporary society is in danger of losing its sense of origins, direction and goals. Much of the dialogue here is highly generalising ('man is man's greatest enemy': Oyedepo 1997b: 12). In scene four, however, humankind invites a Messenger of the Creator to visit earth and to witness a series of enactments of human misery and frustration, and from this point on detail is more sharply etched as Oyedepo depicts a number of characteristic case studies, with the emphasis on Nigeria's social economy.

The device of the witnessing Messenger is not exploited as fully as it might have been, apart from some initial humour (How to make a divine Messenger comfortable? What would he normally sit on?) and the dramatic effectiveness of his increasingly conspicuous silence as each episode is presented. At the end, perhaps predictably, he exits in disgust, insisting to humankind, in the closing words of the play, 'your fate is in your hands' (p. 60). Where the play does come alive is in its individual episodes, sometimes harsh, sometimes sharply funny. Oyedepo is here, as throughout her work, openly didactic (on jobless-ness, one character proclaims, 'Arrest unemployment and many human vices bury their heads': 38). There is – and this is a problem especially in those of her plays that provide panoramic surveys of Nigerian life – a tendency not to explore fully the roots of exploitation, the causes of societal fragmentation, the contradictions that exist between officially stated government policy and real practice, and so on. In each of the episodes in a play like *See!* (as the title suggests) Oyedepo points a finger at a broken-down taxi in the street, at girls in a bar rebuffing young men not wealthy enough to treat them lavishly, at the blandishments of a corrupt charismatic preacher. After initial recognition no very significant understanding of the structure of these abuses, crimes and anomalies is established, and Oyedepo's dramaturgy is sometimes inert when it comes to inviting approaches to problem-solving. Thanks, however, to the sharpness of her recognitions and, in this play and *Worshippers of the Naira*, her skills as a satirist, Oyedepo does here provide material that could (in a produc-tion geared to that end) be used to provoke exploration of the issues involved, and even a participatory approach to problem-solving.

V One final play of Oyedepo's I wish to discuss is *The Rebellion of the Bumpy Chested*, a play that remains (as far as I know) unpublished, despite the fact that performances in Nigeria have been widely publicised. Subtitled 'A feminist manifesto' in the Ibadan production programme, this is a piece on the idea of an organised rebellion by women against male domination – a scenario that has previously been explored in the Nigerian theatre, notably in adaptations of Aristophanes' *Lysistrata* (see Dunton 1998: 86–7).

Oyedepo's approach here is in part didactic. For example, in the second part of scene five, in which the women's leader Captain Sharp outlines the manifesto of the Bumpy Chested Movement (BCM) to two concerned husbands, covering such issues as chauvinist prejudice against women holding high office, the sharing of childbearing responsibilities, and so on (one of the husbands responds with a speech on natural order somewhat along the lines of Ulysses' 'degree' speech in *Troilus and Cressida*, a favourite mine of quotes for Nigeria's conservative governing elite). Mostly, however, Oyedepo adopts a freer dramaturgy here, using dance and song (in, for example, the play's typically arresting opening scene, depicting a BCM training session) and some effective satire in depicting the husbands' responses to their wives' revolt. There are, throughout, some striking theatrical *coups*: especially startling, perhaps, for audiences from southern Nigeria where palm wine is a staple, the moment when BCM-member Rebecca enters with tapper's rope and a gourd of palm wine for the women which – in this hallowed grove of man's world – she has tapped herself. Most effective of all is the last scene, in which two of the husbands enter into role-reversal, the first borrowing his wife's clothes, making himself as pretty as possible, the second entering with a child strapped to his back, revealing he is making a successful living as a rice-seller. The humour here might seem to approach burlesque (the rice-seller turns to the husband in women's clothing and proclaims, 'If I met you on the street, and I didn't know of your new mode of dressing, I would make a pass at you. Allah! I would make an instant approach!'). On the whole, though, what makes this scene startling and theatrically daring is the sense that these men are not involved in travesty, that they are not putting on some kind of retributive parody; rather, as they enthusiastically discuss childraising and prospects in the food-selling business, they are genuinely undergoing some change in their sense of their allotted roles. How does this scene relate to the main body of the play, and what is the general ideological orientation of *The Rebellion of the Bumpy Chested*?

What is perhaps most notable is that although the play shows signs throughout that it might end by declining a radical perspective, by objectifying the activities of the BCM as in some way ill-motivated or unrealistic, in the end it does not do this. Certainly there are indicators that this is what it might do. Captain Sharp, leader of the BCM, is characterised as 'a hunk of beef with a stentorian voice ... grim-visaged and of stern mien'; towards the end of the play, a former suitor claims it is Captain Sharp's arrogance and overbearing nature, and the fact she has been jilted eighteen times, that have led her to form the BCM. Other distancing elements emerge: in the opening scene, the uncompromising insistence that two women, one of them lactating, the other pregnant, keep up with their BCM training; or, in scene four, the harsh treatment of BCM member Sarah, who has concealed her membership of the organisation from her husband and who at home still acts the dutiful wife, terrified of conflict. These plot elements provide a tension that is not, however, exploited to undermine the validity of the BCM manifesto, and this fact gives the play an urgent, troubling quality that is sustained throughout. It is a play that effectively energises audience empathies and antagonisms, but that does so in a way that does not invite easy, unproblematic allegiances. The final moments of the play remain open-ended as two of the women, Salwa and Tara, discuss the struggle, first agreeing that equality is perhaps an unrealistic goal and that the confidence of the BCM is hubristic; then recognising the primacy of true love in human relations; finally, however, agreeing that, if not the struggle precisely as defined by the BCM, then the struggle to identify new and far more just ways of organising relations between men and women must continue.

VI Since the untimely death in 1995 of Nigeria's pioneer female dramatist Zulu Sofola, the chief focus in critical writing on drama by Nigerian women has been on the work of Tess Onwueme, whose output is truly remarkable in terms of its range, ambition and sometimes explosively inventive dramaturgy. Other female dramatists who have produced work of real significance include Chinyere Okafor, Onyema Onyekuba[5] and Stella Oyedepo. Oyedepo, in her immensely prolific output, sometimes seems only to toy with the challenges offered by her subject-matter and by the ideological implications of the issues she addresses. In her weaker work her approach to dramaturgy seems somewhat constrained, falling back at times on a shallow melodrama. But in her strongest work there is an energy and inventiveness that provides actors and producers with significant opportunities to contribute to the vitality of Nigerian theatre.

NOTES

1. Oyedepo's published play texts give the author's name either as simply Stella, or as Stella 'Dia Oyedepo.
2. Amongst other prominent Nigerian dramatists working in Ilorin at that time – though in these three cases based at the University – were Zulu Sofola, Olu Obafemi and Akanji Nasiru.
3. Though the horror this play confronts is that of South Africa's apartheid regime (the play was commissioned by Nigeria's National Committee for Action Against Apartheid) and is one of a considerable number of Nigerian plays on this issue (see Dunton 1998: 284, for a listing of these), a current preoccupation of Nigerian public debate has to do with the recognition that whilst since 1994 South Africa has entered into a new era of liberty and (however compromised) social and economic justice, for the Nigerian State these goals still seem elusive.
4. At no point do I want to make a case against didacticism *per se*.
5. For an account of the work of Sofola, see Dunton (1992: 32–46, 154–9). For Onwueme, see Dunton (1992: 95–107, 177–80; Dunton 1998: 178–88; Obafemi 1997: 260–4). For Okafor and Onyekuba, see Dunton (1998: 162–3, and 188–91), respectively. Although Okafor has only published two volumes of plays to date (both in 1996), she has continued to produce important work, especially in the fields of developmental theatre/theatre-for-conscientisation (amongst recent plays is *The New Toyi Toyi*, produced in Swaziland, where Okafor is now based, in 1998).

REFERENCES

Dunton, Chris, 1992, *Make Man Talk True: Nigerian Drama in English since 1970* (London: Hans Zell).
——, 1998, *Nigerian Theatre in English: A Critical Bibliography* (London: Hans Zell).

Erinola, Olu, 1979. *Initiation and Sacrifice* (Ado-Ekite: Bcomgboye & Co.)

Obafemi, Olu, 1997, *Contemporary Nigerian Theatre: Cultural Heritage and Social Vision* (Bayreuth: University of Bayreuth).

Omotoso, Kole, 1976, *The Curse* (Ibadan: New Horn).

Oyedepo, Stella, 1988, *The Greatest Gift* (Ilorin: Gbenle Press).

—— 1994a, *Don't Believe What You See* (Ibadan: Caltop Publication).

—— 1994b, *Worshippers of the Naira* (Ilorin: Delstar Publication).

—— 1997a, *Doom in the Dimes* (Ibadan: Caltop Publication).

—— 1997b, *See!* (Ilorin: Delstar Publication).

—— unpublished, *Our Wife is Not a Woman*.

—— unpublished, *The Rebellion of the Bumpy Chested*.

—— unpublished, *A Sacrifice to Mammon*.

—— unpublished, *The Twelfth Wife*.

—— unpublished, *A Storm in the Purse*.

—— unpublished, *The Days of Woe*.

—— unpublished, *Survive, We Will*.

—— unpublished, *Beyond the Dark Tunnel*.

—— unpublished, *Burn the Fetters*.

—— unpublished, *Mourning for the Land*.

p'Bitek, Okot, 1984, *Song of Lawino* (Oxford and Johannesburg: Heinemann).

Who Can Silence Her Drums?

An analysis of the plays
of Tess Onwueme

OMOFOLABO AJAYI

With the publication of *Shakara* (2000), Tess Onwueme confirms she is a talented, socially committed and serious political writer. With themes ranging from overhauling backward traditions (*The Broken Calabash*, 1984 included in *Three Plays* (1993) with *The Reign of Wazobia* and *Parables for a Season*), rejecting destructive innovations (*Tell It to Women*, 1992, revised 1997), lambasting Western imperialism and greed (*The Desert Encroaches*, 1985), women's rights (*Parables for a Season*, 1993), exposing racial injustice (*Riot in Heaven*, 1996), to identity issues (*The Missing Face*, 1997), Onwueme's critical eyes are constantly on the pulse of her society, investigating and advocating change where this is relevant and beneficial. Limited neither culturally nor geographically, her plays ask individuals, nations and international communities to turn a searchlight on themselves and conduct a critical self-appraisal.

Even as a fledging playwright, Tess Onwueme proved she was not afraid to take on difficult, even taboo, social issues. One of her earlier published plays, *A Hen too Soon* (1983), attacks the tradition of arranged marriages, especially between young girls and much older men. Although by the 1980s the practice was meeting with some isolated resistance, it was still commonly considered acceptable. Onwueme presented the matter as a woman's rights issue at a time when this area was still politically delicate and socially unexamined in many African countries. The repeated criticism of that play, and the thematically related *The Broken Calabash*, as 'facile feminism' (Olu Obafemi 1994, 1988) vividly underlines this point. Let me quickly point out that Obafemi's criticism of the two plays as stylistically contrived and structurally weak is valid, although these are not unusual faults for an inexperienced writer. The point is that feminism was virtually taboo and seen as another form of colonial imperialism being promoted, this time not by their men but by Western women. For an African woman to subscribe to feminist ideals was considered an almost treasonable felony.

Passionate and committed, Onwueme continues to write prolifically. In addition to her published plays, she has a body of unpublished poems and has recently added a novel to her credit, *Why The Elephant Has no Butt* (2000). With each play she hones her craft as a playwright, improves her dramatic techniques, perfects her style, broadens her horizons and thematic complexity, and becomes more daringly experimental. She has come a long way from being 'A writer too soon' (Osofisan 1985), to emerge as an accomplished and internationally recognized writer.

How has Onwueme attained this status? Using five of her most recent plays *The Reign of Wazobia, Tell It to Women, The Missing Face, Riot in Heaven,* and *Shakara,* I will look at the following: (a) socio-political themes, (b) women's liberation movements and (c) dramatic techniques. The attempt to break up her thematic focus into just two broad categories is somewhat arbitrary. Her themes intersect and interweave, but I have decided to give the women's issues separate attention because, in addition to making women and women's issues pre-eminent in her works, Onwueme specifically devotes a play, *Tell It to Women,* to the feminist discourse. Regarding dramatic techniques, I will discuss the quintessential Onwueme dramatic style.

Towards social and political transformations

In *Parables for a Season* and *The Reign of Wazobia* (*Three Plays,* 1993), Onwueme expands her vision of social transformation beyond the tentative *A Hen too Soon,* and focuses on the social oppression of women with mature vigour. *Three Plays* (the trilogy is completed with *The Broken Calabash*) attempts a sustained argument against patriarchal systems that stifle women's potential, breed corruption, and lock affected societies into bankrupt traditions and stagnation. *The Reign of Wazobia* (*Wazobia*), the last in the trilogy, especially argues that not only do women want to lead, but they are also capable leaders and visionaries who seek to move their communities productively forward.

Even as she preaches social change, Onwueme maintains that any credible change must come from within, and not be imposed externally. It is for probably this reason that Wazobia, the eponymous protagonist of that play, ascends to the throne of Ilaaa in Anioma kingdom according to an ancient tradition. Tradition requires that a female regent be chosen, by ritual means, to rule for three years, or seasons, after the passing of the Ogiso, the king, before a new man is elected. There is a nagging question, however, as to the origin and purpose of this tradition. Why is the interregnum needed? Is it to allow women to taste power no matter how briefly? Or is to discredit them since they have not been groomed for leadership and are chosen, not through an assessment of their abilities, but by a ritual process? Whatever the reasons, Wazobia proves that in spite of her humble origins and youth she is intelligent and capable. She also likes the taste of power and the authority it bestows, declaring, 'I, Wazobia, have tasted power and *will not go*' (p. 131 author's emphasis).[1] However, for Wazobia staying in power does not mean enriching herself and terrorizing her subjects, as has become the norm for a number of contemporary African leaders. She stays in power to fight those determined to keep the kingdom chained to the past as well as to effect changes for the benefit of women. Her strength of character and the support of the women, especially the Omu, the

'King' of women, see her through the tribulations of gender inequity and disgruntled plotters, both male and female. A manifesto she proclaims reads in part,

> ... We all, man, woman, child must be schooled. To actualize these potentials for full benefit, for all with none posing an obstacle to another, with the left washing the right, and the right washing the left. Henceforth, women will have equal representation in rulership. (p. 153)

Easier said than done. The play is not set in a feminist Utopia, and Wazobia has to motivate the passive women encountered at the beginning of the play. The women not only participate in a mock battle against the men, they actually form a semi-circle of protection around their regent against the men's uprising. However, the women cannot effect the necessary changes by themselves, they need fellow male citizens like Ozoma to join with them in building a new, invigorated society. Equally important are the priests and the Omu, whose roles are set and defined by tradition. The priests prove to be the incorruptible voice of the gods and so help in thwarting the chiefs' schemes against Wazobia. Moreover the Omu herself becomes a convert and a pillar of support for Wazobia's agenda. Unlike the Ogiso, the Omu is a *grassroots* women's leader, and is able to mobilise the female citizenry in more effective ways than Wazobia could have on her own.

To Nigerians and those familiar with the country's politics, the title of the play strikes an immediate chord. Popularised by Victor Olaiya, a highlife musician, the term 'wazobia' is a common expression that captures the multicultural and multinational make-up of the country. It is a composite word meaning 'come' in the country's three major languages: *wa* (Yoruba), *zo* (Hausa), and *bia* (Igbo). As a composite word, wazobia means 'come together', signifying the desire for national unity. The interface of feminist politics with national politics shows how crucial the participation of women is to national unity.

With *The Missing Face* (1997), and *Riot in Heaven* (1996), Onwueme joins the small but hopefully growing group of African writers who examine the issue of slavery and the relationship between Africans on the continent and in the Diaspora. Among the few who have charted this course are Ousmane Sembene (*Tribal Marks*), Ama Ata Aidoo (*Anowa* and *Dilemma of a Ghost*) and Femi Osofisan (*Tegonni*). The reluctance of Africans to revisit this painful past is not limited to creative writers, politicians generally give it a wide berth too.

Onwueme attempts to discuss the issue in the appropriately titled *The Missing Face* (1997). The symbolic missing 'face' or question, is represented by an *Ikenga* sculpture broken in two, with one half 'lost' on either side of the Atlantic. Although the institution of slavery is not explicitly examined in the play, either in its European transatlantic form, or the Igbo variant, the *osu* caste system, it is implied in the split Ikenga. The Ikenga, explains the author in her foreword to the play, 'signifies the Igbo ancestral symbol of manhood and personal achievement'. The Ikenga then becomes the critical dramatic vehicle driving both the plot and meaning in this highly allegorical play. The allegorical form is couched as a 'rite of passage' encompassing on the one hand, the more obvious identity quest, and on the other, a more subtle but significant subplot about manhood and achievement.

The quest for identity is initiated and undertaken by Ida Bee, an African-American woman. With her son, Amaechi, she travels to Idu in Igboland, Nigeria, to trace the relatives of her father, Meme, and her son's father, Momah. Momah abandons mother and child after he completes his studies and returns home to Nigeria. Apparently he believes that as a descendent of enslaved Americans, Ida Bee is the equivalent of the Igbo *osu*, and socially beneath him. Meme too has disappeared, demoralised after being laid off at work without compensation and unable to get another job. The only memento of Meme that survives the fire, and which Ida Bee now carries with her to Idu, is a broken Ikenga he gave her on her twenty-first birthday, saying, 'Hold on to this Ikenga. Some day, you will mend the splinted [sic] face of our people, and we will be whole again' (p. 7). Broken on the night he completed his manhood initiation rites and as he was being kidnapped and spirited to America, the sculpture is also Meme's only keepsake of his homeland. In a dramatic surprise, the baby he leaves behind in his homeland turns out to be Momah, Amaechi's father.

Intricately interwoven into this journey of self-discovery is an underlying question about manhood pertinent to both Africans and African-Americans. In contemporary America young black men are an endangered species for a myriad of reasons. Among these are institutionalised racism and corporate capitalism that throws people like Meme out of jobs, while hopelessness and lack of motivation drive young African-American men to resort to guns and gang terrorism.

Many Africans are like Momah who has completely internalised colonial propagandist values and believes that anything meaningful must come from America and Europe. Stripping himself of his heritage, Momah declares: 'Black-out the black past, backward in time and space. I mean, it is time we in Africa shortened our long-winded names to JACK, TOM, DICK and HARRY' (p. 30). Indeed by the time Ida Bee meets him, he has abandoned his name 'Momah', associated with a way of knowing among his people, and adopted the meaningless 'Jack'. The sum total of his manhood is ridiculous and unfulfilled dreams. And how can they be fulfilled when he trashes his legacy as worthless and repudiates his identity? Obviously, it is not only the Diaspora that needs an identity check-up. Faced with such a crushing, negative sense of self, how does an individual become a responsible and productive member of his or her community? Ida Bee undertakes her journey so her son can know there is another life-style and process of attaining manhood; however, Momah, his father, must first learn how to be a real man. He must accept and take responsibility for his son on the one hand, and on the other, be a responsible citizen to his people.

At a much deeper level of interpretation, *Face* is a political call for Africans and the Diaspora to know their heritage, recognise their related identities and unite. To make this a reality, there is need for both to undergo a rite of passage *together*. The past, symbolised by Meme, will inform and instruct the present, represented by Momah, on how to guide the next generation, represented by Amaechi, to a productive and meaningful future. Crucial to the ritual process is the Ikenga. A split Ikenga is impotent and must be made whole again. With Ida Bee initiating the process, the Ikenga becomes whole and the rites are carried through. Meme, the spirit of the ancestral past, appears as a masquerade to witness his son and grandson attain real manhood.

It is indeed a new beginning. Momah and Ida discover they are siblings and Momah in particular learns an important lesson that both the so-called slave and the *osu* are social, political and economic constructions; neither is innate, genetic or hereditary. Significantly, Ida Bee's arrival in Idu coincides with the celebration of Iwu festival, an ancient Igbo festival of communal renewal. Her questioning presence injects an urgency sincerely to observe and realise the objectives of the festival and not simply go through the motions.

Although published a year earlier than *Face*, *Riot in Heaven* (1996) seems to take off conceptually where the former ends. It appears logical that having overcome their differences in *Face*, the African and the Diaspora will team up to demand reparations from their oppressors. As one people, their intertwined destiny and the commonality of their struggle is indicated in the hyphenated names of the characters. Coupling the names of freedom fighters and political activists on both sides of the Atlantic, Onwueme signifies this double identity/ one people/one goal in characters like Traveler X (Malcolm X), Marcus Mandela (Marcus Garvey/Nelson Mandela), Winnie Idia (Winnie Mandela) and the gender-bender Sojourner Nkrumah (Sojourner Truth/Kwame Nkrumah). Inferentially, the coupled names of notable Western historical figures like Jefferson Lugard (Thomas Jefferson/Fredrick Lugard) and Stanley Livingstone (Henry M. Stanley/David Livingstone) suggest there is no major distinction between the colonisation of Africans and the enslavement and discrimination suffered by the Africans in the Diaspora. Cultural representations in the form of *griots* and soul train; religious icons like the ancestral grotto, Church, Jah Orisha, St Peter and Amadioha; and political references such as affirmative action, new [world] order, collide, confront and converge in the exploration of African affairs and Western imperialism.

The major action of the play takes place where Traveler X finds himself in his journey through life, at the crossroads of earth, hell and heaven. Crossroads, 'the junction that confuses the stranger in town' is another cultural image powerfully deployed in the play.[2] It is a critical moment as only one choice leads to salvation and future empowerment, and not surprisingly, Traveler X is lost and confused physically, mentally and spiritually. The first choice is the path of inaction and empty rhetoric that provides no salvation. The second is through whining and begging to be allowed into a mythological heaven where God is on vacation and justice has taken flight. Enthroned instead are racism, power hierarchy and unbridled materialism, and the traveller who takes this road must be satisfied with crumbs and subservience. The final choice leads to true freedom and empowerment, but unfortunately the track, represented by the freedom train, is broken down. Before the train can function again, there must be cooperation among black people and between the genders. Guarded by Sojourner Nkrumah, the freedom train becomes a metaphor for a struggle that must be sustained through time and space to attain real freedom and meaningful power.

Riot is an excellent and spectacular piece of drama. The language, imagery, allegories, symbols, songs, music and dance come together like a complex jigsaw puzzle. Onwueme's use of music, especially the Negro Spirituals carefully inserted at strategic moments in the play, is perceptive and powerfully evocative. The chorus of the Unseen that brings together the wisdom and experiences of the African and Diaspora ancestors adds to the play's dramatic effectiveness and meaning. The play is indeed, as its sub-title proclaims, a 'musical drama for the voices of color'. The excessive repetition that often bogs down Onwueme's work is minimized. And if character development appears sacrificed, the connection with immediately recognisable historical and political figures helps make the characters full and rounded. It seems Onwueme packs her whole creative self into this work and excels herself ideologically, structurally, aesthetically and politically.

Shakara: Dance Hall Queen (2000), also described as 'a play about Mothers and Daughters', deals with a more localised, but no less socially relevant issue. The play, woven around two female-headed households, confronts a very real contemporary social malaise – the 'get rich quick' syndrome. Set in a city in Nigeria, *Shakara* may also be read as a discussion of the social and economic tribulations of single mothers abandoned by their husbands and of daughters neglected by their fathers. The mothers, Mme Kofo and Omesiete, each in her own way, struggle to give the best to their daughters. Unfortunately, their choices run counter to their children's expectations and beliefs. Omesiete is a poor woman determined to bring up her two daughters, Shakara and Kechi, to be morally upright, dignified and with a healthy sense of self in spite of their dire circumstances. Kechi, a 'born again Christian', looks to heaven for deliverance from poverty, but Shakara is restless, and seeks to define herself outside her class. Her model is Mme Kofo, her mother's boss, and a wealthy, class-conscious woman of the world. Ironically Dupe, Mme Kofo's daughter, admires the simple, dignified and honest life of Omesiete, but in her attempt to get close to her idol, Dupe gets drawn to Shakara's dissolute life-style. Meanwhile Mme Kofo, a drug trafficker, keeps her daughter on a tight leash as a way of protecting her from her unsavoury way of life and the disappointments she suffered in her own youth. Bringing the play to a climax, each daughter rejects her mother. Dismissing what she perceives as her mother's lack of ambition, Shakara eagerly volunteers to carry Mme Kofo's drugs to Europe after her mother refuses, and Dupe repudiates her mother's ways of life by reporting her to the police when she discovers she traffics in drugs.

Mothers and daughters are reconciled in the end through tears of forgiveness and repentance. Parents will in the future be enabled to use their power and wisdom to guide, not stifle the growth of the younger ones, and the younger ones will use their new forms of knowledge, not to destroy, but to inform and improve the old order.

Shakara is fast paced, with well-balanced scenes, and credible characters. The detective format of the play, however, creates stylistic problems and some scenes drag. Perhaps because of this, Onwueme's attempts at creating gripping dramatic suspense and surprising revelations are not very successful. Also Onwueme's attempt to make the play a morality tale in the story-telling tradition often seems contrived.

Critics have previously commented on the influence of the playwright Femi Osofisan on Onwueme, in particular her similar use of the anti-illusionist play-acting as a dramatic technique (Obafemi 1996: 264). The play-acting device is well used in this play. If imitation is a form of flattery, Onwueme pays Osofisan homage in *Shakara*; his influence is visible throughout the play. For example, the detective structure of the play recalls moments in Osofisan's *The Chattering and the Song* (1977), and the humanistic denouement of the suggested class conflict echoes *Once upon Four Robbers* (1991) and *Morountodun* (1982).

Spotlight on women's liberation movements

Ultimately, the question arises for Onwueme, as it does for most contemporary female writers, where does she stand on women's rights issues? Clearly, Onwueme privileges women and their concerns in her plays. Each play features women in prominent roles, and their characters are well developed even when they are not the protagonists. At every opportunity, Onwueme asserts that women are critical to any wholesome community.

In her 1992 (revised version 1997) play *Tell It to Women*, Onwueme confronts the controversy surrounding women's movements. While she does not focus specifically on the labelling factor, she examines the concept, content, context and relevance of feminism to contemporary African women. Appropriately, the quest starts as a research project in an American classroom. The play opens with a rather boisterous, half serious, half playful discussion of the project: 'To reassess the FEMINIST MOVEMENT', but the group soon settles down to the business of scholarly research. The first level of the research, carried out as a brief skit, concludes that feminism has failed. It has alienated men, and its claim to sisterhood rings hollow.

The second leg of the research shifts the play from the American classroom to Idu, Nigeria. Beyond simply moving the play to a different locale, the travel to the African continent is also a dramatic device operating at two significant levels. On the one hand, it echoes Western researchers who routinely travel to Africa to 'observe the natives' and collect 'raw materials' to develop theories that Africans must use in order to be understood in Western discourse. On the other, it questions if the West is the first, last and only word in women's struggles against patriarchal oppression. Do other cultures not have their own means of combating patriarchal domination? Ebony, a female student who appears to be the one of the voices of the author, gives a foretaste of what the answer will be:

We're going to the East, and then South to Africa! Africa is our destination. Now let's go on a cruise to the West. When we come to Africa, you will see the difference. Here in the North West what have we been exploring? It's been conflict ... conflicts upon conflicts of tension between men and women. We'll soon go to Africa and then you'll see the place of DIFFERENCE. There, our focus is *difference* not *conflict*. (p. 44)

What are the differences between the African and the Western women's movements? Are there no conflicts in the Southern hemisphere's version? Upon 'entering our world', in Idu, 'the class of twelve' encounters a gathering of rural women patiently awaiting their 'daughters', Ruth and Daisy from the city, to enlighten them about modern ways. Daisy and Ruth are in Idu during the celebration of the New Yam festival, to launch the government programme, and the First Lady's pet project of 'Better Life for Rural Women'. The gathering becomes another classroom forum to examine and assess Idu patriarchal structure and undertake a comparative analysis of Idu and Western women's roles and status. The women all agree that each gender has its role to play in the family and in the community, and question the purpose of global feminism. Even though the system places more value on the boy-child, the girl-child is recognised and appreciated as the real backbone of the family. Although they do not deny that as women their lot is not easy, they are quick to point out motherhood as the uncontested area of power and prestige for women. Adaku affirms:

Adaku This is no laughing matter. For me, motherhood is the ultimate power and I don't know any man yet born of woman who can boast of that power to conceive ... I mean create and carry another life. In Idu, men are outsiders in the process of giving birth. (p. 97)

The women's complacent unity becomes shaken however, when Yemoja, a young married woman, is chosen by the *Umuada* to be Idu women's representative for the First Lady's project. It turns out that the power hierarchy of the society is not merely gender-based, it is *both* inter- and intra-gender-based. Moreover the intra-female power structure sustains and perpetuates the patriarchal system. The *Umuada*, as 'daughters of the clan' traditionally claim power over those who only married into a village, becoming 'wives of the clan', with less say in clan affairs. Yemoja is willing to serve, but Ajaka, her mother-in law, objects on behalf of her son. The following exchange between the two is revealing:

Ajaka Why Yemoja? Why should it be my son's wife who must leave my son and children. Why must it be my own who will wander into the city to be the ears of Idu? I reject your choice!

Yemoja I have heard you mother-in-law. As Ogwashi people say, the ruling Obi has spoken, but it is left to Ogwashi to hear. If the women have chosen me to be their eyes in the city, I, Yemoja will go to the city. Yes, if the world calls for a new masquerade I shall be the new masquerade!

Ajaka (*alarmed*) Obida hear! Is this what a wife bought here for my son with my own money has to tell me? (*silence*) Yemoja, you have forgotten you are just a wife?

Yemoja I have forgotten nothing. My people gave me to your people as wife, not as slave. A wife is a wife, not a slave! And if the women of Idu make me their choice, I accept to be ...

Ajaka What Yemoja! (*silence*) You? Have you lost your mind? (*silence*) Are you losing your head before a crowd? (*silence*) You have forgotten you are just a wife in Idu. And not even a daughter who has a stronger status? (*silence*). Yemoja, think of what you will be losing if you disobey us, your in-laws. (p. 50)

The conflict widens as Ajaka storms out to appeal to higher authorities – father, husband and other men. In the ensuing showdown between the women and the patriarchs the value of gender division of duties is upheld. The women will decide on this matter as, although this is a patriarchal society, it is to the *Umuada* that traditon delegates power to settle domestic problems among women. Men cannot dictate in this area. The debate then moves on to consider two important issues in this review of feminism: (a) the destructive consequences of meaningless modernisation represented by Ruth and Daisy, and (b) the regenerative qualities of traditions shown through Yemoja and Sherifat, Daisy's mother-in-law.

Daisy and Ruth are prime examples of how not to go about changing society, people and ideas. Often referred to as *oyibo* (Europeans), their role is to expose the shortcomings of Western feminism imported wholesale to a different environment. The only knowledge they acquire from their sojourn in the Western hemisphere is how to devalue and oppress those they believe are 'uncivilised'. Ruth, who was sent to America as a teenager, is the most culturally alienated of the two. A research acholar, she is *the feminist*, and a declared man-hater. Meanwhile Daisy, a civil servant and married with children, is Ruth's lesbian lover and eager feminist student. Once in the city Daisy turns Yemoja into a maid and treats her as a chattel.

Both Yemoja and Sherifat reveal the dynamic nature of Idu culture. Standing respectively for the new form of knowledge and the old ways of knowing, both women demonstrate a constructive and meaningful way of revolutionising society. Yemoja sets the tone even before arriving in the city. In the following excerpts from an exchange with her father, Yemoja argues for an overhaul of the culture that privileges boys over girls.

Okeke ... Yes daughter, we sent the men first to school to learn the white man's ways just the way we send them to hunt in the forest to bring back the goods to add to our riches. We do not lead our daughters on to shores we are not sure of. Why? Because daughters are the eternal treasures of our land...

Yemoja I too want to be a hunter of values with my brother! I too seek to bring back new treasures. How can I always remain here to receive from the hands of my brother? I too have my hands and can fetch the world out there! (pp. 63–4)

When Yemoja's brave venture into the city almost destroys her confidence, Sherifat comes to the rescue. Together they reverse the terror tactics of the feminist duo and the soul-destroying effects of an impersonal city to change the course of events. Their co-operation provides the base for the rural women to storm the city and redefine themselves as women in contemporary society on their own terms.

The moment of change is effected subtly but significantly through a dance and music routine. Throughout the play dance and music function effectively as dramatic elements and cultural symbols. But one of the most powerful moments is when the women realise they do have power to end being pushed around. Left to rehearse a marching drill to a military tune in preparation for the launching of the Better Life for Rural Women project, Yemoja and Sherifat find their own rhythm, change Daisy's music to Idu sounds and substitute new dance steps.

Yemoja You see, our mother! We can change the steps!
Sherifat We can! Thank God for our daughters ... (p. 148)

An elated Bose, Daisy's daughter, joins in the rehearsal, thereby completing the cultural education she has been receiving from both Sherifat, her grandmother, and Yemoja, her surrogate mother. As the youngest, her recruitment completes a three generation-cycle, the past, the present and the future, to echo a similar pattern in *Face*.

Women is truly as the author describes it, 'an epic drama for women'. It is a play of ideas. Like the research project it is set out to be, it attempts to debate many issues affecting women and rebut the various misrepresentations and misconceptions Western feminists have propagated about African women. It is a monumental task and a worthy research project, but as a creative enterprise, it is another matter entirely. In order to cover as many bases as possible, repetitions are rife, the action becomes laborious, and readers have an overload of information. There are also a number of inconsistencies; such as Dede's German wife who speaks French, or when stage directions indicate Okei is aware of the lesbian relationship between his wife and Ruth but his actions and pronouncements do not reflect this.

Dramatic techniques in Onwueme's plays. Language drives ideas; proverb is the horse of discourse

Even in her very early plays, it is evident that Onwueme is not only thematically and technically ambitious, she realises and handles both areas effectively (Obafemi 1996: 264). In Onwueme's plays technical devices are intricately interwoven with her thematic focus. Over the years she has perfected what

Obafemi describes as her 'employment of the allegorical mechanism as a symbolic and metaphoric route to social satirisation and dialectical inquiry of contemporary society' (1994: 93). Her works are replete with creative use of symbolic representations, metaphoric allusions, vivid imagery, masks, verbal puns, proverbs and comedy that drive the plot, enhance meaning and underscore the message. They are like the Yoruba proverbial horse that guides a conversation to a smooth conclusion.

Onwueme's plays constitute total theatre in the tradition of classical African theatre. In its original form the dramatic action in African total theatre is realised predominantly through the non-verbal language of symbols, movement and music; the spoken element is minimal and is usually sung or chanted. Although the verbal predominates in Onwueme's plays, as is common in contemporary theatre, the non-verbal arts have significant presence and are well integrated. Music and dance are crucial dramatic vehicles for her plays. Movement through performance is the language of the theatre. Performing arts in their own rights, dance and music enhance the performativity of other arts by infusing them with their audio-visual and tactile-kinetic qualities. Onwueme, like any self-respecting practitioner of a total theatre shamelessly milks these qualities to bring out the best in her works.

In addition to the already discussed role-playing technique frequently used, ritual and travel motifs are two other significant trade-marks in Onwueme's dramas. Rituals help to validate established traditions, but also create new ones because they have 'built-in structures to cope with new crises, and to initiate and create new concepts thereof' (Ajayi 1998: 46).[3] Onwueme uses the ritual medium in this very fundamental sense. In her works, the ritual functions in a transformative process critical to the protagonists and what they represent thematically and ideologically. Central to the ritual signification process in Onwueme's approach, is what I call the 'arc of ritual wholeness'. Recurring either as a full or semi-circle, the arc symbolically fuses the three aspects of the ritual process – the past, the present and the future. The resulting wholeness brings about a healing process and resolution to the individual, generation, communities, or cultural, socio-political and ideological issues.

The travel device functions as a quintessential thematic metaphor often interwoven with the ritual in a more mundane way. It serves as a more rational complement to the ritual process. As Onwueme's protagonists move from one point to the other, they encounter events and/or people that alter their lives for the better: Traveler X teams up with Sojourner Nkrumah, and together they realise their dream of freedom, the 'class of twelve' travels to the African continent to learn about another type of feminism, and the rural women of Idu journey to the city to take control of their lives in a rapidly changing society.

Conclusion: people are powerful ideas

The concept of power with its implications for human relationships is a single thread that runs through and connects Onwueme's works. Whether she is exploring gender issues, racial equity, feminist movements, international politics, parent–child or interpersonal relationships, her recurring question seems to be, 'how can a balance of power be achieved?' If change must come and without any 'riot in heaven', there must be an honest examination of the past by the present, and between the powerful and the oppressed. As Odozi expresses it, 'When will you ever learn that the present must see a reflection of self in the contorted face of the past!' (*The Missing Face*, p. 43).

Early analyses have attempted to categorise and perhaps limit Onwueme as a feminist playwright (Obafemi 1988), but she is a writer who is not limited to one subject or to a single perspective (Amuta 1989; Obafemi 1994, 1996). People provide the impetus that drives Onwueme's creative ideas, and people are not one-dimensional. There is no question that her foremost concern in this respect is Africans, their relationship with the African Diaspora, and their empowerment in the global context. Onwueme highlights the black woman in her plays, but having committed herself to scrutinising the distribution of power, how can she afford to ignore black women, the most marginalised people in the world?

Onwueme has ideas, issues and causes to explore. Versatile, creative and gifted, she captures human experiences in their various cadences. Young Bose tells Yemoja, the playwright's alter ego in *Women*, 'Sissy, take my pen! Drum with my pen!' (p. 190). Onwueme has picked up a powerful drum, and with the big stick of her pen she is beating out relevant sounds and pulsating rhythms. Who can silence her?

NOTES

1. Unless otherwise indicated, all emphasis in quotations from the play will be the playwright's.
2. The crossroads is the public abode and shrine of Esu, the Yoruba trickster deity and messenger of Ifa-Orunmila, the deity of fate and the divination system. See Femi Euba (1989) and Omofolabo Ajayi (1998: 39) for further discussions.
3. See also Victor Turner (1982: 79–83).

BIBLIOGRAPHY

Ajayi, Omofolabo, 1983, 'Women in Transition: Zulu Sofola's Plays' *Nigerian Theatre Journal*, 1, 1.
—— 1993, 'Thoughts on Double Patriarchy: Black Feminist Criticism', *Journal of Dramatic Theory and Criticism*, Spring, 24, 3: 41–149.
—— 1998, *Yoruba Dance* (New Jersey: Africa World Press).
Amuta, Chidi, 1989, 'The Nigerian Woman as a Dramatist: The Instance of Tess Onwueme', in *Nigerian Female Writers: A Critical Perspective*, ed. Henrietta Otokunefor and Obiageli Nwodo (Lagos: Malthouse Press): 53–9.
Caraway, Nancie, 1991, *Segregated Sisterhood: Racism and the Politics of American Feminism* (Knoxville: University of Tennessee Press).
Cleage, Pearl, 1993, *Deals with the Devil and Other Reasons to Riot* (New York: Ballantine Books).
Collins, Patricia Hill, 1991, *Black Feminist Thought: Knowledge, Consciousness and the Politics of Empowerment* (New York: Routledge: Chapman & Hall, 1990).

—— 1996, 'What's in a Name? Womanism, Black Feminism and Beyond'
http://www.sistahspace.com/nommo/wom509.html : 1–9.

Emecheta, Buchi, 1997, Interview quoted in *Gender in African Women's Writing: Identity, Sexuality and Difference*, ed. Juliana Makuchi Nfah-Abbenyi (Bloomington and Indianapolis: Indiana University Press): 7–9, 12–46.

Euba, Femi, 1989, *Archetypes, Imprecations and Victims of Fate* (New York: Greenwood Press).

Obafemi, Olu, 1988, 'Tess Onwueme's Plays', in *Perspectives on Nigerian Literature*, ed. Yemi Ogunbiyi (Lagos: Guardian Books).

—— 1994, 'Towards Feminist Aesthetics in Nigerian Drama: The Plays of Tess Onwueme' *Critical Theory and African Literature Today*, 19: 84–100.

—— 1996, *Contemporary Nigerian Theatre: Cultural Heritage and Social Vision* (Ilorin: Joe Noye Press/Bayreuth: Bayreuth African Studies).

Ogundipe, Molara, 1984, 'Nigerian Women,' in *Sisterhood is Global*, ed. Robin Morgan (Harmondsworth: Penguin).

—— 1994, *Recreating Ourselves: African Women and Critical Transformations* (Trenton, NJ: Africa World Press).

Osofisan, Femi, 1977, *The Chattering and the Song* (Ibadan: Ibadan University Press).

—— 1982, *Morountodun* (Ikeja: Longman Nigeria).

—— 1984, 'A Writer too Soon: A Critical Review of Tess Onwueme's *A Hen too Soon*', in *Nigeria Magazine*, No. 151: 93–5.

—— 1991, *Once upon Four Robbers* (Ibadan: Heinemann).

Turner, Victor, 1982, *From Ritual to Theatre* (New York: Performing Arts Journal Publication).

Walker, Alice, 1983, *In Search of Our Mother's Gardens* (London: Women's Press).

WORKS BY TESS ONWUEME CITED

Onwuema, Tess, 1983, *A Hen too Soon* (Owerri: Heins).

—— 1985, *The Desert Encroaches* (Owerri: Heins).

—— 1993. *Three Plays* (Detroit: Wayne State University Press with Heinemann Educational Books, Nigeria).

—— 1996, *Riot in Heaven: Musical Drama for the Voices of Color* (New York and Lagos: Africana Legacy Press).

—— 1997, *The Missing Face* (New York and Lagos: Africana Legacy Press).

—— 1997 [1992], *Tell It to Women* (Detroit: Wayne State University Press) (previously published as *Go Tell It to Women* (New Jersey: African Heritage Press).

—— 2000, *Shakara: Dance Hall Queen* (San Francisco and Lagos: African Heritage Press).

—— 2000, *Why the Elephant Has no Butt* (San Francisco and Lagos: Africana Legacy Press).

Noticeboard

Compiled by JAMES GIBBS

The Noticeboard section provides opportunities for the sharing of information about theatre in Africa and by Africans. As will be seen from the pages that follow, a variety of sources, including Internet sites, correspondence and newspaper cuttings have been used in attempts to draw attention to issues and achievements. Submissions of relevant contributions for future issues of this publication are warmly invited.

651 ARTS AND AFRICA EXCHANGE

Founded in 1988 and housed in Brooklyn's Majestic Theatre, 651 Arts is a major 'African American performing arts presenter'. Africa Exchange, part of 651's international programme, was set up in 1995 and is funded by the Ford Foundation to 'preserve, transmit and nurture African culture'.

Africa Exchange organises conferences and makes it possible for African theatre-people to work in America with US-based artists. The first three conferences it promoted were INROADS: AFRICA 1996; Africa Exchange: Conversations on World Culture (1998); and Global Interchange: Artists in Conversation (1999). Theatre-people supported include Bode Sowande (Nigeria), Hassan El-Geretly (Sudan), Souleymane Koly (Côte d'Ivoire), Styx Mhlanga (Zimbabwe), and a number of South Africans: Walter Chakela, Yael Farber, Duma Ndlovu, Aubrey Sekhabi and Mbongeni Ngema.

As an example: over a one-year period Koly collaborated with Bernice Johnson Reagon, artistic director of Sweet Honey in the Rock, on a new performance work for Abidjan-based Ensemble Koteba. Theatre directors/playwrights Sowande and Sekhabi spent May and June 1998 at the Lincoln Center in New York interacting with directors from around the world through workshops, seminars, readings and productions. Sowande's work has spanned decades; Sekhabi is emerging as an important post-Apartheid voice which has been heard both at home in South Africa and abroad. His play about domestic violence, *On my Birthday*, was part of the Heritage Africa Festival Washington, DC (1997) and *Not with my Gun* drew large audiences to the main theatre at the Market Theatre, Johannesburg in 1998. Chakela has written more than ten plays since the early 1970s and is director of Hillbrow's Windybrow Centre for Arts.

Moving into 2000, 651ARTS produced evidence of the work of Yael Farber with Thembi Mtshali on *A Woman in Waiting*,

which seeks to show South African history through the eyes of one woman. In January 2001, Nii Yartey started the second part of his exchange with C.K. Ladzekpo hosted by East Bay Center for the Performing Arts, Richmond, CA. It is encouraging to note the extent of these programmes, particularly in view of the problems encountered by the Ubuntu movement
(See www.651ARTS.org/africaexchange)

UGANDA BRITISH COUNCIL

The kind of theatre activities promoted by the British Council have changed radically since the 1960s, when tours by classical performers were predominant. For British Council activities, for example, in Uganda. (See www. britishcouncil.org/uganda/arts) Following that link, we read (in late 2000):
'This year, the British Council is arranging for a playwright from the Royal Court Theatre UK to come to Uganda. The objective is to continue to build on the skills of the playwrights which have developed over the 4 years of this project and also to guide them towards writing plays on Good Governance themes like:
- fighting corruption and combating economic white collar crimes like embezzling funds
- proper records management
- educating the girl child
- protection and prevention of Child Abuse
- women's empowerment
- alternatives to imprisonment for petty offenders (training magistrates to actively ensure that this is executed)
- Penal Reform – improving the conditions of prisons in Uganda
- creating a more informed citizenry

(Civic Rights Education like voting)
- Encouraging the citizen to vote
- Consulting the citizen
- Engaging the citizen and informing the citizen
- The problem of street children
- Raising awareness of HIV/AIDS in prisons (working in partnership with the Uganda Prison Service.
'These plays whether as full-scale performances or in scenes will be used as the basis for workshops in communities, to help sensitise people in both rural and urban areas on the importance of Good Governance.
'As part of this project, the British Council will provide support for the publication of the play *A Time of Fire* by one of Uganda's leading playwrights Charles Mulekwa.'
The commitment to the Good Governance projects reflects the energy that Rose Mbowa and others put into participatory approaches to development. Those interested in getting a glimpse of Mbowa at work might obtain the video that forms part of Alice Welbourn's *Stepping Stones* package. The training manual and video tackle HIV/AIDS, and gender issues, communication and relationship skills. They grew out 'of a need to address the vulnerability of women and young people in decision making about sexual behaviour'. The work has been supported by the African Medical and Research Foundation (AMREF), Norwegian, Swiss and British government bodies, UN organisations, and a heavenly host of church agencies including CAFOD, Christian Aid, Secours Catholique and Norwegian Church Aid. The impressive list of backers also includes HIVOS, Memisa Medicus Mundi, OXFAM, Redd Barna, and World in Need.
Stepping Stones, published by Actionaid, is distributed in the UK by TALC

(Teaching-aids At Low Cost), and costs about £50 (£20 for the Manual and nearly £30 for the video). (Contact TALC, PO Box 49, St Albans, Herts. AL1 5TX, UK; talcuk@btinternet.com www.talcuk.org)

BBC AFRICAN THEATRE TO AFRICAN PERFORMANCE. THE LEGACY

Writing in *Research in African Literatures* 30 years ago, Shirley Cordeaux looked back on the involvement of the BBC with African Theatre. She listed the plays broadcast on the BBC's Africa Service between 1959 and 1970, beginning with Edward Scobie's *The African Roscius* and ending with *The Trial of Busumbala* by Gabriel Roberts. She drew particular attention to the links established with the Third Programme in the UK, which meant African plays were broadcast to British audiences as well as in the African Service. Her list of over a hundred plays by title and author bore eloquent testimony to the benefits of working with the BBC: it included a roll-call of a generation of African writers.

The BBC has encouraged authors by running competitions, offering advice, broadcasting work, and paying royalties, and the year 2000 marked around 40 years of involvement. The Millennium Competition for what is now, significantly, 'African Performance' (rather than 'African Theatre') attracted scripts from more than 500 writers, and from these a short-list of 20 was submitted to Ugandan playwright Charles Mulekwa for final adjudication.

Charles Mulekwa

Author of *Nothing Against You*, which won a BBC competition, and *In Time of Fire*, Charles Mulekwa has not been given the critical attention he deserves,

and there have been few attempts to place him in the context of Ugandan theatre. Interviewed by David Stead for a programme that went out on the World Service shortly before his prize-winning play, Mulekwa talked about the Ugandan theatre and his own life in it.

He was, he said, one of many with a growing interest in drama who was discouraged by Idi Amin's assault on the theatre, an attack epitomised by the murder of Byron Kawadwa, the Artistic Director of the National Theatre. That terrible event was accompanied by the persecution of other artists, that led to Ugandan writers avoiding controversy (and death) by writing slight farces. For years the theatre in Kampala was the victim of fear, and it wasn't, it seems, until power was in the hands of Yoweri Museveni (1986–) that, in Mulekwa's words, 'people began to say everything they had wanted to say for a long period of time'.

The influences on Mulekwa's writing and his eventual decision to make a career in the theatre have been various. He told Stead of the significance of his exposure to different traditions of drama in Uganda – he speaks and writes in four Ugandan languages, and he recognises the merits of improvised drama. He indicated that he had responded to the challenge he encountered on moving to Kampala where there was a vigorous theatre culture with over 200 fiercely competitive drama companies.

For several years drama was largely an amateur activity for Mulekwa, and it was only when he took up a teaching appointment at King's College, Budo, that his professional brief came to include theatre. He was put in charge of drama in the famous school and, in 1990, wrote his first play, *The Woman in Me*. This he described as being on the theme of 'boy meets girl and the parents don't like it'.

The following year that play was produced at the National Theatre and began to earn Mulekwa recognition as a playwright.

He had long been familiar with the work of pioneering Ugandan dramatists and theatre activists, such as Robert Serumaga and Rose Mbowa. Indeed *The Monitor*, (Kampala), carried his description of Mbowa that should be recorded beside the obituary this publication has carried. He wrote: 'She lived, breathed, professed, taught, shared, expanded, led, administered, promoted, encouraged, upheld, supported, had enthusiasm for and believed in the potential for theatre as a way of life that should not be ignored.'

Mulekwa was also influenced by imported traditions, by visitors, and by exposure to theatre outside his homeland. For example, his horizons were widened when he took part in a USIS-backed production of *Fences* by August Wilson, and when he attended a playwriting workshop, where he met Gabriel Gbadamosi. Gbadamosi helped to loosen his 'writer's block', and the result was *The Eleventh Commandment* about 'men sexually abusing young children'. The importance of this play was recognised in Kampala, and during 1994, benefiting from the scheme that links the Royal Court Theatre with Uganda, he took up a residency at Royal Court Theatre, London.

While in London, Mulekwa was exposed, in his words, 'to very accomplished playwrights', and he took part in sessions on directing and acting. In 1995, he wrote *Nothing Against You*, which exposed the troubling ways in which bride price and the law sometimes operated. This play was produced by the BBC and opened more doors: Mulekwa moved on from London to do a postgraduate degree in playwriting in Manchester.

What has become his best-known play, *In Time of Fire*, was produced in Birmingham during 1999, and is being published with the help of the British Council. Having written it out of personal experience and the tribulations of friends during war, Mulekwa says he wanted to show 'to what degree war can dehumanise somebody'. While the play is written in English, the stage directions indicate that the characters are thinking in KiSwahili. Language (as the BBC well knows) can never be separated from politics, and in Mulekwa's Ugandan context, KiSwahili is, among much else, the language that Amin and his brutal soldiery used. It was, Mulekwa says, the tongue people learnt so that they could plead for their lives.

In selecting the winners from the short-list of 20 prepared by African Performance, Mulekwa said he looked for a strong narrative line, a clear plot, psychological characterisation and 'the light and shade' of dialogue. He gave first prize to *Before the Rain Comes*, which turned out to be the work of a veteran actor-playwright who put 'Ade-Yemi Ajibade' on the cover of his text. London-based Ajibade should be better known. He has had a long career combing acting with writing. His plays include *Parcel Post*, produced at the Royal Court Theatre, London, in 1976, and *Waiting for Hannibal*, staged by the Black Theatre Co-operative at various venues in the 1980s.

Eunice Wanjiru and Philip Parker
Second prize in the BBC's competition went to Eunice Wanjiru, a student of Economics at the University of Nairobi, who was 19 when she wrote her play. Wanjiru responded to the challenge issued by the BBC by composing *The Fortune Teller of Babubu*. Long fascinated by those who claim to look into the future, she wove her play around the

encounters of a fortune-teller and the profits that can be made from manipulating the credulous.

Third prize in the African Performance competition went to Philip Parker, a student in Jos whose play, *My Uncle George*, included several well-turned domestic situations, and presented the problems caused by impotence, sudden access to money, and the presence in the home of a second wife. Impotence has featured in several African works, but this time the new, blue tablets, those stamped 'Viagra', have a part in the drama.

For those interested in contacting the BBC, note the following address: BBC African Performance, PO BOX 76, Bush House, London, WC2B 4PH. (Note also african.performance@BBC.co.uk)

Gogol in Liberia and *Hobe Rwanda* in Kigali

That the BBC does not always work from scripts and that it is justified in the change from 'African Theatre' to 'African Performance' was clear from the following worthwhile projects.

Historical circumstances, some going back centuries, others a product of the 1990s, have conspired to make English a common language for important minorities in Liberia and Rwanda, and to allow the BBC to work in areas where 'London' had little influence in the past. In both cases the style of performance selected by producers enabled local performers to make a considerable contribution through improvisation.

Gogol

The production improvised by an eloquent, observant, Liberian cast in idiomatic Liberian English followed the broad outlines of Nikolai Gogol's *Government Inspector*. While general social situation was 'given', telling changes of detail were made. For example, Gogol's allusion to Pushkin was replaced by the Liberian impostor's (rather expansive)

claims to friendship with film stars and politicians ('Tony Blair?' 'Sometime we even go for fishing'), and the admonition that ends the play was taken from a policeman and given to a Town Crier. The production revelled in the much-loved, much-adapted, much-produced Russian original that makes itself at home wherever there are corrupt local bureaucrats and quick-witted, protean individuals.

Hobe Rwanda

The relative positions of major European languages in Rwanda is a sensitive issue, and charges of linguistic imperialism should be borne in mind in analysing recent events there. BBC producer David Stead worked with Anglophone young Rwandans who had spent time, in some cases almost all their lives, as refugees in Uganda in a programme entitled *Hobe Rwanda* (Embrace Rwanda). The returnees and their producer opted to allow the trauma of the recent past and the tensions of the present to provide a loose structure for the programme, one that accommodated autobiographical narratives, songs, dramatised reconstructions and improvised scenes prompted by a love affair that crossed ethnic divisions. Attempts to explore the feelings of those in prison for murder, and Hope Azeda's painfully honest report on negative reactions to a play intended to promote reconciliation were particularly poignant.

The pain involved in attempts to come to terms with what it means to be Rwandese was not avoided. At one point in the programme, an authority figure said 'Since 1994, Rwanda has no history', and one could understand the impossibility of incorporating genocide within a coherent narrative about the land of a thousand hills. The four young people involved in the production, Azeda, Eddie Rwema (journalist), John

Agumba (hotel assistant) and Evin Mutesa (student), were not prepared to accept the 'no history' escape clause. Their willingness to subject divisive experiences and nightmarish memories to scrutiny was impressive. It will not be possible for anyone to 'Embrace Rwanda' for a long time, but perhaps Hope Azeda was not misnamed: a tentative handshake with the national legacy is a beginning.

FROM NASA TO SIYAYA ARTS THEATRE, ZIMBABWE TO UK

The Nostalgic Actors and Singers Alliance (NASA) was founded in Zimbabwe during 1989 by the late Mike Sobiko and four companions. Their base was Makokoba, a township of Bulawayo that had already spawned significant performing groups, including Black Umfolosi, Amakhosi and Sunduza. Over time, the use of the acronym 'NASA' was found to be both necessary and confusing. It was necessary because few could bother with the full title. It was confusing because some within Zimbabwe thought the group must be linked with the National Social Security Authority (NSSA), and some outside the country wondered whether the USA's 'Space Administration' (NASA) was backing the group for some underhand purpose.

At the end of the 1990s, when a change was felt to be necessary, rebranding went hand in hand with a sense of history, a determination to acknowledge roots and achievements. The name chosen to take the group into the new millennium 'Siyaya' (also 'Siyaya Arts', and 'Siyaya Arts Theatre') came into use in September 1999. ('Siyaya' can be translated as 'we are going ahead'.) Even as the new identity was assumed, the following 'past productions' were listed:

Zwelethu (*Our Country*, a history play set in a fictitious southern African state), *Makinte* (on educational issues), *Theresa* (on AIDS awareness and reproductive health), *Victim* (on child abuse), *Jive Sinjonjo* (1993, on the birth and growth of the group), *Skeleton Life* (1993, about family planning), *Another Negative Case/ANC* (1994, on the need for artists to organise themselves), and *No Difference* (1992/3, which focused on the distance between rich and poor).

In the Summer of 2000, Siyaya Arts Theatre took *Kokoba Town*, 'the working title of an innovative package of township theatre shows', on an international tour. Put together under the artistic direction of Saimon Phiri, *Kokoba Town* was performed at a variety of venues including Aberdeen and Edinburgh, where they were booked in to St Bride's Centre, Orwell Terrace, which has a reputation for hosting companies from abroad during the Festival. The 'package' included *Zwelethu*, described in this context as a 'dramatisation of Africa's battle to protect and celebrate its cultural heritage', about which one reviewer wrote: 'Although offset by more than a little humour and ultimately optimistic, this (is) a dark play (that reflects) oppression and death.' In *Umhlola – The Cry*, written and directed by Saimon Phiri, can be seen 'the plight of Zimbabwean schoolchildren yoked to an archaic education system'. Near the end of a tour, the hour-long play was performed at the University of the West of England (Bristol).

It was astonishing to have such a large company, some 15 performers, on tour, and it would seem that they are only able to support such a number because their appeal is partly as a music and dance group that attracts bookings from festival organisers. *Umhola* picked up themes from the past, including the resentment felt by those who lived in the forest and fought for independence only to find that the fruits of their victory went to those who stayed in school. A major target, one that made it a suitable choice for a student audience, was the kind of education given in Zimbabwean schools. It seems surprising that the syllabus has not been modified since Mugabe came to power, and that the call to study work by Achebe, Soyinka and Marechera has not been heeded.

The performance was based on a text. It was presented before a back-cloth and between wings. But in other respects, in, for example, musical idioms used, in movement and in gesture, it drew inspiration from Shona resources. Indeed the switching between English and Shona was balanced so that an English-speaking audience felt the performance was open and enriching, perfectly comprehensible and fast-moving. In the heady and purposeful cocktail it was possible to detect links with South African theatre of the 1980s and early 1990s for Zimbabwean drama, like anti-Apartheid theatre, is fuelled by anger and a belief in the power of performance. It came as a surprise to hear, in the exchange between audience and performers that followed the final admonition from 'the stage', that some Zimbabweans think the theatre was responsible for bringing down Apartheid. On tours Siyaya has been appreciated and earned awards. But despite plaudits from foreign audiences and despite support from such bodies as the Commonwealth Secretariat, members of the group often feel inadequately appreciated by their home government. Dedicated, disciplined, accomplished 'cultural ambassadors', they do not share the rewards accorded run-of-the-mill foreign-office personnel. In part they are suffering along with under-resourced performers elsewhere, in part they are

being punished for being Bulawayo-based and primarily Shona-speaking.

Siyaya Arts, PO Box 1919, Bulawayo, Zimbabwe; c/o nasa.theatre@prontomail.com

CONFERENCE ON INTER-CULTURAL THEATRE

Nigeria was very well represented at the Common Grounds: Theatre and Interculturalism Conference held at Northampton (14–16 April 2000). Femi Euba, Harry Garuba, Biodun Jeyifo, and Femi Osofisan made particularly noteworthy contributions, and much of the debate found a focus in the Jawi Collective's staging of Osofisan's *Once upon Four Robbers*.

The emphasis was not entirely surprising since the Northampton faculty includes two Nigerians, Jumai Ewu and Victor Ukaegbu, key members of the Jawi Collective, who took major roles in organising the event. *Once upon Four Robbers* has been on the syllabus at Northampton for some time, and the production (see Ukaegbu and Awo Asiedu in *African Theatre: Playwrights and Politics*) provoked considerable discussion. At a special conference performance the response was strengthened by Nigerians other than those already mentioned, including Rufus Orisayomi, editor of *Kayode*, a London-based African Arts bi-annual. The discussion of issues that Osofisan insists on towards the end of his play was particularly vigorous and, given Jeyifo's authoritative presence, inevitably trenchant.

The deepest division within the conference was between those who were regarded as using the language of inter-cultural theorising to mystify, and those who were engaged in theatrical productions rather than in talking about them in recently invented terms.

SYNCRETIC THEATRE CONSIDERED AT CONFERENCE IN GERMANY/BELGIUM

The theme of the 23rd annual conference of the Association for the Study of New Literatures in English (ASNEL), held at Aachen and Liège (31 May – 4 June 2000), was 'Towards a Transcultural Future: Literature and Society in a "Post"-Colonial World'. In the place of Northampton 'Inter-Culturalism', ASNEL preferred the time-tested 'Syncretism', and papers were presented at a series of panels on 'Syncretism in Theatre'.

The programme included Lorenza Coray-Dapretto on 'The Reshaping of South African Artistic Community'; Haike Frank on 'The Revival of Story-Telling in Post-Apartheid South African Theatre'; Thulaganyo Mogobe on the Botswana experience of Syncretic Theatre; Peter Paul Schnicrer on David Lan's trilogy *The Winter Dancers, Sergeant Ola* and *Desire*; Stuart Marlow on 'Limits of Representation' in South African and Northern Irish Traditions', and John Tiku Takem on 'Early Post-Independence Cameroon Drama: Anglophone Marginalization or Poverty of Radical Ideology'.

Their reservations were made concrete by a contingent of anglophone Cameroonians who preferred to show rather than talk and who put on part of a production, so bringing a whiff of Douala, or more accurately Buea, to the conference. It was clear that anglophone Cameroonians felt their theatre has not been given the attention it deserves by comparison with that of their francophone fellow Cameroonians.

(Their position has, I think, become untenable since the publication of *Matatu* 20, a selection of papers presented at Mandelieu in 1995. Under the title *New Theatre in Francophone and Anglophone Africa*, editor Anne Fuchs included papers by Hansel Ndumbe Eyoh and Godfrey B. Tangwa that redressed the existing imbalance.)

GHANA

Readers may be interested to know that the organisation 'Mbaasem' is 'a non-profit foundation to establish and maintain a writing place for women'. In an advertisement carried by the *Daily Graphic* on 12 September 2000, women writers resident in Ghana interested in 'being in touch with other Women Writers' were invited to contact PO Box TF 525, Trade Fair, La- Accra, to call 021 505 510, or to e-mail mbaasem@ghana.com.

December 2000/ January 2001 saw the appearance of *FonTomFrom*, a double issue of *Matatu* devoted to 'Contemporary Ghanaian Literature, Theater and Film'. Dedicated to the memory of Efua Theodora Sutherland, the 383-page volume includes a previously unpublished play by Sutherland, *Children of the Man-Made Lake*, reprints her important but elusive statement about the Ghana National Theatre Movement, 'The Second Phase', and includes Anne V. Adams 'Revis(it) Ritual' which examines *Foriwa* and the work of Werewere Liking. Other items linked with the theme of this volume of *African Theatre* include Kofi Anyidoho on Efua Sutherland, a bibliographical round-up of work by and on her, and essays on romantic fiction and on Aidoo's *Changes*. Kwaw Ansah is interviewed about Ghanaian theatre and film, and

Mohammed Ben-Abdallah talks about 'Plays and Playwriting'. The volume is co-edited by Kofi Anyidoho and James Gibbs.

e-mail: orders-queries@rodopi.nl
http://www.rodopi.nl
ISBN: 90-420-1283-8 bound US$85.00
ISBN: 90-420-1273-0 paper US$28.00

TANZANIAN ELECTIONS 2000 WOMEN'S PARTICIPATION IN A NEW DEMOCRACY

In October 2000 Tanzania had its second ever multi-party election. Ann Shrosbree and Bill Hamblett from Small World Theatre, a Wales-based theatre company, were in Tanzania during the run-up to the election collaborating with a group of Tanzanian performers to find out what prevented people, particularly women in poor communities, from participating in the election by voting and standing as candidates. The project was funded by the British Council in Tanzania.

The use of participatory theatre as a research tool and the introduction of life-size puppets of women into the process enabled people living in poor communities around Dar es Salaam to create stories which reflected their lives. These became part of performances which the actors later replayed to larger audiences. Audiences joined in the forum style performance, changing the play, arguing with the characters and each other, and generally exploring the nature of democracy.

A larger than life puppet figure, 'Bwana Democracia', chaired the proceedings and provided factual information about who was eligible to vote, how and where to register. As the large puppet head was revealed, the actors arms in the puppet's sleeves started to move and his voice boomed out, the younger members of

the audience scattered with squeals of fear and delight. While those of voting age heard how Mr Democracy was weak and had come to find out why the people of Tegeta, Kunduchi, Kawe or Mbagala were not interested in voting. He became strong only when people participated. The performance that followed used characters created by the community and included real stories such as:

- A woman with a small business selling doughnuts from a roadside stall who waited for a long-promised loan until a road widening scheme destroyed her modest enterprise.
- Another woman who was furious when she had her lighted cooking stove stolen from outside her house when she went inside to fetch a pan. Fierce debate within the audience as to the reasons for an increase in petty crime usually followed.
- A young woman teacher wanted to stand as a candidate but had a hard time convincing her father that women could be leaders. Some women in the audience supported her and others said it was unnatural for a woman to have demanding work which took her away from home.
- Fishermen held an auction with mimed fish on a real beach which drew 800 or so people to participate by discussing the pros and cons of fishing versus voting on polling day.
- A performer playing a corrupt politician bribed the audience and made impossible promises. For example he vowed that beer would flow from the taps (the taps are dry in some of the communities) and that the direction of the wind would change (to blow away air pollution from a concrete factory).

The crowds were gathered by the sound of drumming and singing, and by that

international trademark of electoral campaigns – the squeaky megaphone! Expecting a political speech or partisan message, people in these communities expressed their appreciation of this voter education initiative saying: 'This is a new thing for us. No one came to find out what we thought before. I hope this will be the future.'
The British Council funded the Tanzanian theatre group to continue to perform during the immediate pre-election period. Check:
www.britishcouncil.org/tanzania/arts

WEREWERE LIKING: AFRICA AND EUROPE MULTI-ARTS GROUP KI-YI

Born in 1950 in Cameroon, Werewere Liking has lived in the Ivory Coast since 1978. She is a painter, novelist, essayist, playwright, actress and academic.
She is known to many as the founder of the multi-arts group Ki-Yi, which numbers some hundred artists and has toured widely in Japan, Mexico, the USA, Switzerland and France, as well as in Africa. The group declares itself to be 'a movement for the renaissance of African arts, for the birth of a modern pan-African culture and for the meeting of black cultures throughout the world'. In addition to her plays listed in Banham, Hill and Woodyard (eds) (1994), *The Cambridge Guide to African and Caribbean Theatre*, also note:

Marionettes de Mali, Abidjan, 1987
Elle sera de jaspe et de corail (novel), Paris, 1983, translated into English and Dutch
L'Amour-Cent-Vies (novel), Paris, 1988, translated into English
The Widow Dilemma (play), New York, 1994
Sogolon Kedjau, A Mandingo Epic was first shown in France in September 2000 and there were plans for further development. It explores the story of the eponymous heroine, supposedly 'the ugliest woman in the world', and the divinely chosen mother of renowned Mandingo leader, Sunjiata Keita. A syncretic production, it draws on the music of the Mandingo as well as embracing other African musical forms, and a variety of African languages are combined with French in the production which features the epic chanting of Liking herself. Marionettes combine with human performers in this musical production which celebrates women as the world's peacemakers and the voice of moderation.
Village Ki-Yi were involved in the international MASA (African Market for the Performing Arts) festival, 3–10 March 2001, in Abidjan.
Contacts: Village KI-YI – 08 BP, Cidex 02C21, Abidjan 08, Côte d'Ivoire
Fax: 225 20 22 05 16
E-mail: coffie.randgold@globeaccess.net
(Compiled from notes and information from Village Ki-Yi and Joseph Brunet-Jailly).

Introduction to
Fatima Dike's *Glass House*

MARCIA BLUMBERG

Fatima Dike, playwright, poet, storyteller, was born in Langa Township near Cape Town, South Africa, in 1948. She started writing poetry in 1972 when she became involved in the Black Consciousness Movement. In 1975 she was appointed Assistant Stage Manager at the Space Theatre in Cape Town, and the following year, with the encouragement of Rob Amato, wrote her first play, *The Sacrifice of Kreli*, which dealt with a significant but often neglected event pertaining to her Xhosa people. In 1977 she wrote *The First South African*, a play that exposed questions of identity and explored the pain of racial classification under the inhumanity of apartheid. In the following year she penned a children's play, *The Crafty Tortoise*, her version of an African folktale. In 1979 Dike's *Glass House* premiered in Cape Town as the final production before the closing of the Space Theatre, and later that year it was staged at La Mama off Broadway and the White Barn Theatre in Connecticut. This text and its new version published below form the final part of the discussion in this short introduction. Dike lived in the USA until the end of 1983, when she returned to her homeland, a country she describes as 'burning – just too much violence'.

The year 1990 saw the first production of *So What's New?*, an all-female comedy that situates four women in a Soweto shebeen and offers new possibilities for independent single black South African women who refuse to be restricted to the usual stereotypes of domestic workers, lowly employees or home-makers. In September 2000 the premiere of *Streetwalking and Company* focused attention on black youth caught up in a pervasive drug scene as a source of 'easy' money to satisfy rampant materialism and to escape the harshness of township life. During the 90s Dike wrote plays for voter education and AIDS awareness and continued to teach creative writing and theatre-making at the New Africa Theatre Association. Dike's focus on the empowerment of women and the plight of youth in the townships utilises theatre as a vehicle of awareness-raising. She has given many young would-be actors a chance to be involved in collaborative projects that inspire and motivate them and even initiate new careers.

Finally, I conclude with Dike's *Glass House* and the context that inspired the new version that follows. The play places the spotlight on two South African women, Phumla and Linda, who, despite their respective black and white racial classifications, regard each other as sisters during a period when the political realities of apartheid set the scene for tensions that impinge on both their lives. Since Phumla's parents serve as domestic worker and chauffeur to Linda's parents, the power differentials within the domestic locale, and racial and class differences in the wider societal structures form sites of struggle. The play is set in the present but is interrupted periodically by flashback scenes that stage the girls' developing friendship. Dike revised the play during her five-month tenure as Writer-in-Residence at the Open University in 1996, and directed the new version in Milton Keynes, the King's Head, London, and at the South African Theatre As/And Intervention Conference at the Centre for English Studies, University of London.

The playwright acted Phumla while Libby Anson took the role of Linda. Dike had expressed her eagerness to revisit the play since she felt that she was too close to events when she wrote it – the anger and pain were too raw. Dike has also explained her confusion at the time of constructing the initial version about differing attitudes and motivations for the struggle and has described the 1979 play as 'half-born'.

Revising *Glass House* in a so-called post-apartheid milieu she emphasises that the play addresses racial problems that still exist, and she foregrounds Phumla's words to Linda: 'You know something, as long as I am oppressed, you will never be free.' These words Dike calls the 'real written version of *Glass House*'. Moreover, they still resonate in certain situations in South Africa in 2001, and in any milieu in which oppressive structures exist. Dike's powerful play makes it imperative for readers and spectators alike to address both their own actions and the role that theatre can play within South Africa.

Glass House

FATIMA DIKE

ACT ONE, SCENE ONE

(Phumla is a young black woman in her early thirties. She recalls a conversation she once had with Mr Black, the white man for whom her parents worked.)

Phumla *(Phumla ends up on the sofa)* A profession? ... that is a word people misuse a lot ... something to fall back on? ... like teaching ... Dad, the thought of sixty children in one classroom makes me feel hot and bothered ... Dad ... Dad ... I've watched all my friends who took up teaching, they have aged by twenty years in the last two years. I don't want to grow old before my time ... Nursing? ... Have you seen auntie Mabel's feet lately? She is wearing orthopaedic shoes. Now, I don't want to have feet like that in my old age thanks. Social work? ... I've got nothing against it, it's dignified ... especially if your parents can afford to take you to university ... you'll pay? Well Dad, there's a problem there too which needs to be cured from the root ... we have a social problem that has been created by apartheid ... the haves and the have nots ... the have nots see it as their right to steal, and rob those who have because in their minds they are creating a balance. Now, I will step in and counsel young black criminals not to steal, not to rob, not to sell drugs, but what do I give them in return? ... I am not running away from reality, I am being realistic ... Dad it is not my fault that this country is in the state it is in now ... if I'm going to be a social worker and really enjoy what I'm doing, then the system in this country has to change. You know the other day I was listening to the radio, they were interviewing the matron of Healdtown girls' hostel ... She taught lower primary, then she decided that she wanted to go higher, she went back to school with her husband's blessings, of course, and obtained a P.H. in teaching, she taught at higher primary school level. After that she went back to school and obtained a diploma to teach at high school level. Today she is the matron of Healdtown girls hostel and she did it alone ... I want to do something constructive with my life, you have to give me time to find it, or I will regret any decision that I make in haste for the rest of my life.

(Linda is a white woman in her early thirties. She is the daughter of Mr Black.)

Linda (*Ends up sitting next to Phumla*) Something that Sarah once said to me. 'One day Linda you'll be a woman, and you'll have children of your own. You'll know what it is to be a woman then. Nobody will tell you. Your children will look up to you, but they will also look at you and you will see your strengths and your weaknesses in them. Sometimes you'll wish you could turn back the clock and correct those weaknesses. They will go out of your arms and if you try to hold them back, they will push their way out of your arms. You'll be a woman one day and a good one at that, but not without the pains of motherhood. Your mother is a sickly woman. She leans on me. She knows that I know she leans on you, Simon my husband and Phumla my daughter. Sometimes I see the distaste in your eyes when you look at her. No my child, be a woman. To look down on someone like that is not to learn. I am grateful that I am still able to do things for myself and other people. I know that you and I, Phumla and her father, your mother and your father, we will all go the same way, six foot under the earth. We will all face the same judge. Make yourself pure, before that time comes.'
(*Fade*)
(*Phumla enters the room excited, waving the morning paper in Linda's face: drops newspaper.*)

Phumla (*Sits next to Linda*) Have you seen this morning's paper? Just look at this, isn't this wonderful? The students of Orlando High went to school as usual this morning. After morning assembly, instead of going to their classrooms, they marched out of the school yard carrying a banner that said, 'We do not want to be taught through the medium of Afrikaans the language of the oppressor.' These kids are crazy.

Linda (*Leans over to look at paper*) Carry on reading, there's more.

Phumla 'They were joined by students from Morris Isaacson, then, a little later all the other high schools in Soweto joined in the march. There was no police presence at the time of going to press.' Linda, it's happening. (*They dance around the sofa*) It had to come to an end one day.

Linda Who said anything about the end Phumla? This is just the beginning.

Phumla The beginning of the end. Kunini, how long? I remember in '62 when I was doing standard 7, had to do maths in Afrikaans. I mean maths is difficult in English as it is, how much more if you are doing it in a foreign language like Afrikaans?

Linda Father tried to get you an Afrikaans tutor in boarding school but the nuns wouldn't hear of it, they said it would not be fair to the other students.

Phumla In standard 8 they told us we were going to do commerce in Afrikaans, that year I was convinced that Verwoerd didn't want us to pass. We were doing two subjects in Afrikaans now.

Linda Father decided to hire an Afrikaans tutor for us both. He came to do the whole half term syllabus with you during your school holidays. You felt like throwing up each time he walked in through that door. I used to feel so bad for you.

Phumla Please don't remind me. I know your father meant well, but I really hated him then. Black parents in those days were not interested to see your school work because they wouldn't understand anyway. The fact that you were in high school and in boarding school was more important, and of course you had to pass. I spent a miserable holiday that year because of your father.

Linda I know, but it was worth it. You got an A in your final exams that year and a bursary.

Phumla You know, while we were doing commerce in Afrikaans, the students in township schools were doing geography in Afrikaans because commerce was not in their syllabus. Can you imagine geography in Afrikaans? (*pause*) We stuck it out right through to matric, and now, thirteen years later these kids are showing us that sometimes patience can be a sign of cowardice ... Suddenly I feel nauseated with myself ... my generation.

Linda At least you had an education then. They don't have an education now. Today a black child in standard 10 is the equivalent of a white child in standard 6.

Phumla Oh come on Linda don't talk like a white woman now. When was Bantu education an education? It was bad then, it's worse now. It's going to be interesting to hear the views of the people on the train this evening.

Linda Ja. I think I'll hang out in the township with you after work, I'd like to hear what the gang has to say about this.

(*Black out*)

ACT ONE, SCENE TWO

(*Flashback: Phumla and Linda when they were about 7 years old buying sweets from Jackson's Cafe.*) (*Behind the table*)

Phumla Hey, which sweets do you want ?

Linda I can't see, lift me up.

Phumla There's sharps, sunrise toffies, nigger balls, bulls eyes, marshmallow fish ...

Linda I can't see, lift me up.

Phumla Hey uya dika yazi.

Linda And you too.

Phumla (*Getting down on all fours*) Come on, get up and be quick. I want to buy too.

Linda No, you buy.

Phumla Bhut' Jackson I want sharps with all this money.

Linda Hey, I didn't say I wanted sharps.

Phumla Hey wena, make up your mind maan.

Linda I didn't tell you to buy sharps. I want sunrise toffies and nigger balls.

Phumla Bhut' Jackson could you please change these sweets for sunrise toffies and nigger balls? ... it's not me it's Linda ... she's not a whitey she's a little girl.

Linda What's he saying ?

Phumla He's being rude ... bhut' Jackson we want our sweets ...

Linda Come now bhut' Jackson give us our sweets we want to go ... I'm not madam, my name is Linda ... What's he saying?

Phumla He says uliciko.

Linda What's that?

Phumla It means you're a speaker.

Linda What's that?

Phumla It means you're a speaker. You know when the old people have a meeting to talk about naughty children and all the other things that are wrong in the township? The person who speaks at the meeting is called iciko.

Linda INCIKO. Do you think I will be inciko when I grow up?

Phumla If you can say iciko properly ... here comes our sweets speaker ... Hey Linda give some of those sweets here.

Linda You chose sharps and I chose sunrise toffees and nigger balls, so get off my back.

Phumla Hey, even so, we must share equally. You can't have more hayi bhut' Jackson, it's not me it's Linda, she's cheating ... (*To Linda*) You heard what bhut' Jackson said ...

Linda I won't because you're being nasty.

Phumla Hey bhut' Jackson says if you don't do as he says he'll take all those sweets from you.

Linda He won't. I bought them not him.

Phumla Bhut' Jackson says bring those sweets to him and he'll divide them for us.

Linda I won't. I bought them, not him.

Phumla We bought them.

Linda It was my money.

Phumla It was mine too.

Linda Mine.

Phumla Mine. (*Phumla lunges forward and grabs the hand holding the sweets. The two girls fight for the possession of the sweets, but when they see Jackson coming round the counter, they get up and run off together.*)

(*Black out. Phumla remains behind the table. Linda goes centre stage.*)

ACT ONE, SCENE THREE

(*Linda sits, waits for fade up, then picks up her mike and walks to centre stage.*)

Linda The police arrived in Soweto with one intention, to break up the march. The march was about a mile long, with thousands and thousands of students who were joined by township residents by then. At first, the police intimidated the students by taking pictures of the march and the marchers. When that failed to disperse them, they resorted to arresting them, picking four or two at random and throwing them into the back of the police vans. The students resisted arrest since they felt they were not breaking any law, they wanted to know what they were being arrested for. At this point the police lost patience and started to use force. The students also lost patience and started to throw stones. The police took out their tear gas, bird shot and rubber bullets started firing into the crowd. Someone must have been using real ammunition, because a woman in the crowd cried out in horror when she lifted her shirt and discovered that a bullet had gone through her stomach. The crowd started to run for cover, a boy of about thirteen was shot, someone managed to pick him up in his arms and run with him, unfortunately the boy died before he could be helped. In return, all the liquor outlets in Soweto were burnt to the ground because they were owned by the government. People looted them first. Public transport was withdrawn from the townships, and the only means of travelling was by train. The police sought the help of the army to try and control the violence that had taken over Soweto. Some of us wonder if this was to be the government's response to the educational problem which had been ticking away like a time bomb for more than twenty years. If it was, it could expect tougher opposition from the black students.

(*Comes round the table to centre stage*)

Phumla It was very strange the following morning. The township was quiet as if it was watching the whole situation behind closed curtains. The burnt out shells of vehicles told the story of yesterday's madness.

(*Linda moves clockwise to stand behind the table, Phumla moves anti-clockwise to join Linda behind the table.*)

The beerhalls were still smouldering from last night's drinking. Some primary school kids did not know whether to go to school or not; they were waiting for an order from somewhere, but definitely not from their school principals. When the order came it was crisp. 'THIS WAR IS FOR HIGH SCHOOL PUPILS ONLY. ALL CHILDREN IN PRIMARY SCHOOL MUST GO BACK UNTIL FURTHER NOTICE.' It was signed by the comrades.

Phumla (*Flashback. Light change*) 5:40 a.m. The bell rings. The tractor is still ploughing the fields. It's been going on all night. The morning is cold and blue. The tractor goes past the dormitory pulling a trailer behind it. It stops at the hospital. Thomas and brother Richard jump off. They go into the hospital and come out carrying a coffin between them. Four hands slide it to the back of the trailer. They go back and come out with another one. Back and another one till there are six of them in a row like loaves of bread ... T.B. victims. The tractor buries them in the mealie field. The Angelus bell rings. We spill the prayer out, the bell punctuating our lines. Mother superior lipreads every word. The bell rings three times. I kneel at the altar, stick my tongue out. A yeastless disc sticks to the tip of my tongue. I swallow. I'm afraid to chew the body of Christ. The precious wine comes in a gold cup. I drink the blood that washes the sins of man. (*The bell rings*) Good morning sister. Good morning girls. In the name of the Father and of the Son and of the Holy Spirit amen. Hail Mary, full of grace the Lord is with Thee, blessed art Thou amongst women and blessed is the fruit of Thy womb, Jesus. Holy Mary mother of God, pray for us sinners now and at the hour of our death amen. Take out your English books. (*The bell rings*) Good morning teacher. Good morning girls. Hail Mary full of grace the lord is with Thee, blessed art Thou amongst women and blessed is the fruit of thy womb Jesus, holy

Mary mother of God, pray for us sinners now and at the hour of our death amen. Take out your Tswana books and turn to page ... (*The bell rings*) Good morning sister. Good morning girls. Hail Mary full of grace the Lord is with Thee, blessed art Thou amongst women and blessed is the fruit of Thy womb, Jesus, Holy Mary mother of God, pray for us sinners now and at the hour of our death amen. Take out your Afrikaans ... I was washed many times. I was forgiven many times. Now, I want to think and feel sister. (*Slow fade*)

ACT ONE, SCENE FOUR

(*Mr Black is reading a newspaper. Phumla is reading. Flashback to a conversation between Phumla and Mr Black.*)

Phumla Daddy what is a chauffeur?

Mr Black A chauffeur is a man who is employed to drive a car.

Phumla Are you a chauffeur?

Mr Black No.

Phumla But you drive a car?

Mr Black Of course I drive a car because I own one. A chauffeur drives a car that belongs to somebody else and he gets paid for doing it.

Phumla Why?

Mr Black Sometimes the person who owns the car can't drive or he doesn't like driving.

Phumla Why would you buy a car if you can't drive or hate driving?

Mr Black If you have money, you can do almost anything you like. You can buy a car even if you can't drive because you can pay somebody else to do it for you.

Phumla Daddy, do you have a chauffeur?

Mr Black Yes.

Phumla Is my father your chauffeur?

Mr Black Yes.

Phumla Can't you drive Daddy?

Mr Black Of course I can drive, but I hate driving.

(*Flashback to a conversation between Simon and Linda*)
(*Simon goes to pick Linda up in chauffeur's uniform*)

Linda Simon.

Simon Yes Miss Linda?

Linda I wish you wouldn't call me Miss. Why do you call me Miss? We call our lady teachers at school Miss.

Simon Well ... you know ... a sweet little thing like you is a Miss.

Linda You never call Phumla that and she's sweet too.

Simon Of course I do. I call her sisana.

Linda What's that?

Simon It means 'Little Miss'.

Linda Simon, Phumla is big as I am. If you call me Miss, then I don't see why you can't call her Miss too.
(*Quick black out*)

ACT ONE, SCENE FIVE

(*August 11th: The beginning of the student revolt in Cape Town.*)

Phumla I was getting ready to go to work. In the middle of my cereal I hear this song. Outside. A powerful song. The kind of song that drags you out of your house onto the street. Once you're outside, you keep hearing the song getting stronger and stronger but you can't see who is singing it. I ran to the corner where our street meets the main street. I looked right, there was nothing. I looked left, the students from Langa High School were marching. They were coming down the main street, dressed in full uniform, marching four in a row. They had a white banner which read, 'AFRIKAANS DOES NOT EDUCATE. IT OPPRESSES.' There were other banners and posters which expressed their feelings. I read them all as I ran through their ranks. Looking into their faces, there was a solemn intention on them. As if Soweto had not happened. As if no one had died in that first attempt at protest. This one was fresh, with fresh faces and fresh determination. I knew most of the kids in the march, but that morning, I did not. There was a hardness in their faces. A coldness in their eye. Maybe it was there to distance us from them or the other way round.

I heard the songs, some were new, they were songs of protest. Where did they come from? Some were traditional songs dressed in new lyrics. Others were hymns questioning the right of the government to shoot innocent people. Others were down-right aggressive songs that challenged the government to mess with the rights of the masses and see what would happen. We were mad, mad with the power of numbers, mad from the intoxication of the music. I smelt freedom, for the first time in my life I smelt freedom.

(*Linda starts her dialogue from the table and moves downstage*)

Linda Later that morning, the police arrived. Followed by the army. At first they did nothing. They watched the march from their vehicles, made a couple of calls on their two-way radios, got instructions from their seniors. Then, they started taking pictures of the students as they marched past. They drove slowly, looking at each row of students as if to memorise their faces, they were intimidating them. Suddenly, one policeman jumped out of the van, ran into the march and arrested two students. They kept doing this at intervals, but the march was not distracted until one of the students resisted arrest. The police had to use force.

(*Stops down stage. Phumla walks down stage.*)

Phumla At that point, the students disbanded. They went to stand across the street at the Methodist Church yard and held a brief meeting. When they returned, they marched to the police station, but they were locked out by the policeman on duty. They were asked to state their reasons for wanting to come inside the police station yard. One of the leaders said they wanted to know why their fellow students were arrested, and, if they were arrested they should be charged, given a date to appear in court and released.

Linda The policemen inside the yard told them that they should speak to the station commandant.

Phumla The leader then told the police that if they could open the gate and let them come inside the police station, they would be willing to talk to the station commandant.

Linda The police told the students that the station commandant was not in.

Phumla When the students asked when the station commandant would be in, they were told that nobody knew when he would be in. Maybe after they stopped rioting. So, they decided to keep vigil at the gates of the police station.

Linda I suppose the police got tired of sitting there staring at the faces of the students. They tried to disperse them, but they would not go. They shot tear gas at them, but they would run to the houses nearby, throw water on their faces and come back. This went on for sometime, in fact it became a game between the students and the police. Someone on the student's side decided to give the police a dose of their own medicine, when they shot tear gas into the crowd, this boy picked up a cylinder before it exploded and threw right back into the police station yard.

Phumla One of the policeman inside the yard spotted the youngster. He came out of the yard and chased him, grabbing him by his school jacket, but the boy pulled off his jacket and the policeman was left holding it. We laughed and cheered because the boy had out-smarted the policeman. When the second round of tear gas was shot into the crowd, the boy did the same thing again. The same policeman came out of the yard and chased him again, this time catching hold of him by his shirt, and the policeman was left holding it, again we laughed and cheered. When the third round of tear gas was fired into the crowd, the boy did the same thing, but this time the policeman did not chase him. Instead, he pulled out his service revolver, took aim. When the boy saw this, he started to run. The policeman pulled the trigger and the bullet went straight through the back of the boy's head, slicing it into two. We watched his brains spinning upwards, then spreading out in the wind on their way down. Gravity. The boy was still running, he managed to cross the street, but, as he put his foot on the pavement, life went out of his body. He fell, hitting the pavement with the back of his head, spilling what was left of his brains on the street. There was silence, the silence of death. When he did not move all hell broke lose. Men, with stones in their hands, women, with stones in their hands, children with stones in their hands screamed for blood. Inside the police station yard, guns were shocked to a stand still. The school teachers went to pick the body up, but eight automatic sub-machines guns were cocked into action immediately. The boy was state property, he was under arrest. A dog from nowhere, walked into the tension and began nibbling on the bits and pieces of brains next to the body. (*To Linda*) It was a game.

Linda (*Puts sunglasses on and faces Phumla*) To you maybe. To us he was threatening the security of the state.

Phumla With what, the very tear gas that the state was firing into our midst?

Linda Oh no my dear, the tear gas was a culmination of these events. This protest against Afrikaans is a communist plot to undermine the rule of the Afrikaaner in this country. Our forefathers died for this country.

Phumla Our children are dying for this country too. That man ... that policeman is old enough to be his father. Maybe he has a son that boy's age. When he goes home tonight, will he able to look his son in the eye and not think about the black boy he killed this afternoon?

Linda He was doing his job.

(*Black out*)

ACT TWO, SCENE ONE

MRS BLACK'S MONOLOGUE

(*Flashback to Linda's mother when she was pregnant with Linda.*)

Mrs Black It's difficult baby ... it kicks and pummels in the night, makes me nauseous in the mornings ... my body is swelling ... I'm looking uglier by the day ... can't wear my beautiful gowns anymore ... Lester doesn't allow me to eat junk food anymore ... he only wants the best for this baby ... men have it good all the way ... the pleasure is his ... the pain is mine ... but I do have my stolen moments with strawberry ice cream in the evenings ... and I hope the brat enjoys it ... Lester doesn't love me anymore. To him I'm just a machine that makes replicas ot himself.

(*Black out. Bright light on Phumla. Interrogation lamp is on during Phumla's speech.*)

Phumla After the boy was killed all police vehicles were stoned. Russian cocktails were thrown against the walls of the police station. People tried to burn the old pass office down. They were burning tyres on street corners to deter the police vans from moving about freely. By the end of the afternoon, I was lying down at my house in the township recovering from the tear gas, when Mr Black drove to my front door. I was very upset that he had come into the township at that time because I was afraid that someone might try to harm him, but he reassured me that the police were not far. He told me to pack a bag quickly and go with him. I told him that there was no need really. I was safe as long as I stayed indoors, but he wouldn't hear of it. So, I packed a few things and went with him. The police followed us to the entrance of the township. When we got on the highway, they turned back. We must have been driving for about two minutes, when a rock broke through the windscreen. It missed both of us, but the glass cut me a little on my hands. The car hit a mini bus taxi in the next lane and swerved back to the right lane hitting another car, skidded on its side then rolled over on its roof and carried on sliding down the free way till it hit the concrete wall on the side of the road ... I don't remember what happened after that.

(*Back to normal lighting*)

Linda Father is dead Phumla.

Phumla How?

Linda The steering wheel ...

Phumla I don't know what got into him to come into the township today of all days.

Linda Father would have walked through fire for you. Did you recognise anyone?

Phumla (*Shakes her head*)

Linda You need time.

Phumla If they think I saw them, they will be looking for me now.

Linda They can't get to you now because they know that the police have spoken to you.

Phumla They'll want to know what have I told the police. They will want me more than ever now.

Linda Are you sure you did not see anyone?

Phumla (*Shakes her head*)

Linda Then there's nothing to be scared of.

Phumla There's plenty to be scared of. They don't know if I saw any of them. Even if I told them that I didn't tell the police anything they wouldn't believe me. If the police suspect for one moment that I might have a clue, they'll suck it out of me, you can be sure of that. So, they cannot trust me.

Linda So what's the plan?

Phumla I don't have one. All I can do now is to try and get some information through the grapevine.

Linda How?

Phumla By going into the township myself.

Linda You're asking to get yourself killed.

Phumla Not if I can help it. I trust no one right now. So whatever has to be done, I will have to do it myself.

Linda I can help. I know all our friends and I know how to contact them.

Phumla Thank you, but no. I have one death on my conscience and it's enough. Besides, this matter concerns your father. If you get information that can lead the police to the killers you won't be able to keep it to yourself, you'd want to go to the police with it. The killers will still kill me anyway.

Linda If you tell, you get killed. If you don't tell, they go free.

Phumla Don't. Don't do this to us.

Linda It's the truth though isn't it?

Phumla It's not as simple as that and you know it. This is a war. You kill one of us, we kill one of yours in return. Who is to say those children had no right to act the way they did? And who is to say the police were wrong to shoot them down. Here, it is wrong to point out the wrongs of society if you are black. It is right for the police to shoot and maim and kill to protect the state. Who will arrest the police? Who will arrest the government?

Linda Who will identify my father's killers so that they can be brought to justice?

Phumla If we had the answers to all these questions, we would solve this problem wouldn't we?

Linda You are pathetic, do you know that?

Phumla I know. I wouldn't be in this shit if your dear father had not been so concerned about my welfare. Why can't you people let us be, why can't you stop interfering? I did not want this. I do not want this.

Linda You wait a bloody minute miss. My father cared about you. I cared for you.

Phumla What do you know about caring? You mother people, you smother people, with your hand-outs.

Linda You call my father's contribution to your well being a hand-out?

Phumla No, I don't call it a hand out, I call it an expensive hand-out. I'm in this shit because I'm black, under-privileged, and could have been under-educated if my parents' employers, your parents, were not liberals.

Linda I hate your black guts. Get out of my house.

Phumla It's not your house, yet. (*Exit. Flashback light*)

ACT TWO, SCENE TWO

(*Sarah, Phumla's mother remembers Phumla's birth. Flashback.*)

Sarah We waited ten years for you. Your father and I had given up hope of ever having a child, but you came. I didn't know that I had conceived till four months had gone by. When I knew you were inside me, I couldn't wait to tell Simon. He did not believe me. When you arrived, he slaughtered a goat, for our our ancestors to bless you and protect you. Mrs Black did not understand any of this, because in all the years that I had worked for her, I had never left her alone, unless there was death or sickness in my family. Mr Black understood. For three days and nights we sang and danced, ate meat and drank beer till there was nothing left but bare bones, which your father and the other men at the feast burnt and buried at the bottom of the garden when it was all over. I remember the night you were born. It was 9.30 in the evening. Somewhere in the township I could hear the heartbeat of the Zionist Church beating through a drum. It was a diffcult birth. I kept getting cramps in my legs, but the church music eased the pain. It was as if the Lord was in that room with me in those painful moments. When you arrived you were smooth and whole. (*Slow fade*)

Phumla The struggle was getting intense. Violence was spreading. The frst adult person to die was not killed by the police directly. It was an unknown person who had gone to loot. When the man came out of the bottle store hugging six bottles of gin, he came face to face with a police van. The man ran back into the burning building and was burnt to ashes still hugging the six bottles of gin which had exploded from the heat of the fire by then.

Linda After Phumla had gone, I could breathe. I had space to move, to think, to reassess the whole situation on my own, sanely. I did not want her out of my life. I needed time. I knew that she had not gone far, she just went out for a walk to get rid of her anger, to get away from me. This country is a trap, for black people, for white people too, all of us have had a black person in our lives. The maid is always there to mother you in the absence of your parents. When you came home from school, the maid was always there. If your parents divorced, it didn't matter whether you went to live with your mother or your father, the maid was always there. Phumla was always there, we left the house together, we came home together. This government, that has brought us together, is tearing us apart. I went to look through the window in the hope of seeing her in the yard, instead I saw a car which had not been there before and every hour I went to look, it was still standing there and Phumla had not come home. She was seen leaving our house and they had sent a car to follow her. The car outside was to protect me in case Phumla came back with her comrade friends and decided to finish me off. My phone was tapped in case the comrades tried to contact Phumla.

Phumla After leaving the scene of the bottle store, I headed for the older part of the township via my house. I jumped the fence from my neighbour's side, entered my house through the bathroom window, fumbled around in the dark till I found my father's old coat and skull cap, I put them on and headed for the location. As I turned into Church Street my eyes blew my mind out. The whole street was sitting outside drinking liquor that was stolen from the municipal bottle store. Several guys were sitting on the roof of the bottle store soaking it in petrol, they set it alight. Someone ran to the station to tell the police that bottle store in Church Street was on fire. When the army arrived, the whole street was busy moving their possessions from their houses in case they caught fire. My friend Sindiswa had to be carried out on her bed because she had passed out long before the fire started, I decided to spend the night on her lawn watching over her in case some sex-hungry bastard decided to do something to her while she lay there senseless. I took two bottles of Smirnoff from my friend's stock, wrapped myself in one of her duvets and warmed myself to sleep with a straight of vodka, courtesy of Cape Town municipality. VIVA!

ACT TWO, SCENE THREE

(*Phumla sits at the table Linda is on the sofa.*)

Linda Phumla and Sindiswa were picked up by the special branch the following morning and were detained, I was scared to be involved, but I realised that I was involved. I called my father's lawyer and told him that Phumla had been arrested and I needed help. At first he was not interested, he blamed her for father's death. Later he decided to appoint a young man who was fresh from university to take my case on. I was happy for two reasons: he was going to prove himself. Secondly, his sympathies would be with the under-privileged. I engaged him immediately. He was able to get them both out on bail within a month on some technicality. (*To Phumla*) You've been sitting in that same spot since you came back this morning.

Phumla I'm fine thank you.

Linda No, you're not fine. What did they do to you ... did they hurt you ... Phumla talk to me ... I'm Linda ... you can talk to me ... did they hurt you?

Phumla Are you going to hurt me?

Linda Me hurt you? ... Oh Phumla no, never ... Are you alright? Maybe I shouldn't have brought you straight home, I should have taken you to a doctor for a thorough check-up.

Phumla Please don't call the doctor, I've been very good today, I did not move, I sat in one place, I did not wet myself, I did not make a mess. Please don't call the doctor, look I'm going back to my seat. I'll be quiet. Please don't call the doctor.

(Linda puts a white smock on. A picture of Phumla, head and shoulders.)

Linda Phumla Hlophe, black female. The x-ray taken of her skull shows that while she was in detention she was taken to the interrogation room, strapped to a chair, her head and face were covered with a wet burlap sack and she was hit over the head daily with a cane for long periods of time. Under hypnosis, the patient revealed that she was raped several times by white male wardens. Her head was banged against the wall to help her remember the day Mr Black died. It will take a highly experienced psychiatrist to heal this woman. It will take God's love for this woman to relax in the company of men. Marriage is something that she cannot even think about now or in the distant future. Having children is out of the question. Finally, she was hypnotised to get her to remember the day Mr Black was killed, and the faces she described under hypnosis were arrested in the township. She was taken to a line-up and shown the people that she had identified as Mr Black's murderers. This poor woman did not know fact from fiction, day from night. She was taken in and out of solitary confinement so frequently she lost all sense of reality, Phumla Hlophe has suffered enough.

Phumla When you are a political leper, you have no position in your community. You become a soulless body. People wonder why you still remain in the community after it has been proved that you are the telephone line that passes political secrets to your white masters for money. They say sheep, you have a price. You have no sense of black pride. You have been mentally retarded by oppression, you are nothing. You don't have self-respect. You are despised. You are discussed. You are something that is nothing. Even little children who are not old enough to be physically involved in the struggle, but who know what the comrades are doing and can give the black power salute know you, they say, 'There goes sis' Phumla the mpimpi.' Impimpi means 'sell-out'. People who don't know you will ask, if she is a mpimpi why is she still alive, why is she still in the community with you? They will say, 'She is not alive, she is dead. Her white masters used her and used her and when they were done with her they spat her out. This is what is left of her, now, she lives with her conscience.' In the meantime, none of them know the truth, you and God are the only ones who know the truth. I was never an informer, the whites were never my masters, it is the way the government has presented the truth to the people. But God's truth is a funny thing, 'You can rock the truth, but you can never sink the truth.' Truth will rise one day like a drowned body and float toward the shore, nobody will ignore it then. 'Truth can never be hidden forever.'

So, while some people were convinced that I was a sellout, others were but they too did not know the real truth. One day, the comrades needed my help. But they were afraid to come to me directly. You see things were changing in the struggle. People were being arrested and jailed without trial, so people wanted to escape, to make connections outside the country. People needed to arm themselves.

(Phumla and Linda are playing snakes and ladders)

Phumla How much longer am I supposed to play this childish game?

Linda You're getting better. Well, we can call our doctor and tell her that you're bored with playing snakes and ladders and maybe she will promote us to draughts.

Phumla I can count, I read, I can go to the toilet alone. Maybe I must start cooking or doing some adult chore.

Linda Someone called Thami phoned and asked to talk to you. I told her you were sleeping. I took her number.

Phumla Thami, who could that be?

Linda Here's her number.

Phumla I'll call her and find out what she wants with me.

Linda Whatever you do, don't answer any questions.

Phumla Don't worry I won't, I'll listen and when I'm done I'll tell her, 'I'll think about it and call you back when I've decided.'

Linda Good girl.

Phumla Linda, I'm not mentally impaired, I'm emotionally impaired.

Linda I know, and you know me, I can't help worrying.

Phumla I know, but please relax, because if you are, I will relax too. Now, pass me that phone, thanks, do you know this is my first phone since …

Linda I know, come along now, make that call before we lose our courage.

Phumla The local civic hall has been burnt to the ground. Spectators are to be dealt with severely. If you are black, you march. Whether you know the reason behind the march or not. Because when freedom comes it will be for you too. Those people who choose not to go to protest marches can no longer stand at their gates and watch others going to fight for their freedom. If you do you are courting trouble.

Linda The comrades announced their first Black Christmas that year. For the first time, white business realised the value of the black consumer. The comrades made sure that black consumers supported black business.

Phumla There would be no celebrations, black people could not buy groceries from the white owned supermarkets in the city. We had to support our local black shop owners.

Linda O.K. Bazaars, one of the biggest chainstores in the country, decided to use unmarked shopping bags for gutless and less patriotic blacks.

Phumla The comrades got wind of that and started to search plastic shopping bags as they came off the trains, buses and taxis.

(Flash back to Mrs Black's death)

Phumla The grass is alight with glow worms, I cupped one in my hand and it went out just like that.

Linda Autumn here is unlike autumn anywhere else in the world.

Phumla Look at the moon, it lights that cloud up so heavenly, shuu'. We spend so much time looking around us that we miss the beauty of the heaven.

Linda Mother is fading ...

Phumla Yes.

Linda I wish she would go. I wonder if Daddy ...

Phumla Your father will accept it.

Linda Ja, he is going to need their support more than ever now. They have been pillars of strength to us during mother's illness, but now he is going to need us more.

Phumla I look at your father, and I look at your mother, no two people could be more different, yet they met, fell in love, married, had you and lived happily ever after.

Linda Opposites sometimes make the best couples.

Phumla Ja, but your mother.

Linda What about her?

Phumla Your mother never came to terms with the fact we are people. Human beings you know. All these years she still treated us like servants. And your father ... ah well your father is a ... unique person. To me he is colourless, skinless ... he's just a ... a father ...

Linda Some people transcend certain things. My father transcends problems of race. He was born politically correct in his white skin. This is not something that he picked up during his lifetime, he was born with it. It's a gift.

Phumla It's a virtue. Your father has a unique quality, black people always smell racism, but, when your father walks into a company of any people, black, white, yellow, in between, he blends like sugar into milk.

Linda Whereas my mother is extremely the opposite. My mother is English ... upper crust... she can't help herself ... she would die before she can admit to being friendly with the servants. Class comes first. That is proper.

Phumla I know that, it's just that I find it hard that she maintained that awful custom all these years. There's something called trust, you develop trust with people you have lived with most of your life.

Linda Familiarity breeds contempt.

Phumla BULL! I know what's wrong with your mother. All these years she had a crush on my father. And she had to sit on her feelings. Because, if she let her frozen heart melt, the emotions locked inside would destroy your father, my mother and the two of us and we would end up with a half-breed sister between us.

Linda I think your father fancies my mother. And every morning, before he takes her tea into her bedroom, I have seen him drenching himself with Brut aftershave.

Phumla You see when my father takes your mother tea in the mornings, count how long he takes to come out of your mother's bedroom (*Pause*). Exactly, they are doing it. Quick sex!

Phumla Mrs. Black is gone. No emotions were spent. We didn't follow her coffin to the graveyard, there was no corpse, just ashes in a vase. Her buddies chatted right through the memorial service. Afterwards they shook Mr Black's hand. Someone gave him a kitten, I suppose as a substitute for Mrs Black ... or perhaps it was a forget-me-not present ... anyway I can't see Mr Black sitting by the fire with an angora shawl over his knees stroking a cat yet.

Linda I loved my mother.

Phumla You could have fooled me.

Linda Mama was beautiful and fragile. Everything about her had to be beautiful. She was elegant. I was ordinary. I hated our weekly visits to the hairdresser. I hated the silk stockings she forced me to wear. She was beautiful and had to have beauty. I didn't care. I was happiest in my jeans and running shoes.

Phumla Designer jeans and running shoes I might add.

Linda When she died, she was the most beautiful corpse I had ever seen. She deprived the worms the taste of her beauty. She couldn't bear the idea of her beautiful skin falling off her face. Her body rotting in the stinking depths of the earth. Her hair falling, to disintegrate into the satin lined coffin. She chose fire.

ACT TWO, SCENE FOUR

Phumla We have just come back from the reading of Mr Black's will. I had no idea that I was mentioned. Mr Black left me this house and all his cars. How do I explain this to my people? What will they say?

Linda Why don't you sell it?

Phumla Sell this house, are you crazy?

Linda This house is yours now and you can do with it as you wish.

Phumla Will you buy it?

Linda Buy my home, are you crazy?

Phumla You're right, how can I sell you your home?

Linda Sell it.

Phumla You white people have no respect. This is your parents' house, you were born here. You and I were brought up in this house. Your mother died in this house. This house has your memories and my memories. Sell this house? Never.

Linda It's just a house. Phumla. Property. Do you have any idea how much money you can get if you sold this house?

Phumla Hogayi, right there. Linda, this is our home.

Linda Oh no, I'm not going through that again. Either you stay or you sell.

Phumla I can't sell this house, it has too many memories for me.

Linda No problem, you can go back to your parents' house in the township.

Phumla And get killed.

Linda Then shut up and stay here. Things won't always be this way forever.

Phumla Your mother doesn't have a resting place, and personally I don't think I want to have her staying with me on the mantelshelf.

Linda Poor Mum, she's been kicked out of her own home.

Phumla She's lucky she's dead, she can't feel anything.

Linda Her spirit will.

Phumla Not for long, she will join her husband at the graveyard and they will be together again in death as they were in life.

Linda Amen. (*Pause*). You're not selling the house then?

Phumla Not on your life. Over my dead body.

ACT TWO, SCENE FIVE

Phumla This house is too big for one person!

Linda You'll get used to it.

Phumla I'll never get used to it.

Linda It's yours now.

Phumla Linda, I can't live alone in this house, it's too big.

Linda Just try it, for one week.

Phumla Where will you go?

Linda Oh, I wont be far, I've rented a cottage on the beach front in Camps Bay.

Phumla Are you having an affair?

Linda Phumla, I am not having an affair.

Phumla Then why are you leaving.

Linda Why can't you accept the fact that you can have twenty rooms to yourself, to have space and not feel guilty about it?

Phumla The first day was fine, I cleaned the bottom floor thoroughly, the following day I did the windows and the curtains, the day after, the cutlery, and so on until the whole house had been spring cleaned. I spent the next week recuperating on the sofa with the remote control cemented to the palm of my hand ... it was in heaven on earth. I phoned the video company and all the movies I wanted to watch were delivered at my door.

Linda I was introduced to a young man who was a freelance journalist who was working for a French television company, he was from Mitchells Plain. He told me that he was reporting on the student revolt and went into the areas where the action was. I went with him to the funeral of a black student who was killed by the police in Paarl.

Reporter Police cover political funerals for many reasons. People tend to give themselves freedom of speech at these funerals. Comrades pass information to other comrades at these funerals.

Linda We drove along the N2, not far from one of the coloured townships, two coloured students came out of the bushes, a boy of about nineteen and a girl of the same age, they were dressed in school uniform. My friend stopped to pick them up and we drove on in silence. We entered a black township, the two students at the back lay flat on the seats, we reached a taxi rank, the two got off without saying a word or looking back. A double decker bus came down the street, followed by a single decker. Suddenly petrol bombs and rocks hit both buses as they raced down the street. The two drivers decided to abandoned them and fled on foot with the youths hot on their heels. The buses were driven away by some of the youths.

Reporter See those mini taxis across the road, that is the black taxi industry struggling to be born, the bus company monopolises the transport industry in the black areas because it is being subsidised by the government. They don't want to give the black taxi owners a piece of the transport pie. The black taxi owners have made an agreement with the students to disrupt the bus company so that it does not operate comfortably in the townships. In return the taxi owners have promised to give them free transport when they ...

Linda Did you plan all of this?

Reporter Plan what?

Linda The performance that I've just witnessed: We know that you reporters pay these kids to do things especially for you so that you can send gory films overseas because that is what sells South Africa abroad.

Reporter The performance you have just witnessed takes place every day if you frequent this particular spot. The comrades know me, I know them, and if I'm going to cover a funeral it's normal for me to pick them up. I ask no question. Because if you don't know what is going on, what can you tell the police?

Linda Our discussion was interrupted by a commotion to our left. Same time. A meat truck stopped outside the butcher shop, I saw a look pass from one youth to the next as they watched the meat truck. A policeman came out of the back of the truck, he had a rifle. The truck driver and his side-man got out, went to the back of the truck and began to take meat carcasses to the butcher. Once they were inside, the youths attacked the policeman. One minute they were all over him, the next minute they were gone. The policeman was left with a knife sticking out of his neck, the youths had taken his rifle. When the truck driver and his side kick saw what was happening, they jumped into their truck and were about to drive off when a brick, followed by a petrol bomb, smashed through the windscreen of the truck. They abandoned the truck and were running back to the butcher. The woman closed the door in their faces and when we last saw them they were running in the direction of the police station.

Phumla I missed my home. I missed the township. I missed the life, the noise, the music, the dance, the anger, the joy, neighbour leaning over neighbour's fence. I missed ubuntu. The following week, I received a message on my answering machine asking me to get in touch with comrade Nkuhlu at an address in Gugulethu. I phoned Linda, but she was not home. I left a message telling her where I was going and she got in touch with her reporter friend immediately. When the comrades call, you go, because if you don't you have something to hide. If you don't go, they will find you anyway. The comrades wanted to know. Why was I living in the white man's house as if I owned it? Why did the white man's daughter move out?

Linda It never stops in this damn country. If it's not the police, it's the comrades.

Reporter Listen, there's no time to waste, Phumla could be in a kangaroo court by now. So, I'm going in there, I'm going to contact some friends who might be able to tell me exactly where they took her.

Linda I'm coming with you.

Reporter I don't think so, things might get sticky. You stay next to the phone because if things get bad I might need you to run around for me.

Linda Keep in touch.

Reporter Fortunately, Phumla had given us a clue. The name of the comrade who had asked her to come out. I found her in a kangaroo in the next township. This particular court was run by government spies who had infiltrated the student's movement, so I couldn't call the police. So, I went to the real comrades in the area and filled them in on what was happening. I gave them the address of the kangaroo court where Phumla was held. Nkuhlu and his lot were taken to the real comrades court, tried and sentenced to death by necklacing.

Linda This country is sick. (*Pause*) I'm leaving.

Phumla You are leaving?

Linda Yes, there's nothing here for me.

Phumla There's everything here for you.

Linda Just give me one good reason why I must stay here.

Phumla Freedom.

Linda Your freedom you mean?

Phumla Our freedom.

Linda I'm free.

Phumla Oh no you're not.

Linda I can pack my bags, get on a plane and leave any time.

Phumla As long as I'm oppressed, you will never be free.

Linda It's my life. My sanity. I am leaving.

Phumla No, you're not. We are in this shit together.

Linda Stop me!

Phumla The world hates South Africa. Hates white South Africans. I wonder if you be able to tell people that you a white person come from South Africa? Just go! See if I care! Go!

Linda The necklace killings came and went. The influx control laws fell by the wayside, then, one day, the president announced that the pass and it's laws were no more.

Phumla When the announcement was made, it was as if we had not heard it. It fell on deaf ears, because we did not go on the streets and celebrate the death of one of the most evil laws made by man this century. Instead, the government supported its announcement by posting notices on bill boards all over the country in black area The ads read, 'HAMBA DOMPASS'. Go away passbook.

ACT TWO, SCENE SIX

(*Flashback to Sarah's funeral.*)

Phumla The coffin was in the living room. The lid covering the head and shoulders was leaning against the wall next to it. Someone tiptoed into my bedroom to call Linda and I. Gentle hands guided us to the coffin. Uncle Edward was standing at the head of the coffin. He took my hand and placed it on Mama's forehead, it was frozen, empty, she was not there. I looked at her, she looked strange. Her eyes were closed, but they had sunk into her skull. Her face was lifeless, it looked like a statue. Her hair was short and snow white, I had cut it six months earlier and it had not grown, it had stayed at the same length till she died, that was strange, because Ma's hair was always long. I stroked her, it was dry like the bristles of a brush.

Linda I remember the night she died as if it was yesterday. I was frantic, I drove to Aunt Ellen's, her best friend, then my father arrived, we sat around her bed. She thanked my father for the beautiful life he had given her. Then she asked him to take care of Phumla.

Phumla Mr Black was white, he was my mother's master. I looked into his face, a thick vein ran down his forehead between his left eye and nose, it was throbbing, his eyes were red, he kissed mama with sticky lips. Mr Black was white man, he was my mother's master.

Linda When I saw the peace of death on Sarah's face, I just curled up and disappeared into my father's armpit. Sarah, my Mother was dead.

Phumla They are all gone now, it's just you and me babe.

Linda Yes, it's you and I babe. We have come a long way from the day when it all began. The day I saw my father's face smashed in by stones, I hated you. The day I saw his face caked with dry blood. You had just come back from hospital, you were lying in your room, in my father's house and you were black. I could see your head on that white pillow, it was a black woman's head. It was whole. I went into my father's study, pulled out his gun and cocked it. I could see your skull wallpapering the walls of that room in black and red. You were black, my father was caked with blood. Your face, your hair were plastered all over that room and you were black.

Phumla We must never forget what happened here, you and I. We must tell our children, they must tell their children that what happened here must never happen again. (*Pause*) You see, I'm a believer, somewhere inside here, I have pride and trust. I'm proud of who I am, I'm proud of you, of us. I trust you to trust me to hold you dear to me forever. Because I care about you and you care about me.

Linda We must never forget what happened here you and I. You will always be here for me and I will always be here for you, because I love you and you love me.

Phumla And now, because we are equal, I think we should also take our first step to freedom together. I have reserved us two seats in the front row to watch Mandela walk to freedom on television.

(*They sit in front of the TV and watch Mandela walk to freedom and his inauguration speech as the first black president*)

THE END

Book Reviews

Every attempt has been made to provide full bibliographic details with the help of the Africa Book Centre, 38 King Street, Covent Garden, London WC2E 8JT. UK prices have been provided where available. All editions are paperback except where otherwise stated.

Wale Ogunyemi, *Queen Amina of Zazzau*
Ibadan: University Press, 1999, 89 pp.
ISBN 978030567X, £4.95/$8.95

Akinwumi Isola, *Madam Tinubu, The Terror of Lagos*
Lagos: Heinemann Educational Books, 1998, 117 pp.
ISBN 978129390X, £4.95/$8.50

Amanda N. Adichie, *For Love of Biafra*
Ibadan: Spectrum Books, 1998, 112 pp.
ISBN 978029032X, £4.95/$8.95

(The three titles above are distributed by African Book Collective Ltd, 27 Park End Street, Oxford OX1 1HU, UK)

Patrick Mangeni wa'Ndeda, *Operation Mulungusi* and *The Prince*
Kampala: MK Publishers, 2000, 171 pp.
ISBN 9970405738, n.p.

Wale Ogunyemi is long established as one of Nigeria's foremost playwrights, and *Queen Amina of Zazzau* is typical of his work – well-crafted theatrically, fast-moving, intelligent and entertaining. Ogunyemi has often chosen historical themes, but always invested them with contemporary meaning. This is true of the present play. Queen Amina was the legendary queen of Zaria in the fourteenth century, a warrior-queen who pacified and protected large areas of Hausaland, and who was reputed to take lovers in all the places she conquered, killing them when she left. Ogunyemi's fascination with Queen Amina centres not only on the tales of her extraordinary exploits, and her strengths as a woman, but also on her role as a peacemaker and unifier. Here the contemporary message is played, with Amina calling for 'a humane society where no one is oppressed by those in positions of power'. (This seems to exclude her lovers.) Ogunyemi sets the play on a simple stage devoid of any permanent setting, allowing dance, movement, song and music to create the panoramas of historical action. This is a splendid, accessible drama that invites imaginative acting and staging.

Akinwumi Isola's *Madam Tinubu, The Terror of Lagos* again takes a historical figure as its subject. Madam Tinubu was a powerful Lagos trader in the middle of the nineteenth century and a thorn in the flesh of the British Consul Campbell, in his efforts to manipulate the Oba of Lagos and impose British authority. Isola's excellent play has no hesitation in portraying Madam Tinubu as a formidable fighter against colonialism and a dangerous woman to antagonise. A large cast of characters, some historical, some fictional, carry the drama strongly through the tumultuous events leading up to the exclusion of Madam Tinubu from Lagos. Isola, on his own admission, takes some liberty with the facts in making Madam Tinubu's banishment to Abeokuta a voluntary action, but he has produced a fascinating portrait of his heroine and a lively and provocative staging of an important episode in Nigeria's history. Though only recently published, the play was staged as a convocation play at the University of Ife in 1978. Its scale is somewhat formidable – a company of at least fifty seems to be necessary – but the playwright has excellent dramaturgical control over his large subject, and writes sharply, observantly and wittily. The play belongs to a fascinating and successful movement in Nigerian theatre, where plays are the vehicle for re-presenting history from an indigenous perspective.

Amanda N. Adichie's *For Love of Biafra* is a heartfelt play from someone who, though she is too young to have experienced the Nigerian civil war, wishes to remind audiences of its human and political destructiveness. A simple love story about the relationship between an Igbo girl and a Hausa boy is set in the days when the Igbo inhabitants of northern Nigeria were persecuted and chased from their homes, with the subsequent secession of the Igbo homeland in the name of Biafra. As any chronicle of these events has to be, this is a moving drama. Metaphorically (and somewhat evangelically) the Biafran flag is waving strongly at the end of the play, but its essential purpose is to call for humanity and unity and to deplore division and ethnic cleansing. Structurally the play is often rather awkward – too many short scenes moving loosely between locations. In this respect it shows more the influence of television drama rather than the stage in the playwright's experience and technique.

Patrick Mangeni's two plays *Operation Mulungusi* and *The Prince* are effective moralities – the first with a present-day setting, the second within a traditional past. Both, directly or obliquely, refer to real events. Operation Mulungusi was the code-name for the invasion of Tanzania by the Ugandan ruler Idi Amin in the 1980s. Mangeni, himself Ugandan, allows this act of aggression and immorality to stand as a symbol for a wider moral corruption in Ugandan society. *Operation Mulungusi* is set in a context of the personalities of an evangelical 'born-again' church in Uganda. Despite their spiritual pretensions, the characters are tempted by corruption and greed, subject to jealous rumour, and constantly plotting against each other. The discovery that the Pastor of the church has AIDS, and its alleged source in his seduction of his young wife, creates havoc within the community. False prophets, either devious traditional healers or American preachers who proclaim that God has healed AIDS, feed on the misery. It is only the appropriately named young wife, Hope, who offers any positive way forward. In a comment that draws together the central message of the play – that Ugandan society, having been traumatised by brutality, has to find the moral and political strength to go forward – Hope says 'our future is the awareness that we have lost it in ways that we could have possibly avoided … A positive attitude towards our life will benefit those to come, and in this way, we will have lived our future.'

The Prince is a shorter and simpler play, telling the tale of a young Prince in a traditional community who rebels when his assumed succession to his father's throne is frustrated. In a lively and engaging morality story, the virtues of unity are preached as the 'banana' and the 'yam' people learn to live and grow together, and the Prince, albeit at his death, acknowledges that a King is made by the choice of the people and not by autocratic right.

Martin Banham
Emiritus Professor,
University of Leeds

Duncan Brown (ed.), *Oral Literature & Performance in Southern Africa*
Oxford: James Currey; Cape Town: David Philip; Athens, OH: Ohio University Press, 1999, 243pp.
ISBN 0-85255-554-7 ISBN 0-86486-395-0 ISBN 0-8214-1309-0, £11.95

This book brings together essays on the principal themes of research in oral literature and performance from a variety of disciplines. The essays are uneven, they do not represent southern Africa as the title claims, but they take discourse on orality beyond the departments of Anthropology, Sociology, Languages and Folklore into departments of English or Literature and others, where the issues have been anathema from the onset of colonialism and apartheid. The book reports research by literary critics, anthropologists, ethnomusicologists and others in such a manner that the direction of future discourse on the subject is conveyed. I have only a few minor complaints to make. One of these days, some reviewer must boldly tell some South African scholars to start looking at what African scholars in universities around southern Africa have already published to avoid repeating what was going on elsewhere as 'Bantu Studies' under apartheid. For instance, the editor's expectations of the relevance of the essays to current trends in scholarship are patently over-rated and in some cases dated.

Duncan Brown (p. 1) expects this collection 'to grant oral forms and research greater visibility and stature'. He hopes it will help 'to undermine the often artificial separation of oral and literate forms' and the 'intersection of performed and printed forms'. He believes that these essays 'can reenergise and reconceptualise cultural, historical and political studies in Southern Africa'; that they can throw light on the 'remarkable resilience of many oral forms to the colonising forms of print, and the transformative power of orality on literate discourses'. It must be pointed out, however, that these objectives apply mostly to the English or Literature departments of those South African universities which have lagged behind in research and discourse (largely because of their 'apartheid' syllabus) in these areas. It is clear, from Isabel Hofmeyr's (pp. 18–26) succinct *resumé* of recent trends in research in other departments in South Africa, that orature acquired the academic visibility and stature denied it by colonialism and apartheid long before the publication of Ruth Finnegan's *Oral Literature in Africa* (1970, OUP), to take one pertinent instance. Research has now moved to the conceptual level, whether one believes in cognitive models or not, where discourse concerns the nature of 'knowledges' as partly sketched by Isabel Hofmeyr and exemplified by Karin Barber's paper (pp. 27–49).

For the English or Literature departments in other southern African universities, research and discourse in these areas, and the interface between oral/aural/verbal texts/utterances and written texts and/or their utterances either in African languages or in colonial languages like English, French or Portuguese, has informed most undergraduate and postgraduate courses for some time. Scholars in the universities of Zimbabwe, Malawi, Zambia, Tanzania, Uganda, Kenya, Somalia, Ethiopia and others (some of these countries constitute parts of southern Africa and are not represented in Brown's collection) have published numerous critical essays in journals, books and dissertations on the subject. Some of the exciting work in the field is currently being published from the Institute of African Studies, University of Bayreuth, Germany. For scholars, who followed their West African counterparts in their comparative examination of such African epics as *Sundiata*, *The Mwindo Epic*, *Shaka*, *Muyaka* and *Ozidi* and taught them alongside Homer's *Illiad*, *The Odyssey* (even John Milton's *Paradise Lost*!), the issues raised by some essays in this book have already been exhausted. Scholarship has now moved to the stage where, as Karin Barber (p. 28) claims, 'the conventions in accordance with which the text/utterance is generated and in the light of which the intended audience secures "uptake" of its meaning' is at the heart of the inquiry.

It is not visibility that oral literature and performance requires, and therefore it is not taxonomic/prescriptive/descriptive presentations that are needed. What is required is the search for Afrocentric theory or some hybrid thereof, which has the most explanatory adequacy and which should be at the centre of scholarship. Discourse on African 'orature' (thanks to the late Ugandan scholar Pio Zirimu who coined the term to resolve the apparent contradiction inherent in the treatment of oral/aural/verbal text *vs* the written text) and its performance has gone beyond the all-pervasive Parry–Lord model (cf. Leroy Vail & Landeg White, *Power and the Praise Poem: Southern African Voices in History*, 1991, James Currey and The University of Virginia). The 'home grown' or 'hybrid' models have begun to be mapped out (cf. Henry Louis Gates, Jr, *The Signifying Monkey*, 1988, OUP; Valerie Lee, *Granny Midwives and Black Women Writers: Double-Dutched Readings*, 1996, Routledge). So, now that apartheid is gone, let black and white South African scholars, whose extensive 'knowledges' (Hofmeyr, p.18) of orature and its performance is probably the richest in the southern African region, immerse themselves in orality and take the lead in its ('original'?) discourse. For, as Karin Barber (p. 28) claims, 'The more an outsider the critic is to the text ... the greater the need for him/her to immerse him-herself in the genre's conventions, instead of simply imposing expectations of how texts work which were formed in the course of exposure to another tradition.' Therefore, let the critic seek the structure, that might lead to theory, first from the text/utterance before imposing a familiar one from outside.

The essays in this book may suggest new directions of discourse in oral literature and performance. It might be worth pointing out, however, that Liz Gunner's (pp. 50–59) cogent discussion of 'pre-election praise poetry' and 'post-election praise poetry' would probably have been richer if the place of 'election-praise poetry' (cf. Mzwakhe Mbuli, Lesego Rampolokeng and others) had been considered. The trouble with studies in pre- or post- anything (I dare say, including postcolonial theory!) is that they tend to be blind to or unnecessarily erase the essential middle. And I am not convinced about the existence of the laws of logic for the narrative of the western style autobiography which Coullie (pp. 61–86) uses as a point of departure. Would a comparison of *izibongo* in Zulu to autobiography in Zulu produce the same results? I find the quotation in Biesele's (p. 161) paper fascinating. If 'Different People Just Have Different Minds', this surely suggests that discourse must move to an examination of those minds, that is, at the cognitive level rather than the dated morphological configurations with which Biesele grapples. This is why I find the most stimulating essays to be Hofmeyr's, Barber's and Opland's, which would need a fuller critique to do them justice. These minor criticisms aside, this book is welcome; for those puzzling about the nature of orature and performance studies, this book is worth purchasing; for established scholars in the field, the book provides matters to which they are bound to respond.

Jack Mapanje
University of Leeds

Geoffrey V. Davies (ed.), *Beyond the Echoes of Soweto:*
Five Plays by Matsemela Manaka
Amsterdam: Harwood Academic Publishers, 1997, xiii + 244 pp.
ISBN 90 5702 161 7, ISSN 1049 6513

Barney Simon, *Born in the RSA: Four Workshopped Plays*
Witwatersrand: Witwatersrand University Press, 1997, xxvii + 193 pp.
ISBN 1 86814 300 7

Jane Taylor, *Ubu and the Truth Commission*
Cape Town: Cape Town University Press, 1998, xviii + 73 pp.
ISBN 1 919713 16 6

These three publications are an amazing tribute to the extent to which South Africa has broken silence. The shift from play texts which are performed to their being published indicates a new freedom to make stories more widely available. The profound significance of The Market Theatre for South African theatre is evidenced insofar as most of these plays premiered there.

The first two collections of plays workshopped by Barney Simon and Matsemela Manaka both appeared in 1997, but cover plays produced from the late 1970s to 1989, thus they represent key plays created and produced during some of the most tense time in South Africa.

Ubu and the Truth Commission was created and performed in 1997, published in 1998. The decade between the plays' productions provides a frame through which one can measure the distance South Africa had travelled from disbanding Apartheid to facing some of the consequences of it. The earlier plays provide individual stories which outline the experiences for diverse South Africans in an abhorrent system. *Ubu* provides a satiric critique of South Africa's official attempt to break silence through the Truth and Reconciliation Commission (TRC), and the many paradoxes of this as a process. *Ubu* has been performed in South Africa, Europe, America and Britain, and much has been written about it in reviews, academic journals and on web sites.

Jane Taylor's introduction outlines how *Ubu* evolved from the original Alfred Jarry text, and how it intersects with the South African context. William Kentridge's notes contextualise *Ubu* in relation to other plays by the Handspring Puppet Company, while looking at the specifics of doing a play about the TRC. He directly addresses the ethical question related to the use of victims' stories in the play. He argues that the use of puppets obviated the problem of having an actor play a real individual. These puppet scenes are most powerful. Basil Jones and Adrian Kohler explain how the puppets are developed, and how they relate to the exploration of 'the era of trauma the play describes' (xvii).

This text, like all the others reviewed here, comes out of a workshop process. Jane Taylor wrote the text as the company improvised the scenes, Kentridge created the animation and back projection and Basil Jones and Adrian Kohler worked on the puppets. What emerges is a powerful combination of live actors playing Ma and Pa Ubu, and puppets who portray all the other South African figures.

As with most African theatre, the play is much more than words: the mime, back-projections, use of sound effects, song and dance are key to the total experience. The text engages creatively with these non-linguistic aspects of the play by including photographs and sketches of back projects that are reproduced on the pages opposite the text, sometimes with written explanation of how the images work in relation to the scene.

This play has had such impact because it addresses some of the more complex issues of the TRC – the purpose and justice of a system which allows amnesty for gross violations of human rights. It also unequivocally exposes some of the raw horrors of Apartheid: both the attitudes and actions of apparently 'decent' people who may have been one's husband or neighbour. The real power of the play, though, is its ability to both face the very personal and specific, and universal issues. A Romanian woman's response to the play was: 'It's so local. So local. This play is written about Romania' (xv).

Within the frame of 'telling the hidden stories' I turn to Barney Simon. More of his plays have been published than have those of Manaka. The collection of Barney Simon's collaborative work begins with *Black Dog/Inj'emnyama* (1984), rather than *Woza Albert!* and *Cincinatti*. The collection is foreworded by tributes to Barney Simon's memory by Mannie Manim, Athol Fugard, Lionel Abrahams and Nadine Gordimer. The plays are introduced by Pat Schwartz, who knows the Market Theatre and knew Barney Simon well. She traces Barney Simon, the man and his vision, from the 1950s to his creation of The Company and Market Theatre with Mannie Manim in 1976.

Barney Simon was a storyteller, profoundly interested in people and their stories. His work was characterised by the workshop process. Schwartz acknowledges some of the complications of this process when she says that 'the shaping of ideas in his particular way frequently led to bitter words about credits, arguments about royalties and accusations of intellectual pilfering from writers and actors who believed they had been short changed – accusations which hurt him deeply and which he passionately denied' (xvi). This, along with the tracing of Simon as a 'profoundly non-political man' goes largely uncontested and is not problematised in the introduction. It would be wrong to convey the idea that Barney Simon's plays did not radically challenge South Africa under Apartheid. However, it is perhaps the collaborative voices which give weight to the varying degrees of the challenge in the different plays.

The plays vary greatly in power and thematic focus. What they have in common, though, is their interest in the individual stories of those on the margins.

Black Dog/Inj'emnyama (1984) parallels the stories of a white English paratrooper and a black ANC freedom fighter. It explores the complexities, anger, confusion and cost of the ideological war in terms of individual people, who love, fear and dream. While it is by no means one of Simon's best plays, it has a power and directness as it unpicks the binary oppositions so easily assumed about Apartheid South Africa.

Outers (1985) explores white people who have become vagrants in Joubert Park. While the performers spent time with the vagrants in the park, there is not enough biography to make the characters in the play real people, rather than symbols. The play is difficult to read as a text, as there is a lot of street language and a minimal story-line.

Born in the RSA is one of Barney Simon's best known plays. It is written like a docu-drama, a living newspaper, blending techniques of journalism and theatre with backdrop video images. The play is about commitment and betrayal – to individual people and to a greater Cause. The play is structured as six cubes each with a person inside it. In very specific, individual terms we see the suffering and cost of the South African system.

Score Me the Ages (1989), meaning 'What's the time?', is about two 'rent-boys' and two of their clients: a gay middle-aged, wealthy advertising executive returned from London to his brother's funeral, and a working-class hospital porter. The fifth character is a pregnant woman alone in her flat, contemplating abortion as her husband is in prison. Each of these figures suggests how many people in South Africa are isolated, marginalised, coming from broken families with unfulfilled dreams. The play touches on taboos in South African society, but gives no real sense of the complexities and pain of a homosexual life, or of prostituting oneself. The abortion issue is more clearly explored than other issues in the play.

My main criticism of the collection is that there is no real contextualisation of these plays for the reader outside South Africa. There is no glossary for the many Afrikaans, Zulu, Xhosa or slang words and phrases which characterise the plays. I would like to have seen the editor rise to the challenge of contextualising these plays in the post-Apartheid South African context. Rather than summarising Barney Simon's life, Schwartz could have explored Simon's contribution both for his time and in the period to come. Nevertheless, the collection pays tribute to Barney Simon and the high regard in which he is justifiably held in South Africa. This collection is an important collation of work by Barney Simon created at the Market Theatre in the 1980s.

And finally, the collection of five of the fourteen plays written by Matsemela Manaka between 1977 and 1991. This edition, collated by Geoffrey Davies, is a splendid academic achievement. Besides editing and publishing plays of which I had only seen *Pula* in print, Davies has included a 31-page introduction with diverse scholastic references. He gives the reader some sense of Manaka's thinking between 1980 and 1989 via position articles written by Manaka on Theatre of the Dispossessed, The Babalaz People, and Theatre as a Physical Word; interviews with the author by Davies and Ann Fuchs; and a statement made by Manaka, 1989. Davies has included reviews of productions in the 1980s from South African newspapers such as *The Sowetan*, *City Press* and the *Rand Daily Mail*, resources beyond the access of most European or American scholars. Photos from archives of the Market Theatre and *The Sowetan*, as well as Manaka's private collection give one a visual sense of the performers and productions. The collection includes footnotes translating idioms or languages other than English. This is crucial to plays which signal their diverse cultural contexts in their multilingualism.

Davies acknowledges Manaka as a visual and verbal artist by including two colour prints of Manaka's own paintings. Throughout the plays one is aware of the centrality of the physical image to the themes of his plays in his use of theatrical images – like the steel chains around the two workers necks at the start of *Egoli*, and the mime in *Egoli*, *Pula*, *Children of Asazi* and *Toro*. Manaka's interest in music and dance is evidenced in the combinations of traditional African and European musical instruments and dance: in *Gorée* he uses both the African *djembe* and European violin, he 'combined Venda, Tswana, Xhosa, Sepedi, Tsonga, Ndebele, Swazi, Ghanaian, Nigerian, Senegalese, ballet, contemporary and jazz dances' (p. 237, Victor Metsoamere).

His commitment to the Black Consciousness and pan-African visions are seen in his plays' themes and management: the plays are scripted for all-black casts, and the few white characters his plots require are always negative portraits, usually of white authority figures who are mimed by black artists with the use of pantomime noses and spectacles. His work is managed, designed, lit, produced and directed by blacks. Manaka is one of the South African artists who has seen the need for relating their work beyond the borders of South Africa to the whole continent of Africa and the diaspora. His plays deal with the major issues of Apartheid, both in terms of the poverty of rural areas and the results of urbanisation: detribalisation, the migrant labour system, forced removals, social disintegration in the townships and crime.

Egoli (1978) is Johannesburg, city of gold. The action is set in a mine compound for migrant labourers, and thus exposes the implications of the industrial system for black workers: the poor living conditions, the daily exposure to violence, the brutalisation and dehumanisation, the harshness of separation from their families which often results in their turning to prostitutes, being restricted to manual labour and the unsafe working conditions. The choice is starve in the rural areas or die in the cities.

Pula was first performed in 1982 in Soweto by the Soyikwa African Theatre group. All the characters are played by four male actors who transform themselves through speech and movement. The title means 'rain', and the play traces what happens when the rain does not come: the crops fail, the villagers and cattle die and new-born children are killed to prevent their starvation. Much of the play's movement is carried by the songs, performed as a chorus. Thus the play moves from a simple story of drought to a metaphor for the plight of blacks in South Africa, and the need for socio-political change.

Children of Asazi (1986) is set in a slum in Johannesburg's Alexandra Township. It dramatises the issue of forced removals, using Alexandra as an example. The personal histories add up to a complex vision of the effects of, and responses to, forced removals on a society. The play ends on a defiant note of resistance: 'SONQOBA SIMUNYE' (United we will conquer).

Toro: The African Dream was first performed in 1987 and was much revised after feedback from audiences and critics. The programme described it as a play about 'the search for identity through a cultural collage of drama, dance, music, mime and poetry'. The musical form is problematic when trying to convey a sense of the performance textually. The play depends heavily on the music and dance which reviews suggest strongly convey feelings of celebration, anger and lament. Much of the dialogue is idiomatic, metaphoric, with many similes. Perhaps some of the negative criticism stems from South African reviewers not understanding some of the traditional African oral forms at the heart of this work.

As the title suggests, *Gorée* (1989) is profoundly about liberation. Manaka is challenging South Africa to look beyond its own struggle to recontextualise itself in terms of the larger continent and its struggles. The play looks at the impact of Europe on African culture and identity. It was first staged as a surrealist dream, and thus has many symbolist elements. It traces the story of a dancer who encounters an old woman on Senegal's historic slaving centre, Gorée Island. She helps the dancer find and express her African identity by leading her back to her African heritage – only after self-discovery through recognition of the African heritage is a merging of the two cultures possible – both for the individual and South Africa.

These plays provide a vision of South Africa through the late 1970s and 1980s. Manaka's sense of performance forms beyond South Africa enrich his work. The integration of oral storytelling, music, song and dance make his work profound and inspiring as it experiments with new, syncretic forms.

These publications highlight the unique and exciting theatre which has been produced in South Africa in the late twentieth century. They are important in making this work more widely accessible to people interested in performance and possibilities of experimentation and innovation. One hopes the next period of South African theatre proves as rich as the past two decades have done.

Yvette Hutchison
King Alfred's College
Winchester

Osonye Tess Onwueme, *The Missing Face: Musical Drama for the Voices of Colour*
New York & Lagos: Africana Legacy Press, 1997, 64 pp.
paperback ISBN 157579053X, £4.25, $7.95
Distributor: African Books Collective (ABC) Ltd, Oxford, United Kingdom.

The Missing Face interrogates the dilemma of Diaspora blacks whose feelings of cultural alienation are matched by a longing for identification with an almost mythical motherland whose love they question and ultimately hold responsible for their plight. Set in Idu

(Igboland, Nigeria), a symbolic African kingdom and in Milwaukee (USA) in the late 90s, the play explores the mystical and almost heroic journey of Ida Bee, an African-American woman and her son in search of Momah, her US-educated husband and her son's father. For Ida Bee, the uniting of father and son is a sacred duty; for in the very act of securing Amaechi's identity in Africa lies his salvation from the cultural fragmentation and spiritual vacuity of African-Americans. Armed with the half-face of the Ikenga (Igbo symbol of spiritual authority) and her dead father's instructions to find the other half and unite the sections of her identity, Ida Bee's personal quest becomes the collective odyssey of Diaspora blacks to retrace and restore their African roots. Onwueme foregrounds her interrogation of traditional African patriarchy in Ida Bee's and black women's heroic struggles to sustain family and cultural identities among African-Americans.

This musical drama is divided into seven movements symbolic of the stages of the annual Iwu festival of transition and the passage into manhood. Its tempo is fast, the music ensures smooth transitions and links different chronological periods. Afuzue/Griot embodies the traditional roles of historian and storyteller, and his physical presence bridges time gaps and limits the necessity for explanatory dialogue and extensive plot development. Ida's flashback to Milwaukee and her meeting and marriage to Momah draw the past, present and future into a confrontation resolved only in the enduring strength of Africa's restored roots with her Diaspora citizens. The confrontation depicts the symptomatic failure of Momah's 'Lakunlian' (in Soyinka's *The Lion and the Jewel*) generation for which it is ultimately stepped over in the rights of succession. It is only in the ritual act of collective purification and regeneration that Momah's generation can identify with the recast and stronger bronze Ikenga proudly borne by Amaechi and the future generation.

Though Onwueme's censure of the uncritical imitation of Western civilisation lacks the comic rhythm and biting satire of Soyinka's Lakunle, the complex symbolism of the final meeting of Africa's separated essences is superbly handled. Despite her reductionist approach, Onwueme's dramaturgy still yields enduring theatre enhanced by symbolic representations. Ida's journey and encounters with Africa and her purgatorial banishment and re-integration foreshadow Africa's spiritual re-birth. The foreshadowing imbues the festivities and rituals, the props and the characterisation, with symbolic significance and archetypal stature. Similarly, the play's convincing portrayals of Igboland and Milwaukee; the former in the gripping moment of celebrating its communitas and the latter recalled through the violence of American society, give the play its unique ambience of arresting spirituality and cultural depth, and make it a paradigm of black people's collective search for self-restoration and identity.

The Missing Face draws on such African theatrical idioms as masking, storytelling and ritual. The dialogue combines snappy witticisms and discursive narratives, and the play rushes to a predictable but theatrically rewarding resolution that re-enacts the contiguous relationships in Igbo cosmogony. The reliance on character types limits conflict and character development to a semiotic signing resulting in two unfortunate developments. Firstly, other than Ida Bee and Odozi, the characters lack the depth and stature to match their heroic actions. Secondly, the incest between Momah and Ida Bee is not interrogated as the resolution subordinates this serious cultural abnormality in Igbo society to collective identity. Despite this unfortunate resolution and the unconvincing presentation of Momah's motives, the play is exciting for its proposal regarding African and African-American relations and for its deft and successful integration of African and Western theatrical forms.

Victor I. Ukaegbu
University College, Northampton

Dele Layiwola (ed.), *African Theatre in Performance*
Reading: Harwood Academic, 2000, xvi + 136 pp.
ISBN 90 5755 108 X, £30

This lively and informative volume may be called *African Theatre in Performance*, but it is substantially by Nigerians and about Nigerian theatre. The only exceptions are a piece by Robert McLaren on Zimbabwean Community Theatre, a poem by Tony Lopez, and an article on ritual drama which is by a Nigerian, the editor Dele Layiwola, but which privileges an Ethiopian and a Tanzanian play in its analysis.

The reason for the emphasis is tied in with the volume's sub-title, 'A Festschrift in Honour of Martin Banham'. Emeritus Professor Martin Banham taught at the University of Ibadan in Nigeria between 1956 and 1966, and all the articles in the book are written by now eminent ex-students of Martin's. The two plays are by friends, and his poet son-in-law has contributed the concluding verse. Martin asked me to downplay the *festschrift* aspects of this book, so I will merely state that he has now had three festschrifts in three years – an extraordinary tribute to his seminal contribution to developing theatre studies in Leeds and Ibadan, his role in developing the academic study of African theatre, and to the enormous affection and respect in which he is held by all his many friends, colleagues and ex-students. Finally, I cannot resist noting the many references in this text to Martin Banham's 'flowing auburn hair', I have only known Professor Banham's hair as wild, white and diminishing, but in either state it appears to have made a significant impact on those with whom he has come into contact.

Unusually but happily this text combines academic analysis with creative contributions. The two short plays included are by two of Nigeria's leading playwrights. The sadly recently deceased Ola Rotimi's *When Criminals Turn Judges* is a light-hearted yet stiletto-sharp indictment of abuses of power, both economic and spiritual, and of human hypocrisy. It is a comedy which gets perilously near polemic, sentimentality and tragedy, yet avoids all three as it moves towards the final twists in the tale.

Wale Ogunyemi's *The Hand that Feeds the King* is by contrast a rather incredible polemic parable with the focus, as for so many other Nigerian playwrights, on how the powerful abuse their position. In this case we have a King and a would-be usurper, who both seek to enforce absolute rule by means of terror. The action moves with too much speed to be convincing, as the women take on the role of national saviours. Under the leadership of the priestess Iyaagan they defy the usurper Odidi and use their irresistible sexuality to disarm his soldiers. However this play, which barely masks it's criticism of Nigeria's recent parade of corrupt leaders, comes to a rather limp ending, when all Iyaagan can suggest is that the soldiers be confined to barracks and that no King be enthroned until 'an honest and upright leader ... emerges from amongst us' (p. 89).

The critical essays which make up the bulk of *African Theatre in Performance* build up a mosaic which cumulatively testifies to the range and vibrancy of Nigerian theatre. I particularly enjoyed the sense which emerges of how Nigerians have drawn with a sophisticated and proud relish on their indigenous performance forms to make a theatre which is still rooted in the ancestors and the living earth, but draws freely on international theatrical ideas. The theatre that emerges is syncretic but overwhelmingly socially, spiritually and politically committed whether we are talking about the work of Soyinka; ('Soyinka and Power: Language and Imagery in *Madmen and Specialists*', Frances Harding); the form of ritual in 'Stage and Staging in Yoruba Ritual Drama' (Oyin Ogunba), or a questioning of the place of community theatre in national development ('The Role of Community Theatre in Health Education in Nigeria', Oga Steve Abah).

Now in its third decade, some theatre practitioners and academics appear to have written off developmental theatre as 'discredited' (see Anne Fuchs, ed., *New Theatre in*

Francophone and Anglophone Africa, Matatu, no. 29, 1999: xii). My own argument would be that, like the socialism which has inspired many of its most successful practitioners, so-called community, popular or developmental theatre – the labels are largely inter-changeable – has often been practised by personnel with little understanding of its truly democratic form, and in other instances has too often been crushed by governments frightened of the potential power of such a radical people's form to conscientise and provoke demands for change – see Ngugi in Kamiriithu or McLaren himself in both South Africa and Zimbabwe. In this book Robert McLaren and Oga Steve Abah give us critical descriptions of community theatre projects in which they have played leading roles in Zimbabwe and Nigeria respectively.

McLaren's essay documents the coming together of art and reality around issues of student living conditions and student–police relations, as part of a wider thesis exploring the confluence of performance and actuality in Zimbabwean society. In 1988 drama students made a play exploring the difficulties of student life, consequent to riots over conditions at the University of Zimbabwe. However, the dress rehearsal of *Chokwadi Ndechipi/Iqiniso Yiliphi* (Which is the Truth?) was interrupted by a demonstration, and subsequent performances about the previous protests provoked responses from audiences, which McLaren argues 'seem to suggest they are being relived' (p. 11). A further project then involved police and students working on a performance exploring relations between the two. McLaren admits this is a difficult area as neither side is keen on self-criticism, but art and life again collide when one of the student actors is urgently called to the police station to answer for his role in an anti-corruption demonstration and a policeman-actor volunteers to go with and help the student.

Oga Abah also discusses two case studies. This time both are community plays related to health issues, leprosy and VVF or vesico vagina fistulae (where young girls have their bladders and rectums cut if they cannot accommodate normal childbirth because of their youth). Oga Abah works closely with actual sufferers from the conditions concerned, but he argues that a simple mechanistic information-giving is by no means good enough. The psychological needs of victims of conditions which exclude them from society need to be taken into account. And moreover, Oga Abah, like McLaren, sees theatre and reality as intimately interwoven. His community theatre he says is a means to an end, and community theatre workers must key into agencies and activities which can promote positive outcomes. Only if real linkages which open up possibilities for real change exist can this theatre become more than palliative.

Nigerian theatre is rich in ritual sensibility, and it is therefore not surprising that essays from both Oyin Ogunba, and Dele Layiwola, 'Is Ritual Drama a Humanistic Methodology? Thoughts on the New Theatre', are concerned with ritual and drama. Layiwola's title may be rather a mouthful, but what he is doing is trying to give a new spin to the old debate about where and if boundaries lie between ritual and theatre. What is interesting in a Nigerian essayist is that he chooses the ritual nature of the Ethiopian Tsegaye Gebre-Medhin's play, *Oda Oak Oracle,* and Ebrahim Hussein of Tanzania's *Kinjeketile,* to focus on. It is particularly valuable to have an analysis of the little-known Ethiopian play, and Layiwola is sensitive to the brooding atmosphere of horror in the piece. His argument is that in both plays what he calls 'mythic logic' is inaccessible to man, who suffers a fate he cannot control or often even understand since the gods and spirits operate according to rules incomprehensible to mankind, and where man's very efforts to escape a mythic destiny often only lead him further into terrible disaster.

Later in the essay Layiwola invokes a range of anthropological and cultural theorists in his efforts to define theatre and ritual, but as so many of us have concluded, Layiwola too concedes that boundaries in the worlds of African rituals and performance are often blurred and no satisfactory defining wall can be set up between the two.

I would recommend this book to anyone who has not only a specialist interest in particular essays, but also to those who want a taste of the breadth of concerns and debates in contemporary African, and particularly Nigerian, theatre.

Jane Plastow
University of Leeds

L. Dale Byam, *Community in Motion:
Theatre for Development in Africa*
Westport: Bergin & Garvey, 1999, 216 pp.
ISBN 0-89789-581-9, US$59.95

The series this book has been published in is committed to 'challeng[ing] the current return to the primacy of market values and simultaneous retreat from politics so evident in the recent work of educational theorists, legislators and policy analysts' (p. xi). The Series Foreword continues with its harsh criticism of the present which is said to be marked by 'Social Darwinism', the 'right-wing assault on public and higher education', and a 'resurgence of racism' (p. ix). Followed by a Foreword by Ngugi wa Thiong'o it becomes clear that Byam's study is committed to a socialist-inspired counter-ideology.

Chapter 1, entitled, 'Post-Colonialism, Development, and a New African Theatre', sketches the impact of colonialism on indigenous cultures and art forms, as well as their appropriation by colonialists and missionaries who abused storytelling or theatre as a means of domestication and indoctrination. After independence, the author claims, 'the colonialist's style of education remained intact' (p. 6), and 'theatre in many African countries continued to reinforce colonial values' (p. 6). Explaining the post-colonial situation in Africa with reference to Gramsci and Fanon, the author sets up a dualism that permeates the entire study – on one hand 'petty bourgeoisie leaders', alienated from the people they govern, on the other the so-called 'organic or honest intellectuals' whose aim is to empower the people, people thereby understood in the socialist sense as the workers and peasants.

This clear-cut dualism is upheld throughout the book, as when Paulo Freire's categories are applied, such as the harmful 'banking style of education', working in a top-down manner, versus the liberating 'problem posing pedagogy', utilizing dialogue as a basic means. Theatre is seen as a part of this political division as well: the neo-colonial theatre which aims at maintaining the *status quo* and keeps the masses at bay – examples are the national dance companies set up and funded by many governments, the Alarinjo traveling theatre in Nigeria or other popular theatre experiments brought to the rural areas by theatre troupes from the cities – is answered by the progressive type of anti-aristotelian popular theatre following the pedagogy of Paulo Freire and the poetics of Piscator, Brecht, Augusto Boal and Ngugi wa Thiong'o, encouraging liberation and self-determination.

Chapter 2 covers some of the most well-known projects on TfD in Africa over the last three decades, *Laedza Batanani* in Botswana, *Chikwakwa* in Zambia, the projects of Ahmadu Bello University in Nigeria and *Kamiriithu*, Kenya. Each of the case studies is first described and then analysed according to the Freirean categories as presented in the first chapter.

According to Byam, *Laedza Batanani* did not succeed in bringing about any long-term results, and she calls the experiment pseudo-Freirian (p. 43). Although the TfD projects in Zambia and Nigeria receive a more favourable criticism than *Laedza*

Batanani, the main goals of TfD are seen as not yet achieved: Whether *Chikwakwa* theatre in Zambia or the various projects carried through by Ahmadu Bello University –they too are considered pseudo-Freirean because in Byam's opinion they failed to fully involve the community and, both having been initiated by universities, they were not really firmly based in the community and therefore did not yield long-term benefits.

Byam claims that *Kamiriithu* in Kenya was the first project on TfD in Africa which could be rightfully called Freirean. The basic difference to all earlier projects is seen to be that the community had the authorship over the play that was being developed. Constantly being re-assessed and remodelled through the community members involved, the play and the performance was given enough time from research and thematic investigation to rehearsals, organization and performance. It was here, Byam claims, that a truly authentic African theatre was created, based on local history, communal art forms such as mime, song, dance and the indigenous language. Moreover, Byam considers *Kamiriithu* as the first project with long-term results which, although forcefully stopped in Kenya, was able to live on in another country – Zimbabwe.

After the destruction of the Kamiriithu Education and Cultural Center by government forces in 1982, Ngugi wa Mirii and Kimani Gecau, both involved at *Kamiriithu* and now exiled, contributed to building up a community theatre movement in Zimbabwe which was based on the ideals of *Kamiriithu*. Zimbabwe, Byam claims, was perfectly suited for the setting up of a successful community theatre movement because the country had an explicit socialist ideology, and – more important – had witnessed the effectiveness of mass participation and community activity through the experiences of the liberation war where theatrical forms such as the *pungwe* (an all-night gathering between freedom fighters and community members in liberated or semi-liberated areas that combined conscientisation and discussions on the political situation with festival elements such music and dance) had laid a sound foundation.

Byam sketches the most important steps in the development of community theatre in Zimbabwe, from the Zimbabwe Foundation for Theatre with Production (ZIMFEP) with its educational programme for ex-combatants and the 'community based theatre project', to the establishing of ZACT, the Zimbabwe Association of Community Theatre, in 1986/7. For the rest of the book, ZACT's development, its structure, work and impact are scrutinised as it succeeded in becoming a nationwide body working effectively at national, provincial and district levels. The mushrooming of community based theatre companies is described, including various issues such as group structure, age and gender issues, management, and training.

The basic problem with *Community in Motion* is the author's lack of distance concerning more or less anything; scientific sources, subject, research, selection of material or her informants. Nobody will realistically expect total objectivity – however, I can hardly remember another book that could be compared to Byam's study in terms of naivety and even ignorance. Maybe it is the underlying dualistic structure that makes the book and its conclusions so predictable, but even then the pedestal on which Byam puts her theatrical heroes is hardly bearable:

> Ngugi [wa Mirii] personifies Freire's investigator, the revolutionary leader, who has helped to develop an even more significant leader – one who emerges from the community. Also, in the same way that ZACT has gone beyond Freire in its practices, it has also exceeded the government in its mandate and operations – while, for now, finding congruence with both. (p. 198)

In her last two chapters, Byam quotes Ngugi wa Mirii so often, and with so little reflection, that inevitably one starts wondering whether the author has any opinions of her own. Once or twice, Byam mentions that ZACT (or is it not rather Ngugi wa Mirii personally?) does not condone any contacts between ZACT affiliated groups and the other leading theatre body, the National Theatre Organization (NTO), because of the latter's racist history and its practice which is still considered as incompatible with ZACT's ideology. However, completely neglecting an organization that has probably an equally high number of registered community theatre groups as ZACT, among them the country's leading theatre companies, such as Amakhosi in Bulawayo, is hardly justified. Amakhosi and lots of other groups have quit ZACT because of its restrictive policy, its tight control and its interference in what these groups consider their personal affairs.

What we have here is an author fully aware of the pitfalls of political correctness (using the masculine and the feminine form equally), but who has no problem comparing people to animals.

> However, people can live, like animals, in an ahistorical mode, a level of semi-intransitive consciousness during which 'the dominated consciousness does not have sufficient distance from reality to objectify it in order to know it in a critical way'. (p. 21)

The comparing of African people to animals has previously been the preserve of arrant white racism. Considering that Dale Byam dedicated this book to God (!), one cannot help feeling a bit more humility would have been appropriate.

Another shortcoming of Byam's study is its exclusive focus on projects under the guidance of ZACT staff, such as workshops. A workshop lasts between three days and two weeks maximum, and the rest of the year groups have to fend for themselves, and they have to do so in a very harsh economic climate. The author may be right to praise the efforts to establish theatre to escape unemployment, but this issue opens up a variety of new questions and problems, which are tackled nowhere in the book. Many of the communal ideals are incompatible with the present economic conditions, and reconciling communal, non-commercial ideals with economic necessities is a tightrope walk only few groups succeed in. The enormous problems that the community theatre movement in Zimbabwe faces are only very briefly dealt with. The support of foreign donors and health institutions is dealt with in just one sentence (p. 189), yet this is a subject worthy of closer attention, because these institutions have a profound influence on the content and aesthetics of Zimbabwean theatre. Whether justified or not, jealousies are an issue in Zimbabwean community theatre as well, but no criticism of ZACT (and ZACT is not beyond criticism in Zimbabwe itself!) is ever discussed in Byam's study.

To conclude, *Community in Motion* provides a fair survey of the continent's most well-known projects of Theatre for Development, although this has been done much better in books such as Penina Mlama's *Culture and Development: The Popular Theatre Approach in Africa* (Uppsala, 1991), Zakes Mda's *When People Play People: Development Communication Through Theatre* (Johannesburg & London, 1993) or the special issue on TfD in *Research in African Literatures* (Vol. 22, No. 3). Byam offers a more detailed description of the Zimbabwe Association of Community Theatre than has previously been available. However, her biased and subjective style remains extremely problematic.

Martin Rohmer
Munich

Kamal Salhi, *The Politics and Aesthetics of Kateb Yacine:*
From Francophone Literature to Popular Theatre in Algeria and Outside
Lampeter: Edwin Mellen Press, 1999, 448 pp.
ISBN 0 7734 7871 X, £69.95

KatebYacine's life history is intimately entwined with that of Algeria. Born in 1929, he was educated in the French colonial system, attending secondary school in Sétif. When, in the wake of the Second World War, the first Algerian uprising against the French took place in 1945, the sixteen-year-old schoolboy took part in the demonstrations. He was arrested, imprisoned, interrogated and expelled from school. He later said that this experience had taught him the two things which were to become most dear to him: poetry and revolution. He began writing poems (in French) at an early age. His first volume was published in 1946, and when he went to France in 1948 he found many liberal French intellectuals who were eager to help in the development of this precocious young literary talent.

On his return to Algiers, Yacine was able to join the staff of the left-wing daily *Alger Républicain*. Journalism did not pay enough to keep him alive, so he did seasonal farm work in the Camargue, worked as a docker and took other labouring jobs. In between times he travelled widely and published articles in many different papers on both sides of the Mediterranean. Yacine's first major play, *Le Cadavre encerclé*, was published in 1955 in the Catholic journal *Esprit*. As the Algerian war of independence developed, he was championed by anti-war intellectuals (such as Sartre) in France as an exemplary spokesman for free Algerians, though this oversimplified his position. He began to work with Jean-Marie Serreau, a director who had a very important role in empowering dramatists from many of the French colonial territories in Africa. Serreau put on the first production of *Le Cadavre encerclé* in 1956, first in Tunis and then in Brussels when it was subject to a government ban in Paris. In the same year Yacine's novel *Nedjma* was published and this won him an international reputation, being widely translated.

In the first decade of Algerian independence (following on the Evian agreements of 1962) Yacine was seen in French-speaking circles as the most important literary voice of the young Algerian generation. His work was published, produced in Parisian theatres and generally lauded. In 1970 his longest play, in honour of Ho Chi Minh, *L'Homme aux sandales de caoutchouc*, was published and produced in France. It was also translated into classical Arabic and produced at the Algerian National Theatre, but events in Algeria were developing in a way which caused deep concern to Yacine. This was the beginning of systematic linguistic and cultural repression and the time when the first measures were taken to ban the Berber language. Yacine decided he could no longer afford to enjoy the life of a lionised Parisian writer and that he must return home in order to try to influence events from within his native land. He met up with a number of left-wing theatre people and with them staged his play *Mohamed prends ta valise*. This play is in the form of a satirical comedy with a clear political message, which spoke of the dominant experience of North Africans: having to go to France to find work. This alone would have ensured it an audience among working people in Algeria, but it had an even more important and revolutionary aspect: it refused to bow to official demands to use only classical Arabic, including passages in French, Berber and vernacular Arabic. The touring theatre group responsible for the original production broke up, but Yacine continued to work at developing a genuinely popular and political form of theatre, collaborating with a range of different companies and performers for the next twenty years until his death in 1989. This aspect of his work is very little known because it was not highly valued by the official guardians of culture in Algeria and did not result in poetic texts that could be published and appreciated in Parisian literary circles. But for anyone interested in theatre performance, and especially in a theatre of empowerment which tries to communicate with a popular, often illiterate audience, this is some of the most important work of its time anywhere in the world. It deserves to be judged alongside the work of Boal in South America, but whereas Boal is known and studied everywhere, Yacine is still too little known.

Kamal Salhi does an excellent job in showing how Yacine always refused to be confined to the boxes in which he was placed. Far from being the poet of the Algerian struggle against the French, his early poetry sought to come to terms with the problems of identity experienced by the people of North Africa who had been repeatedly colonised over a period of millennia. Salhi analyses the early work in lucid terms, showing clearly how *Nedjma* was both a mysterious poetic being and a symbol for the Algerian nation, and demonstrating the links between Yacine's writing and other early twentieth-century European and American writers who had sought a poetic voice that could adequately express the complex links between history, land and identity: Claudel, Lorca, Faulkner. Even more important is his long and detailed account of the practical theatre work in which Yacine involved himself after his return to Algeria in 1970. This work was genuinely collective and it threw up 'scripts' which were in a constant state of evolution, changing from one performance to another, and even changing their language, sometimes using Berber, sometimes vernacular Arabic, sometimes a mixture of both, according to the composition of their audience.

This is very difficult territory to handle in a scholarly work, and Kamal Salhi's solution is to devote fifty pages to a chapter on 'The Historical Conditions of Algerian Theatre Growth: Essentials of a Critical Framework', and a further fifty pages to community theatre in Algeria, before getting on to his last 125 pages dealing with Yacine's own practice. If this makes for a rather weighty read, it nevertheless sets the work in its necessary context and demonstrates irrefutably the originality of Yacine's approach and the inventiveness with which he was able to appropriate elements of traditional culture in the service of a truly progressive theatre. Salhi is particularly interesting on the Arab storytelling tradition, the figure of *Djeha*, and the use to which he was put by Yacine. Moreover, when Kamal Salhi gets on to discussing the practical work he proves himself extremely good at analysing popular festive or ritual elements and showing how they take their place in the development of Yacine's political dramas. The discussion of the use of the circle is fascinating. Yacine never used scenery. Whenever possible, he had his audience sit in a circle surrounding the action, the circle having a range of meanings, both festive and communal, and he always had a costume rail prominently placed so that all character transformations were accomplished in full view of the audience. Meaning was conveyed as much through dance and music as through dialogue or dramatic exchange. Here was a theatre combining all possible forms of performance in the search for a genuinely inclusive formulation of popular identity.

Yacine's death coincided with the beginning of the terrible, recent phase in Algeria's history when those who refused to accept the imposition of a single language and a fundamentalist political programme have been silenced by the use of terror and assassination. The plurality of language and identity which Yacine saw as essential, the long historical view he took, which inevitably gave a certain relativism to his fundamental socialism, none of this can be spoken of in Algeria today. Yacine's conviction that, 'Popular Arabic does exist, it is a living language with its own poets and singers, but it is pushed to one side', a comment made in 1988 (a year before his death), sounds like a very mild protest in the light of the intolerant Islamic code imposed by force today. All of this makes the publication of Kamal Salhi's book particularly important. The story of Yacine's life and work is one which should be known far more widely than it is. For this reason, it is all the more regrettable that the author has not taken the trouble to set his subject in the broader context of theatre as part of the struggle for linguistic and political freedom in other parts of Africa and in other continents as well. His frame of reference is exclusively Algerian, with some occasional references to theatre in France, and this makes the book seem unfairly parochial, especially since it is peppered with careless mistakes, such as quoting Genevieve Serreau as if she were a man, or, in the bibliography, attributing *Rabelais and his World* to a certain Mohamed Bakhtin.

David Bradby
Royal Holloway,
University of London

Wole Soyinka, *Death and the King's Horseman*
(with Commentary and Notes by Jane Plastow)
London: Methuen Drama, 1998, liii.+ 89 pp.
ISBN 041136 95506, £6.99

Death and the King's Horseman is the most popular of all of Soyinka's plays that come under the category of 'drama of essence'. It owes its popularity to the beauty of its language and to the opportunity it affords the author to dramatize his pet concept, 'transition'. The play, as first published by Eyre Methuen in 1975 (reviewed by James Gibbs in *Books Abroad*, Vol. 50, No. 2, Spring 1976, p. 458), is unintroduced and unannotated with the exception of the glossary at the end on some Yoruba words and the Author's Note at the beginning upon which critics and readers have relied heavily in eliciting from the play what Soyinka calls its 'threnodic essence'. The present edition follows strictly the structural format recommended by the editors of the Methuen student handbook. It is accompanied with introductory materials nearly as long as the text of the play.

The first section gives a chronological account of major events in Soyinka's life from 1934 to 1997 seen against the background of Nigeria's political history. The somewhat confused story about the beginning and the end of Soyinka's student days at the universities of Ibadan and Leeds is here clarified. This is followed by (sometimes) tedious plot summaries of the play's five scenes.

The next section, certainly the most challenging to the editor and the most revealing for the student, covers four background areas: (a) African theatre, (b) The Yoruba world view, (c) Wole Soyinka and Nigeria, (d) the impact of Soyinka. Jane Plastow allows that drama (both secular and religious) existed in Africa long before the emergence in the 1960s of modern written drama. This modern drama combines the idioms of the traditional drama (mime, music, dance and folklore) and the conventions of European naturalistic drama in the working out of its message; and its mood is overtly political. On the Yoruba world view, Plastow revisits the beaten track of the interdependence between the three areas of existence in Yoruba cosmology: the world of the dead, the living, and the unborn, each linked to the other by the gulf of transition. The focus of 'Soyinka and Nigeria' is largely biographical, portraying Soyinka as a political activist, and repeating much of what is said earlier in the section on chronology. But the real odd man out in this section is the last item 'The impact of Soyinka'. This is an important subject which is discussed with much insight, but as a summing up of the achievement and influence of Soyinka the man and the writer, it ought to have been highlighted separately on its own as a concluding remark instead of being sandwiched here as a sub-theme.

In the commentary section, Jane Plastow makes brief entries on four areas of the play: its history, the characters, the themes and the language. The historical background which is muted in the 1975 edition is here expanded. We are given the identity of the historical Alafin and his horseman, and we learn that Soyinka came to know the story of the Alafin through his friend Ulli Beier. Although the play can still make its impact without this additional material, the text is richer by its availability; the information will certainly help to fix the play's background firmly in the reader's memory. The discussion of the theme is given a political rather than a metaphysical interpretation; it is a refreshing approach inspired by the exchange between Soyinka and Alby James in the interview reproduced in this edition. I find the approach to the discussion of characters descriptive rather than analytical; perhaps this approach is in the very nature of the subject itself, but I believe it is determined by the editor's sympathy for the target audience (the college audience). The discussion on language nearly ran into the same problem but it begins to be interesting in the closing paragraphs where it is integrated into the metaphysical theme.

Alby James' interview with Soyinka offers enlightening commentary on the play, exploring its implications for Nigeria's contemporary history. Elesin, who fails in his duty to his community, is to be seen as the ancestor of the legacy of failed leadership that has plagued Nigeria since independence. These observations have helped the editor to distil a political significance out of the play's heavily ritualistic setting.

The text of the play is followed with a much needed glossary on Yoruba words and some notes on local idioms and expressions and some technical terms associated with colonial administration. The present edition is a significant improvement on the 1975 edition. It is a handy study-guide to a beautiful and deep play, and written in accessible language.

Obi Maduakor
University of Nigeria, Nsukka

Marcia Blumberg and Dennis Walder (eds),
South African Theatre As/And Intervention
Amsterdam & Atlanta: Rodopi, 1999, xii + 293 pp.
ISBN 90 420 0537 8 HB £45, PB £13.50

Loren Kruger, *The Drama of South Africa:*
Plays, Pageants and Publics since 1910
London & New York: Routledge, 1999, xiv + 277 pp.
ISBN 0415 179831, £16.99

In an attempt to review these two books, I am assailed by conflicting impulses. On the one hand I am impressed by the sheer breadth of scholarship and persistent interest in this very challenging area of South African literary and artistic production, on the other I am keenly aware of fissures that the passage of time has exposed in some of the postulations and assertions held by academics represented in *South African Theatre As/And Intervention*. Read from the hindsight of six years into the new democratic order in South Africa, and four years after the conference itself, the essays betray their datedness while revealing anxieties that could not have been apparent to the editors at the time of production. This is a pity, for the analytic freshness of the essays provokes many questions for cultural practitioners and critics as to the myriad challenges thrown up by the 'new' South Africa, and the inability to foretell the future in any meaningful way. Divided into seven sections that treat the following themes, Physical Theatre, early

Fugard, *Valley Song* and Beyond, Performing Race, Gender, and Sexuality, Theatre in/and Education, Theatre Festivals, and lastly Interviews, this collection of critical essays impresses with the multiple concerns that a rubric such as South African Theatre can still command.

My concerns stem from the Keynote Address delivered by Ian Steadman, 'Race, Nationalism and Theatre Reconsidered'. This is unfortunate, for Steadman has been a towering figure of intellectual prowess in South African theatre studies. The keynote address grounds itself in the politics of negation, rather than affirmation. If we are to take the editors seriously when, in the Introduction, they state that 'interventionist criticism and scholarship are as necessary as ever; what this involves is a scrutiny of our own, revisionist critique of recent years' (p. 19), then it behoves the reviewer to interrogate the assertions that Steadman advances.

Steadman lectures South African scholarship on the need to maintain 'critical vigilance at this crucial moment' lest the war against fundamentalism, against essentialism, and against nationalism and racism is lost. These are noble intentions, but it is the convention within which he frames his concerns by virtue of his long association with African-American scholarship that I find objectionable. Because of the 'new' South Africa and all its concomitant uncertainties, there is suddenly a need to guard against 'essentialism, fundamentalism', etc. The use of the Joyce–Gates–Baker debate on the authenticity (or not) of 'black aesthetics' (carried out in the *New Literary History*, 18, 2, 1987) to imply that it may be the bane of South African scholarship to seek to essentialise 'race' and nation is fallacious since it betrays its understanding of South African scholarship as an appendage of the West, as susceptible to uncritical absorption of African-American scholarship which is perceived to hold particular sway over South African intellectuals. By what or whose moral authority does Steadman suddenly become a 'watchdog' of essentialism in South African theatrical studies, and invite others to join him? Steadman is emphatic that the terms Black theatre, African-American theatre, African theatre or South African theatre are crudely nationalistic, extra-artistic terms derived from both 'material and social relations and ideological projections of the State'. 'Black theatre', we are told, 'reflects not a nationalistic image of the politically defined State but a nativistic image of a racially defined essence' (p. 33). The problem with such an assertion is that, by sleight of professorial fiat, it seeks to inscribe Black Africa with the same grand myth of Absence now adopted with glee by luminaries such as Kwame Anthony Appiah,[1] whom Steadman quotes with apparent approval.

For Steadman, the 'nation' must be resisted, an idea which remains problematic because for him it is imperative to 'think constantly of Africa as being part of our thinking about theatre generally' (p. 36). Not once in the entire address does he refer to an African-centred criticism or to any theatrical expertise north of the Limpopo: no, the critics approvingly quoted are Gates, Valentin Mudimbe and Paul Gilroy.

If Steadman has serious problems with the interchangeability of the terms 'African' and 'black' (as exemplified by his criticism of Bhekizizwe Peterson's article[2]), surely we can have no terminology to describe what comes from Africa? It may be that, like Janet Levine, Steadman fears what she sees as triumphant 'black nationalism',[3] which would explain the overwhelming critique of 'black' theatre at the expense of, say, 'Afrikaner' theatre in the address. As it is, the Steadman address provides a sophisticated, erudite reading that betrays embedded ideological predicates. If the 'rigid categorizations' of the past are to be avoided, this should not be at the expense of Africanity.

The subsections that follow offer a rich reading of how South Africans 'play', and may be an invaluable addition to any reading list about theatre studies dealing specifically with the transitional period.

It is inconceivable that a text on South African theatre can fail to have contributions on Athol Fugard, and it is pleasing that this text carries sections on early and the recent Fugard plays. Pleasing precisely because some revisionist re-readings of the earlier and latter plays begin to show the fissures that appear with time. Zakes Mda leads the way, noting that plays such as *Boesman and Lena* lacked a 'spirit of defiance' (p. 6), while Errol Durbach exalts the play that, with hindsight, provides further proof of the ex–South-African Canadian's partiality to liberal humanism. In his reading (or re-reading), therefore, he offers a conscientious understanding of the 'refusal to forget', the 'need to remember', that structures the play. This sort of comprehension of Fugard, as hero and villain in South African theatre studies, can never quite go away, showing the divide that assails scholarship and the lived experience of the country. The pathetic aura of Boesman and his Lena, despite what Dennis Walder elsewhere calls 'the possibility of a flicker of light, of compassion, or dignity',[4] has refused to go away.

That Fugard has been an artist pursuing his art has not satisfied the South African literati. More problematically, his quiet assertion of having been 'a voice' has caused disquiet, for this is interpreted as removing agency from those who struggled and paid the ultimate price. In his interview with Dennis Walder (pp. 219–30), a certain glibness creeps in when he is questioned about being freed of having to 'speak for a silent majority'. The assumption is that there was no other playwrights at the time Fugard's star was in the ascendancy in London and New York. In the new dispensation, the intrusion of personal history tied up in national history becomes embarrassingly self-serving – as in *Valley Song* – precisely because the example of the land invasions in Zimbabwe, and the over-extended reassurances that this could not happen here renders Fugard's supposedly ethnic 'Afrikaner voice' suspect. As Toby Zinman attests, this win-win situation of *Valley Song* has turned 'preachy and saccharine'. It perpetuates white mythologies of land possession as part of the inheritance of the kith and kin of the former ruling class. For Zinman, 'Fugard has intervened between his art and his audience, no longer trusting the medium of otherness; and both his art and audience have suffered'[5] (p. 100). Dennis Walder's excellent paper offers a critique of some of Fugard's theatrical interventions over many years. It sets the tone of what is lacking in the Steadman paper about the possible futures of South African theatre and in postulating the demise of 'protest theatre', it asks what will replace such theatre.

Of course, no study of the transitional period would be complete without Mbongeni Ngema's *Sarafina 2* folly, and Bernth Lindfors painstakingly reveals, using numerous newspaper cuttings, the egomaniac proportions of Ngema's personality. This paper makes for good reading when compared and contrasted with Michael Carklin's, wherein the latter looks specifically at the National Education and Training Forum with its attendant syllabus for both pupils and teachers in the Eastern Cape, where drama is offered as a school subject. For while Lindfors charts the ignoble scandal, at the back of Carklin's paper is an unstated question: what would have been achieved if projects such as those in the Eastern Cape had the kind of interventionist theatrical resources that was stupendously wasted by a crass, base charlatan?

There are critical points raised by the rest of the papers, not least the growth of neglected 'gay theatre'; a pithy discussion of the two arts festivals in a possible resurgence of South African theatre (by Annette Combrink), and instructive interviews with four key playwrights of South Africa: Athol Fugard, Fatima Dike, Reza de Wet and Janet Suzman. All the interviews raise interesting and individual points of development and postulations. It is germane to note that, far from ossifying, South African theatre shows, in this collection, a resilience of spirit that augurs well for the future.

Loren Kruger's *The Drama of South Africa: Plays, Pageants and Publics since 1910* is a very useful addition to South African literary history. Its breadth and painstaking research comes from an academic whose contribution to the field over the years is awesome. It brings a different and fascinating perspective to an area previously ploughed by scholars such as Martin Orkin,[6] and covers aspects also researched by David B. Coplan.[7] In a sense, therefore, it is a useful addition to an entire century of 'making things mean', to use a phrase from Bhekizizwe Peterson. What it does reveal is the identarian contestations drama and pageants have had to negotiate throughout the years, the uses of which are intricately tied to the colonial and postcolonial phases of South African history. Indeed, from Chapter 2 onward, Kruger grapples with the fact that the various publics appealed to by dramatists were participating in postcolonial spaces long before such ideas gained currency. For the Afrikaner component of the South African polity, postcoloniality was a condition for accepting the creation of the Union of South Africa that came into being in 1910. Indeed, the Afrikaner was the prototype of postcoloniality since the very fervour with which the South African War was fought was to be rid of (English) foreign dominance. The hitch, as the Pageant of Union of 1910, and the Pageant of Southern Africa in 1936, reveal, was the difficult curve in attempting to forge two disparate communities of whites together, as the fault lines were over-determined by issues embedded within the Anglo-Boer conflict.

Interspersed with such attempts at nation building were the activities of the 'New Africans' who saw themselves as part of the movement toward 'civilisation'. From the pursuits of groups such as the Mthethwa Lucky Stars, the Darktown Strutters and the Bantu Dramatic Society, it is apparent that they occupied marginal social positions, exemplified by a range of socio-political ambivalences and tensions. Kruger pays special attention to the relationship forged between these groups and impresarios such as, for instance, Betha Slosberg, reflecting, as Peterson does on the obstacles 'faced by African performers attempting to make a living as artists' (p. 33). Such relationships were to a large extent characterised by overweening, patronising attitudes towards the thespians, with impresarios hankering for 'nativist simplicity' and a display of 'splendid savage splendour'. In spite of such restraints, Herbert Dhlomo's plays such as *Dingane*, *Cetshwayo* and *Moshoeshoe* later showed a preponderance of latent 'transition towards a militant nationalism which starts to articulate the need for self-awareness and self-determination'.[8] This of course is an ironic comment on the longevity of Slosberg's legacy when, later, impresarios such as Bertha Egnos made a huge profit on *Ipi Tombi* and similar shows in the 1970s. However improbably, *Ipi Tombi* took off from some of the Lucky Stars' sketches extolling 'idealized images of the past' as opposed to a present fraught with industrialisation and modernity; that is, for all its song and dance, *Ipi Tombi* was nothing more than vulgarised Africana.

My admiration for Kruger's scholarly work extends, too, to the manner in which she brings many little-known plays to the fore, painstakingly weaving into her reading of them the (un)making of disparate communities. For instance, her conscientious reading of Guy Butler's *The Dam* (1953), demonstrates the manner in which unconscious racism needed to be negotiated by even academicians who commanded respect in the world of English Letters. Read in this era, surely Butler's play is hugely embarrassing to him? It is ironic but equally understandable that this play appeared at the volatile time of the tangible beginnings of the African National Congress's Youth League formation and propagation of the Defiance Campaign.

NOTES

1. I am aware of Appiah's argument as advanced in 'African Identities', Linda Nicholson and Steven Seidman (eds), *Social Postmodernism: Beyond Identity Politics* (Cambridge: Cambridge University Press, 1995), 103–15. I have read Mahmood Mamdani's inaugural lecture at the

University of Cape Town as A.C. Jordan Professor of African Studies, 'When does a Settler Become a Native? Reflections of the Colonial Roots of Citizenship in Equatorial and South Africa', *Electronic Mail & Guardian*, 26 May 1998. Further, I have perused Archie Mafeje's 'Africanity: A Combative Ontology', *CODESRIA Bulletin* (2000): 66–71. Concerning Louis Gates Jr's 'signifying monkey', Archie Mafeje has this caveat: 'The fashionable "freefloating signifier" is an illusion in a double sense. First, nobody can think and act outside of historically determined circumstances and still hope to be a social signifier of any kind. Secondly, unlike the illusory "free-floating signifier" it is the historical juncture which defines us socially and intellectually.'

2. Bhekizizwe Peterson, 'A Rain a Fall but the Dirt it Tough: Scholarship on African Theatre in South Africa', *Journal of Southern African Studies* 21.4 (1995): 573–84.

3. Janet Levine, *Inside Apartheid: One Woman's Struggle in South Africa* (Chicago & New York: Contemporary Books, 1988), 255.

4. Dennis Walder, 'Introduction', *Athol Fugard – Selected Plays* (Oxford & Cape Town: Oxford University Press, 1987), ix.

5. Recent events within South Africa bear out the veracity of Zinman's assessment. *The Star* newspaper of 19 October 2000, in a story titled 'Warning of strife over slow land reform', reports that 86% of arable land is still in approximately 60,000 white hands, an unhealthy situation in a country where land equates wealth and well-being. The *Mail & Guardian* story of 20 October 2000 titled 'Nervous farmers turn to the ANC' reports how, in an attempt to forestall Zimbabwean-style land invasions, white farmers are now joining the African National Congress in droves.

6. Martin Orkin, *Drama and the South African State* (Manchester, New York & Johannesburg: Manchester University Press & Witwatersrand University Press, 1991).

7. David B. Coplan, *In Township Tonight!: South Africa's City Music and Theatre* (Johannesburg: Ravan Press, 1985).

8. Bhekizizwe Peterson, 'Apartheid and the Political Imagination in Black South African Theatre', *Journal of Southern African Studies*, 16/2: 231.

S. I. Raditlhalo
University of Venda for Science and Technology

Index

Lightning Source UK Ltd.
Milton Keynes UK
UKOW02f1832181116
287989UK00001B/25/P

9 780852 555965